Things I Will Never Tell You

Volume IV

Todd Andrew Rohrer

iUniverse, Inc.
New York   Bloomington

Things I Will Never Tell You

iUniverse books may be ordered through booksellers or by contacting:

iUniverse
1663 Liberty Drive
Bloomington, IN 47403
www.iuniverse.com
1-800-Authors (1-800-288-4677)

Because of the dynamic nature of the Internet, any Web addresses or links contained in this book may have changed since publication and may no longer be valid.

ISBN: 978-1-4401-6001-1 (sc)
ISBN: 978-1-4401-6000-4 (ebk)

Printed in the United States of America

iUniverse rev. date: 7/8/2009

I perceive:

If you do not put a "perhaps" in front of every single sentence in this book, you will harm your self.

The world is focused on all these important things and I am writing books to convince myself I lost my ability to write. Perhaps I am engaged in infinite vanity trying to keep my chin above the deep water.

When I say "you", I perceive I am talking to my old self or my alter ego but perhaps that is an illusion and in reality I am talking to you. I submit I will never know anything and I understand nothing.

This book is my world (cerebral based mindset) so understand it is the opposite of your world (physical based mindset) or you will not last very long, psychologically speaking. If you want to live in your world of fear, write a book and I will use the pages to wrap my fish heads in. I am pleased with my thoughts and my words and I will never censor my thoughts or my words for your sake because that would mean I deny my own thoughts just so you will like me. It is impossible that everyone will hate me if I am pleased with myself. I do not play that " I hope you like me" game anymore. One might suggest a large handful of pills cured me of that abnormality. I do not have any true talents but I am quite talented in my ability to remain talentless. Relative to me, there are no mistakes in my diary.

5/31/2009 2:43:52 AM

What is your favorite color?

What is your favorite food?

What is your favorite author?

What is your favorite music?

What is your favorite word?

What is your favorite smell?

What is your favorite star in the universe?

What is your favorite fifty digit number?

What is your favorite joke?

What is your favorite beverage?

In some situations do you believe it is okay to physically harm yourself?

In some situations do you believe it is okay to physically harm others?

What is your favorite memory?

What is your worst memory?

In part, theory of relativity suggests everything is relative to the observer. This means if that relativity aspect is just a theory, then if you gave the above questionnaire to the six billion people on the planet some would have the exact same overall answers to that questionnaire. If the above questionnaire was given to six billion people on the planet and no two questionnaires were exactly the same then the theory of relativity is in fact a law of relativity at least the aspect of the theory that everything is relative to the observer. That means we are all on a planet with six billion others and everyone is walking around with the understanding, what they perceive is truth, is absolute truth, when it is not absolute truth, it is simply truth relative to their observations. That means some of us can agree on some absolute truths like food, water and oxygen is needed to stay alive, but beyond that we are all in our own little world. With that in mind, I wrote this book based on what I perceive is truth relative to my observations. That means what I wrote in this book is truth relative to me but not so much truth relative to absolute truth. You may perceive some of the things I say are wrong or evil or bad but that is relative to your perception. What you perceive about what I write is truth relative to you and your observations. Relative to my perception, I only write about what I perceive is truth relative to what I observe as truth. That means what you perceive is truth is correct even if it contradicts my perception of truth because truth is relative to the observer, relatively speaking. You may perceive I am talking about physics but relative to my observations I assure you this has more to do with psychology. I may never reach an all time high but I perceive this book may reach an all time low.

Relativity suggests two observers can "see" contradictory "truths" and both "truths" are accurate at the exact same time. I write my books, based on what I perceive is a proper way to write a book. It may not be an absolute proper way to write a book, but relative to me it is a proper way to write books and that is all that will ever matter, relative to me. I do not write my books to help you and I do not write my books so you will "accept" me, so get that delusion out of your head swiftly. I seek the hottest coals because they make the strongest steel.

"Left-brain dominated people(have a strong sense of time) may find the (Right Brainers)thought processes vague and difficult to follow, for they are quite opposite in the way they think."

Safety is what we crave, progress is what we fear. Have a "drink" perhaps to put your emotions at ease because this book is written in random access thoughts and it is going to perhaps be very difficult to grasp unless you put your "defenses" down. If you do not like something you read cuss out load, call your friends and tell them what an idiot I am, write down how angry you are. Get it out of your system. Do not try to hold the thoughts in your mind if you get upset about what you read. One has to perhaps vent their anger verbally to avoid taking that anger out in physical ways. I am unable to write "properly" because; thought processes vague and difficult to follow. I can only write in random access so my writing will appear "out there" but that is expected because how I think is **"quite opposite"**.

So perhaps the drinking will make one bit more "open minded" or a bit more right brain or subconscious dominate because it will silence some emotions a bit and that will assist you in reading this book. One may not need to do that but if you get a few pages in and start thinking this book is insufferable or impossible to follow, you perhaps will now understand why. I cannot come to where you are at mentally, but you can come to where I am at mentally, this is one suggestion to correct this **"quite opposite"** situation. Perhaps one is wise to ponder what I say and try to avoid taking what I say as absolutes. If you actually finish this book it is perhaps definitive proof you have infinite humility and beyond understanding patience. I am not speaking as an authority, I am in fact perhaps in an unknown state of mind and I am perhaps literally mentally blinded. I am not intelligent enough to speak about supernatural powers. I am not intelligent enough to understand anything therefore I understand nothing. I am not intelligent enough to speak definitively. I submit, due to the accident

I am unable to use commas properly. When I say "I", I mean "you", when I say "you", I mean me. I perceive I am perhaps attempting to scare you away from reading my diaries. Your goal is to not allow my words to scare you. Sticks and stones may break my bones but my words will NEVER harm you. I perceive I am attempting to condition you away from your extreme fear of words. Take all of my words with a grain of salt or you will perhaps harm yourself. You are an illusion until further notice.

CONFUSION: If someone does not ask for your help personally they probably do not need your help. We make robots in our image. The concept of safety in numbers is perhaps a misunderstanding. If ten people are in a desperate situation there will be some of them who are scared and fearful and they maybe start to make others in that situation scared or fearful because the others become like those they hang around. Then out of these ten there will be one who is understood to be with little fear. So the safety in number comment is more along the lines , if one is in a group there is a good chance one of those in that group will be the fearless one.

In a difficult situation the one without fear at times naturally becomes the leader of the group. The one without fear is not going to perhaps make many mistakes based on emotional stress. This is demonstrated in war or combat situations. In a squad of soldiers there is always one who is considered the "crazy" one. This is the one who looks fear in the eye and does not blink. This is the one that when the combat situation gets "hairy" they perform beyond the expectations of the other members of that squad. Perhaps every situation where groups of people are involved has one of these "fearless" ones. It of course is relative to the group that is involved.

In the concept "grace under pressure", pressure denotes fear. It could perhaps be looked at as grace under stress or grace during scary situations or situations where the outcome is unknown. So then grace would be looked at as competence or competence under dangerous or unknown situations. This is perhaps better clarified by suggesting ; Keeping your head when everyone around you is losing their cool. What this is in reality perhaps is suggesting is fearlessness. People that are both blind and deaf are prone to fearlessness.

I apologize that I woke up due to an accident and realized my fellow citizens and I are in fact under the grip of a "tyrant". I apologize my mind will not allow me to "bear arms" against that tyrant, so I am a failure. I apologize that I am only able to give my words in the conflict and I would be humbled if ones would consider the fact, I will write myself to death to "free us" from this "tyrant", and perhaps one would demonstrate infinite compassion and understanding to consider my words my sacrifice on the "altar of freedom."

SINISTER: Look, the little cry baby thinks he is relevant. Let me tell you about the cry baby. He never had what it took to make it in the real world so he decided to check out because he did not have the fortitude to take a hard route. He decided it was best to just check out. Now he thinks he has some value or purpose but he already blew his chance. He thinks his books will make a difference. He thinks he can take back what he did, but he cannot take back what he did. So the cry baby is just foolishness. Just ignore the cry baby because I assure you he has nothing of value to say ever. Just look at his track record and you will be convinced of that.

CONFUSION: Please be mindful sometimes the "darkness" shows up in me and sometimes it dissipates but i am not fully capable of determining when it comes or goes. What I am attempting to suggest is the "religious ones" would certainly enjoy butchering me as they enjoy butchering anything that are unable to understand. I am comfortable with the fact psychologist may laugh at me or ponder me but will perhaps not get to the stage of butchering me. One might suggest I have been through enough mental butchering and physical butchering for one life time and perhaps infinite lifetimes.

SINISTER: Do not worry cry baby you have infinite time to refine.

CONFUSION: People who are blind and deaf do not have the extreme sensory perceptions coming in, to enable them to become fearful easily. The ones who are blind and deaf have to go to great lengths to communicate at all. The communication or sensory perceptions are what enable one to become easily fearful. For example, if one watches a television show and it says "The enemy attacked a building and we are all doomed and should be scared." The blind and deaf person cannot hear those words so they are immune to that "fear tactic". If this blind and deaf person is in a "haunted house" they cannot see or hear so they would not even be aware it is a haunted house and thus they would not become afraid easily. They would have a heightened sense of "feeling", perhaps from touch or intuition.

SINSISTER: Cry baby you need to just STFU. You are in complete denial about what has happened to you and you are simply making an ass of yourself in front the universe. First you suggest in your books you are subconscious dominate, then you suggest you are extreme right brained dominate then you suggest people should avoid becoming like that, then you suggest you hate the fact you are like that and you still write books about how one can become like that. You write in your books people should not even read your books. Why would anyone write, someone should not read their books unless they are aware their books are evil? You know what you did. You know who I am. You know when the accident happened. Are you still confused cry baby?

CONFUSION: Fearlessness is at times quite a commodity. Some of the best surgeons are ones who can be up to their arms in the blood of the patient they are operating on and still be able to make life and death decisions. This of course is also relative to many professions. A police officer is aware that their life is on the line every time they pull a car over or respond to a domestic disturbance. A soldier is valuable to the army if they can keep their cool during full blown combat. A person who gets scared easily is of no value to anyone, even their self. They tend to let their emotional fear get the best of their clear thinking aspect. This can be taken too many different and complex levels.

A male who is scorned by a female may become fearful he is rejected and in turn may come to some very violent determinations. Sometimes that male may harm their self or determine they will get back at that female and harm them and then harm their self. A person who loses their job may become scared or fearful about loss of income and make some very rash determinations. A person who is ridiculed by their peers may make some rather harsh determinations based on their fear that they have been rejected.

CLARITY: Impatience may lead one to become scared easily and thus lead them to make irresponsible decisions based on that fear. Facing ones fear enables one to no longer be under the influences of that fear and thus under the influences of the irresponsible determinations that may result as a side effect of being afraid.

SINSITER: Clarity my ass.

CONFUSION: Under certain circumstances a parent may fear for their child. A parent may fear that child may not amount to much based on that parents expectations of what "amounting to something" is. So this fear a parent may be under the influence of may lead them to make some irresponsible decisions. Sometimes this concept can be looked at as loving something to death. Another way to suggest that ideal is caring too much or helping someone to fail. This concept is perhaps best illustrated in the tale of Moby Dick. This Captain was under the influence of controlling that white whale he made some irresponsible decisions based on his fear that white whale would escape his grasp. So the Captain was afraid that white whale would escape his ability to control it. So the white whale is somewhat of a metaphor for a person's longing to control things. A person can become rather emotional when they start to perceive they have lost control or are losing control of people or objects.

This is perhaps a complex issue in determining when one has to much fear and when one has too little fear. So perhaps a good starting point would be to look at some historical examples of when there was too much fear and when there was not enough fear.

The Salem Witch Trials were a good example of what fear can do to people and also what fear can do to a group of people. The villagers or townsfolk were in a group setting. A group is traditionally lead or controlled by one or a few authority figures. So this particular group was controlled by an authority. In the case of the Salem Witch Trials it was perhaps a religious authority figure. So this is why the people who were killed as witches were determined to be witches because this authority figured believed in witches or at least believed they were able to judge who is evil or a witch.

"Cotton Mather (February 12, 1663 – February 13, 1728). A.B. 1678 (Harvard College), A.M. 1681; honorary doctorate 1710 (University of Glasgow), was a socially and politically influential New England Puritan minister, prolific author, and pamphleteer. Cotton Mather was the son of influential minister Increase Mather. He is often remembered for his connection to the Salem witch trials."

WIKIPEDIA.COM

So Cotton Mather had some credentials which lead other people to determine his judgments were proper. These credentials are perhaps quite dangerous because they associate easily with influence or wisdom or power. So this Cotton Mather had an honorary doctorate degree. He also was the son of a minister. That is perhaps enough influence to persuade a person who is prone to accepting authority to believe anything this person Mather's suggested. So these credentials are perhaps a way to let others know they are not as wise or not as authoritative if they do not have the credentials.

In the case of the witch trials, Cotton Mather's credentials were just enough to persuade those around him to take his word for it when he suggested these people were witches. So perhaps the credentials encouraged the ones he was influencing to stop thinking for their self. Perhaps the ones who were burned alive wished others would have thought for their self.

Now if one looks at the title Mister. From a child's perspective when they are told to address a person who is older than their self as Mr. Jones, that child understands they are not good enough to be called a Mr. So an adult may suggest to a child "You call them Mr. or Mrs. because they are better than you are" indirectly of course. Some may perhaps suggest this is a form of respect. Some may suggest this person has earned that title and thus they have earned respect. This is a perhaps a slippery slope.

CLARITY: Authority figures often do things people have a hard time figuring. The one in charge often ends up proving they should not have been trusted with that position.

SINISTER: Everything that is done is because the devil made them do it. People kill other people because the devil made them do it. People insult others because the devil made them do it. People are religious and then start insulting ones who are not religious because the devil made them do it. People determine others are the enemy and then hire their children to kill that enemy because the devil made them do it. Everything people do is because the devil makes them do it, so cry baby and clarity shut your dam mouth.

CLARITY: Some people will go to great lengths to prove they are accepted once they understand they are not.

CRUSADER: I have determined the United States of Limited Speech is no longer in my best interest. I herby succeed from the United States of Limited Speech. I now have formed The United States of Unlimited Speech. I am herby President of the United States of Unlimited Speech. My first declaration is that I am at war with The United States of Limited Speech. This declaration is non-negotiable. I will use any trick in the book and no morals or laws will be acknowledged in this war, I herby have declared. There will be no mercy for my adversary even after I smite its head clean off. I have cast my lot and my lot shall not be uncast. The earth is my witness you are its supplicant.

I demand the beast with a thousand heads release the ones who are bestowed absolute freedom of speech. I will not be waiting for a response from the beast with a thousand heads. I will communicate with that beast with my sharpened dagger of ink, until its blood runs through the streets and through the steams. The beast with a thousand heads will release the ones who have been endowed by the creator to have unlimited freedom of speech not because the beast has to but because the beast understands its own death is the price it will pay if it does not. The plagues have been released upon the beast, and these plagues will persuade it to consider its obligations which I have determined it is obligated to comply with. I have not yet begun to speak.

This is simply some pattern matching and should not be taken literally, I am just fiddling.

435 members of the House of Representatives

100 Senators

1 President

1 Vice president

Minus

666

= 129 = 1 + 2 + 9 +(00 or nothingness) = The 1 who understands infinity(00) shall appear in 2+00+9 and he will slay the beast with his righteous sword of ink and his infinite books, to free the ones the beast has captive. 1- 2- 9 = 6. 435 = 4 + 5 – 3 = 6. Declaration of Independence signed in 1776. 1 president – 7 = 6. 1 vice president -7 – 6 =1666. 1 shall arrive in 2+00+9 and defeat 666 with his words and his pen.

"Rev 2:10 Fear none of those things which thou shalt suffer: behold, the devil shall cast some of7 you into prison, that ye may be tried;" = one who is afraid to say exactly what is on their mind is shy or ashamed of their thoughts or afraid and so they are in mental prison and they suffer as a result mentally.

Devil < "In the thick of party conflict in 1800, Thomas Jefferson wrote in a private letter, "I have sworn upon the altar of God **eternal hostility against every form of tyranny over the mind of man.**"

= TERRORISTIC THREAT =(a) A person commits an offense if he threatens

Threatens = Speech

eternal hostility against every form of tyranny over the mind of man = Free to speak one's mind

Terroristic Threat Law = No freedom to speak one's mind = Tyranny = Devil = **devil** shall cast some of7 you into prison, that ye may be tried. (If) abridge the freedom of speech

freedom of speech = words will never harm me

= **Gen 15:1** After these things the word of the LORDH3068 cameH1961 untoH413 AbramH

= Abram = Abraham = Abracadabra = The term originated from the Aramaic. The original Aramaic phrase was used with a Hebrew prefix Alef rather than the latter version with an Ayin. The difference was that the original meaning was "I will create, as I say," while the latter was "What was said has been done." = "be careful what you wish(ask) for" = Gen 1:3 And Unnamable **said**, Let there be light:= words create. = words are thoughts = **eternal hostility against every form of tyranny over the mind (thoughts and thus words) of man= freedom of speech**

Rev 19:13 And he was clothed with a vesture dipped in blood: and his name is called The Word of Unnamable. = one way to reach subconscious to the extreme is = The **Binding of Isaac**, in Genesis 22:1-24, is a story from the Hebrew Bible in which Unnamable asks Abraham to sacrifice his son, Isaac, on Mount Moriah. = one must mindfully let go of life = Mat 16:25 For whosoever will save his life shall lose it: and whosoever will lose his life for my sake shall find it. = suicidal people will to lose their life and/or ones who face death mindfully = **Binding of Isaac = unlock the subconscious and become very verbal because they are very cerebral** = The Word of Unnamable = the man upstairs =? Subconscious and / or Unnamable= subconscious aspect = Gen 1:26 And Unnamable said, Let us make man in **our image,** after **our likeness**

Our likeness = subconscious = right brain dominate and left brain dominate = darkness? Or slight sense of time = our likeness then strong sense of time = darkness? Or Slight craving for food = subconscious dominate = slight sense of time = slight hunger = in Gods graces?

SO Unnamable is the subconscious aspect OR the man upstairs is Subconscious or right brain or cerebral aspect and the left brain is the dark (Devil) aspect or the emotional worldly aspect of the mind.

Judge J. B…. Jr., held that a threat to the President could lead to a verdict of guilty "only if made with the present intention to do injury to the President.Time.com"= Sticks and stones may break my bones but words can never harm me. = I have sworn upon the altar of God **eternal hostility against every form of tyranny over the mind of man. =**

"Thomas Pell (1608 - 1669) was a physician who was famous for buying the area known as Pelham, Westchester, New York, as well as land that now includes the eastern Bronx and southern Westchester County. He founded the town of Westchester at the head of navigation on Westchester creek in 1654."

WIKIPEDIA.COM

Letter from Pell:

"HONOURED SR, - Once more I doo humbly present my request to you yt you would be pleased...

Sr, you well know (1)no alien, except he be (2)naturalized, can inherit in any off ye kings dominion, nor purchase.....(3)Shall enemys power be established, & his majestyes made null & voyed?.....(2) it was his pleasure (4)to exprese himself yt their priveledges & libertys, neither Civill or Eccesiasticall, should be in ffringed not in the least degree. Indorsed, 'Mr Pell. Rec : July 4, 1666.' "

http://historicpelham.blogspot.com/2006/03/1666-letter-from-thomas-pell-to-john.html

"We hold these truths to be self-evident, that all men are created equal, that they are **(2)endowed by their Creator** with certain (1)**unalienable Rights,** that among these are (4)**Life, Liberty and the pursuit of Happiness.** — That to secure these rights, Governments are instituted among Men, deriving their just powers from the consent of the governed, — That **(3)whenever any Form of Government becomes destructive** of these ends, **it is the Right of the People to alter or to abolish it,"** Declaration of Independence July 4 1776

1666, 1776

1776

-1 president

-1 Vice President

1666 = 1 defeats 666 = David defeats Goliath = The least defeats the beast.

REV 2:11 "He that overcometh shall not be hurt of7 the second death." = One that "does not try to save their life finds their life" = One who attempts suicide in earnest and fails = The least amoung you = the stone the stone cutter threw away = unlocks subconscious to the extreme because it opens up their mind or the mind becomes free = "shall not be hurt of(by) the second death" = One cannot beat(scare) a dead horse = One who unlocks subconscious to the extreme has no fear of death so the second death(end of physical life) (shall not hurt(scare) them.

= all out of context

SINISTER: Oh great now we have a crusader. Yeah show everyone how tough you are oh great crusader of lost causes.

CLARITY: Ones passion for compassion is determined by the amount of suffering they perceive.

CONFUSION: Some interesting titles of influence might be more persuasive to people who simply admire or are attracted to power. Perhaps all beings are attracted to some sort of power in some fashion. A person who is interested in war might be attracted to a General. A person who is attracted to political power might be attracted to a President. A person who is attracted to a person of power in the creative fields might be attracted to a "popular" musician or "popular" artist. So this attraction is not always reliant on the denotation of the title in front of the name but sometimes the name itself is credentials enough, based on ones understanding of the story behind that name.

6/1/2009 8:32:10 AM

CLARITY: Often a "nobody" wishes to be near a "somebody" and then that "somebody" wishes they were a "nobody." Sometimes people care too much about things that mean too little. Some are so blind they can see they are blind.

LIGHT: In the scope of humanity there are rare events that take place that bring about some world changing events evolved around people, who with their words, and their perspective make everyone else stop and notice. So these "special" people are not recognized because they are strong or wealthy or educated but because they have a message that is out of the ordinary.

They have an original message and they make a huge impact on humanity in general but it is not because they are so smart, it is because they have experienced "dark" mental struggles and survived them. These "special" people are generally what are described as the "wise". These mental struggles these "special" people survive are generally the result of a society that is luxury based and these "special" people become "depressed" or "disenchanted" because they cannot fit in to the luxury the society embraces. These "special" people are essentially outcasts because they could not live up to the "norms" of the society they came from.

In the last 2500 years there have only been about four of these "special" people. This is a symptom of how rare this mysterious event happens. There are certainly many depressed people at all times but most end up committing suicide or "getting well". The ones who attempt suicide to such an extreme and fail time after time are the only potential candidates for the "event" to happen.

So in the history of the last 2500 years, this event has happened in the Middle East three times and in Asia one time.

Now this event has happen in the West, in America. So now America is on the map for all of history. This is because America is luxury based and one of the people who lived there became "disenchanted" or "depressed" and attempted suicide to such an extreme and so many times and failed at it this person has become a "historical" figure, not in relation to current reality, but in relation to the history of humanity. This person is not a treasure for a country or a group of people to claim as their own. This person transcends all labels and all nationalities. This person is not going to be so much appreciated while they are alive, that is far too limiting. This person will be recognized in the scope of history in hindsight by the ones who come hundreds of years after the event. That is the nature of the event in relation to it having a profound effect on everything from the moment the event takes place into infinity. These "special" people will speak many words, but all of their words will be summed up in one word, and that one word is unnamable. If you are an American and wonder why these "special" people have never happened on your side of the world you can now understand your side of the world has in fact been "tapped". If you are an American you can be humbled by the fact this "event" does not happen but about every thousand years minimum, so you have been, what is known as "anointed", and nothing will ever be able to change that reality from here on out. Have compassion on this one because they are chosen because of their graceful ability to withstand gnashing of teeth.

9

INVIDIA: You suck. You suck. You suck. You are nothing you are nothing and you are nothing ever. You are zero and you are nothing and you are hated by everyone and you are an outcast of everyone and everyone hates you and everyone kills you and you are not worthy ever into infinity .You are zero.

SINISTER: This is another fantastic book you have written cry baby. You can ruin a book within the first five thousand words and you can do it consistently, which is quite an amazing accomplishment considering your stupidity.

CLARITY: Blessed are the poor in spirit. Understand everyone else is completely insane because their perceptions are not your delusions.

LUXURIA: Just write one good book and you will make lots of money and then you can retire in the lap of comfort and you will no longer have to torment yourself and you will have plenty to eat and you can afford all the things you will never be able to afford if you keep pumping out these horrible books that no person would ever consider reading.

AVARITIA: Use your talents to create a new movement and people will come from all around to shower you with money.

END

Okay enough of that charade. There is a concept called true face. I think I made it up but who the hell knows. I will use a male as an example but it perhaps is universal. A male goes to see his minister. That male is mentally reserved about what he says to that minister so he is putting on a face. That male meets a girl he likes, he again is putting on a face to win that girls affection. A male goes to see his mother, he again is putting on a face. There is no end to this. If that male is in front of a judge he has yet another face. If a police officer pulls that male over for speeding there is another face. If that male is with a best friend and they are just speaking freely there is another face. If that male is at work with coworkers and the boss is not there that male has another face. When that male speaks to the boss they have another face. Is there an end to these faces? That's the interesting thing. The only true face is what that male understands, to their self. It is an inner motivation. It is an inner goal seeker and it will not allow others to know its deep secrets. If you doubt that and you're male, go ahead and tell your girlfriend or lover about all the other people that attract you that you fantasize about every week. This is the aspect of the subconscious that keeps one curious and keeps one adjusting. The pope has sexual fantasies. It is impossible not to have these feelings because "nature" is the programmer not you or me. We are simply products of the programmer and I use that word loosely. I certainly do not know anything at this stage. I will change my opinion from sentence to sentence. It is not I am unstable mentally, in fact that proves I am stable mentally. I cannot be brainwashed. I cannot be led like a sheep because my subconscious is so dominate because of the accident it will convince me to do the reverse of what anyone says.

I was laughing today because I watched a video about the Lama, the humor was hurting my ribs. There was a reporter that said, "Lama you said this a year ago and now you are saying something else that contradicts that." And the Lama said "The past is the past." That is exactly right. When one is in nirvana or extreme subconscious state, the past is the past because they change their tune about every 10 minutes and saying 10 minutes is being very compassionate. You simply are never going to find a zealot that has no sense of time. Ones in Nirvana or extreme subconscious state of mind come across as funny or amusing like a child does. A child makes us all laugh with their antics. The truth is, when one is in extreme subconscious dominate state of mind they try very hard to do things and they perhaps never really accomplish it because they get half way into a point they are making and then their mind says, maybe the other way is right. So ones in extreme nirvana nearly have to be watched over. They are "innocent lambs" mindfully. They are not going to hurt a fly because they have much effort just with the thought aspect of living. I guess one might say the Lama comes off as being very funny and one who laughs a lot. He is laughing at the fact he is the spokesman for the movement to free Tibet and at the same time talks about how he has no trouble with china occupying Tibet. That is very funny. There is much to laugh about. That is the best mindset one can ever reach considering they are on a small dot in the middle of an infinite universe and no matter what they do, it probably does not really even matter.

I am unable to mentally make a case that anyone is good or bad. I can fake it for about 1 minute. Let's take a bank robber. He stole 10 million dollars and society says he is evil and bad and a thief. Well I see a human being who is doing the best they can to keep up with the status ranking in society of "One needs money to be important." So then one has to say "Well that is the name of the game and you have to play by the rules of the game." Then I would suggest, "Who made up this game and what gave them the right to make up that money game and then tell everyone they have to play by the rules of that money game?" The truth is, the ones who have most of the money made up the money game and are now telling me, I have to play by the rules or I am evil. So my answer would be "I do not have to play by any rules ever because someone said I am free to think and speak as I see fit to achieve what I perceive is a purpose in life." So now I have just negated their mind control game. Let them have their money. That's all they are is money. They are unable to function without money because it runs in their veins. That does not mean I have to buy into their perception that money is important. It is nearly impossible to escape the clutches of the money game but one can mindfully easily escape it. Do not knock yourself out would be a good way to look at it. Avoid playing by the rules and what that mean is, if you feel like knocking yourself out for money do it and if you do not, do not do it. Do not buy into this morals standard. You have your set of morals to live by and to answer to because you cannot live up to the standards of everyone else's morals. There are simply too many morals others suggest. I do not detect any corporations following the law. All the Corporations cheat like hell at everything. I detect all the law enforcement agencies cheat like hell at everything. I detect all the governments cheat like hell at everything. I am uncertain who exactly is telling you they are not cheating like hell, but I am certain they all are cheating like hell. That is human nature or that is the nature of creatures. The lama said clearly I am hesitant to tell the youth the middle way is the way. That is right. This world is full of sharks and they will eat you alive if they detect weakness. All is fair in love and war and civilization is love and war. Love of money and wars to get more money. So simply do not knock yourself out attempting to follow all the rules in a shark tank because you will just eaten by the sharks. Use your mind and think a little. Be creative and find infinite loopholes. All the corporations do. This is how many people are on earth in general. 07/01/09   6,790,062,216.

Is that too many or too few? It appears that we have quite a few people on earth in contrast to how many were on earth 2000 years ago. One might suggest there are a few more today than there was 2000 years ago. One might suggest there is an upward trend happening.

Now, one can do some simple math because that is about all I am capable of is very simple math.

The surface of our planet measures 197,060,800 square miles.

So based on my advanced math skills there is 1 person per 3 squares miles of earth's surface. That is perhaps rather crowded. I am not sure, I divided the population by the earth's surface and got 3. Something. Yeah so you can only go about 3 miles before you start seeing other people. Wait, what that really means is there are 3 people per square mile. So you cannot go any square miles before you see 2 people. It's certainly one of those 2 options. That is dangerous because people have motivations only they know. People do not wear their motivations of their sleeves. We would never elect anybody to be our leader if they wore their motivations on their sleeves. It would never, ever, ever, ever happen. No one would like to know what the leaders main motivation is. Its along the lines of "lie like hell to get elected into power". That's the problem with a leader is they are telling everyone by running for election they want power and then people elect them and the leader perceives it is okay to seek more power. Now this is bad enough if the scientists didn't go around telling us we are lemur monkeys. I simply do not trust lemur monkeys. I do not care if they are a leader or just a normal lemur monkey, I am cautious of them because they are unpredictable because I am uncertain what their TRUE FACE is.

I can attempt to tell you what my true face is. Embarrass myself on a world stage by writing these stupid books in order to condition myself away from fear of embarrassment. That is my purpose, self help. That is a nice way of saying I screwed up. Something happened to my mind and it convinced me I should write books and say stupid things in them and maybe someone will read one and say "You are so stupid." And then I will be able to accept that comment and then something in my mind will happen further. That is where I am at this stage since the accident. My first book as I recall was much more "sane" , my last book was a nightmare, this book is an abomination but somehow my mind is saying, "Good work". I am uncertain how to escape that. I try to stay grounded by reminding myself I sat in my room in depression for 10 plus years and did not really do anything outside of hurt myself and now I write lots of books but I still sit in that room. I cannot even tell if that is really positive change. It perhaps is no change at all. I would like to be able to say I feel important because I can pay a company to publish my books, but I feel no satisfaction or sense of accomplishment from publishing my books. I perceive I am seeking to "feel" again. I laugh about things more now. I do not take anything very seriously for very long. There is a concept about "live a little". I perceive that is not so much about get all these plans and go on all these vacations and relax, it is more about do what you want to do. Do what you wanted to do when you were a child. That is what you want to do. One hears people say "This is what I wanted to do all my life." I recall I wanted to be an archeologist when I was a child, or scientists. I got a microscope when I was young and I just could sit there for hours and look into that eye piece. Maybe this is bad to just want to sit there and ponder what one is seeing. Maybe one has to avoid just sitting there all their life pondering what they are looking at. But I submit that, to me at the time was interesting. I do not really know what the hell I was looking at, so carpet fibers or ants or whatever. I was not trying to solve a problem I was more just trying to figure out what on earth is this thing in this lens. And then everything kind of went black. People started saying "You have to do this." And "You better do this." But my mind was still there asking "What the hell is this under this lens." I understand I started making concessions. To be right up front, I started listening to the voices coming from everyone around me instead of listening to voice in my head. So I blew it. I failed. No one ever wrote a law that said "You have to listen to your own intuition over everything else no matter what into infinity." So I got lost. I forgot that I am here for my purpose. I forgot that I am not here to give other's purpose because they are here for their own purpose.

Since I have to talk about something I will go a bit out of context. I will discuss something that will perhaps make you think a little.

"Black Hawk or Black Sparrow Hawk (Sauk Makataimeshekiakiak (Mahkate:wi-meši-ke:hke:hkwa), "be a large black hawk") (Spring 1767 – October 3, 1838) was a leader and warrior of the Sauk American Indian tribe in what is now the United States. Although he had inherited an important historic medicine bundle, he was not a hereditary civil chief of the Sauk, but was an appointed war chief. He was generally known in English as Black Hawk."WIKIPEDIA.COM

A black hawk can fly to heights where no one can see him. Perhaps you catch my drift. I am quite certain most people in America are perhaps not very interested in this person Black Hawk. One might suggest Black Hawk was somewhat overlooked in American history based on the fact he was just an Indian. Perhaps the ironic thing is long after the average American is gone and forgotten about Black Hawk will still be remembered. Long after the "popular" people have been forgotten about, people will still be talking about Black Hawk. That is a great truth. It is all simply right there in his description. Perhaps it is because his name was Black Hawk. Hawks are not traditionally black. Black is symbolic color because black is the result of all colors mixed together, so black is in fact all colors. I recall in the Lama interview the reporter asked Lama if he was enlightened and Lama said "No." and then the reporter asked "Are you a God?" and Lama said "No I have memory problems and I cannot see well." I am not sure if you get that extreme humor in that but that is hilarious.

I recall I write in one of my other books "I am not God but I may be delusional." I guess one would call that humility or being meek. I will suggest I am not in nirvana even though I have slight sense of time and I am able to understand anything I read, clearly, so that you will understand I am meek and mild. That's the strange thing about it. I submit I may come across as very angry and not make a lick of sense about anything I say in any of books. I am open minded enough to submit maybe nothing I say is right or truth or proper. It is simply hard for me to tell since I cannot even remember what my previous books are about except I understand the 'spirit" of them, and my opinions about things tend to change like the wind. I would not make a good judge of character. I would not be able to put anyone in prison. I would not make a good prison warden because I would let them all out based on some technicality. So in that respect I am simply unable to function in society because for example if I took a job as a salesman I would persuade the customer they should go buy these products from the wholesaler to get a better deal. I keep uploading all my books to download sites and I keep telling readers of my books they can freely copy my books and steal anything I write in them because I will never enforce the copyright I have on my books. I am rather self defeatist because of the subconscious dominate aspect. I perceive I am. I perceive others perceive I am. That is why I suggest I screwed up. As a result of my selfish attempts to harm myself I have been thrown into this mental state of inability to function in a competitive way according to the "norms" of society. If I was in competition I would probably at least have someone proof read my books before I publish them. I cannot proof read my books because I see everything is just fine with them. It is difficult to explain outside of, I go to edit my books and have this "Correct the mistakes" attitude and I "see" the "whole" and it all looks good to me. It is simply impossible it could all be good. So mentally I am extremely biased in my favor. I should win every medal in literature if you asked me but that is a delusion in my head. My books are the worst books ever written in the history of the universe and to top it off I really do not care at all if they are, so what. From my perspective it probably does not matter a hill of beans. I get many laughs out of my books and then I forget about it and start another book. I think that is the main purpose for me writing the books is to look at how silly I am and laugh at that, then publish it and laugh at the fact I actually publish this nightmare called a book. I just make up titles and then I color in certain words in the titles to make inside jokes and I perceive no one even gets the inside jokes but me. So in fact it is natures inside joke. Only I am in on the inside joke, no one else is. I attempt to suggest I unlocked subconscious then some people say no that is right brain dominate, then others say , no that is your sixth sense and then others say, no that is nirvana and then others say, no that is the spirit of unnamable, and then I just say, "I unlocked my subconscious" because I do not really have the slightest clue what happened to me. I am not depressed anymore and I am laughing much more now and my perception has changed but I can't go much further than that. I simply do not know. So I recall I suggested in my last book perhaps my mind snapped. One might suggest my mind snapped out of it or one might suggest my mind snapped completely. Do not ask me because I will perhaps suggest I am a lemur monkey. I do submit women do not like to be called lemur monkeys so you should be very cautious about telling a great truth like that to them. That is my first commandment. So, Thou shall not call women lemur monkeys. I perceive the women and the men can equally see wisdom in that commandment. So, now I have achieved a degree of wisdom and perhaps life will become much easier for me now.

"A 51-year-old man was in a Kansas jail Monday, held on suspicion of first-degree murder in the killing of a physician whose women's clinic frequently took center stage in the debate over abortion, authorities said." CNN.COM

"Abdulhakim Mujahid Muhammad -- a 24-year-old Little Rock resident formerly known as Carlos Bledsoe -- faces a first-degree murder charge and 15 counts of engaging in a terrorist act" CNN. COM

So this is proof we are in a tyranny. One person killed another person. The other person killed a person.

So both men killed 1 person each. Both are charged with 1st degree murder but the other is charged with 1st degree murder and 15 counts of terrorism. One person killed a doctor the other person killed a soldier at a recruiting center. A doctor is just a citizen. A soldier is the arm of the government. The problem is, the government assumes it is not expendable and it assumes the citizens are expendable. So the government has an identity crisis. See if the citizen attacks the government they are deemed a terrorist and if that same person attacks another citizen they are deemed just a murderer. No matter what anyone suggests, both these people acted for political and religious reasons. One killed a doctor for political and religious reasons and one killed a soldier for political and religious reasons, so it is not logical one should be deemed a terrorist and the other deemed just a murderer, unless the government is sending the people a little message along the lines of "do not question us or you will be locked up forever." That quite an effective fear tactic from one who is so experienced at extortion and one who is so adept at using terroristic threats to manipulate money out of the people.

So a citizen is considered cannon fodder in contrast to the government or an arm of the government because the government desperately wants to hold onto its tyrannical grip because, the government is aware it is not relevant to the survival of the land of the free. It is simply not in the plan to survive for any great length of time. The government is expendable at the citizen's slightest whim. Because of this the government has to be very well armed, and it uses the citizen's money to become well armed, so it can kill the citizens with weapons, the citizens bought for the government if the citizens try to abolish the government. It is a very sadistic affair to say the least. The truth is the government is aware everyone is afraid of it so it walks all over them. So once the government has everyone afraid it just does whatever the hell it wants because it understands, it is dealing with a bunch of spineless cowards. That is the truth and it is irrelevant if you do not want to subscribe to that truth. If you get in the governments way they will "love" you and make it look like you are a terrorist. I am counting on them "love"ing me so I entice them because I am what is known as the bait. If they bite on me the one who is holding the pole is going to set the hook on them. I wonder if you understand what that means. Perhaps you have assumed I write infinite books for money. One might suggest once one understands their time is up they throw caution to the wind. I mean once one has become subconscious dominate they lose sense of time and also a capacity for fear as in expected fear or expect consequences so they speak their mind because they are unable to give a dam what anyone thinks. One might suggest it is quite liberating, hint. I was born in the land of the free the government was allowed to exist because of the people and it can be abolished by the people as easily, so the government has serious denial problems at this stage of the game. The "tyrant" assumes everyone has fear because it has fear. One might suggest the governments greatest fear tactic makes me laugh. Perhaps the "tyrant" is not aware the noose is already around its neck. Perhaps that is best, because when the lever is pulled it is going to hurt like a son of a bitch. One might suggest the "tyrant" will not be a tyrant very much longer from the way I see it. When the carpetbaggers own the government and in turn start taking people's homes because the people cannot pay the carpetbaggers fee, there is only one thing left to do, and that is start filleting some fish for the fire. Perhaps the carpetbaggers assume their suggestions of morals are bought by everyone. One might suggest my morals are infinitely exceeded by the blood on my hands. My mouth is black with sticky knives. http://www.youtube.com/watch?v=soGiveUulT4 6/1/2009 10:35:42 PM. I blame it on the rain. I am doomed.

11:36:46 PM - I will put this as plain as I can. I had had an aversion to words and an inability to spell words since the accident and have problems arranging words or my ability to arrange words has been drastically altered since the accident. I perceive words are something more than words. They are some sort of "incantation" mechanism. I won't go any further than that at this time. I will go to sleep now because I understand what that means.11:39:28 PM

6/2/2009 6:05:09 AM - You may perceive I am strange or messed up but in reality, the reason I am uninhibited about what I say is because I went "to the extreme" in unlocking subconscious or to the extreme in right brain dominate. What I mean is, I am not self conscious or embarrassed or have some ulterior motivation like many. Many will say things with an understood outcome in mind. One will sugar coat their words in order to gain a desired effect or response. In my state of mind I am unable to pander to that type of trickery. I am unable to determine why I should write books that people will like and accept, would be a good way to look at it.

Consider a child in line at a supermarket. The child tells the parent in a loud tone "Mom why is that person in front of us so fat." The parent, just about faints from the child's comments but the child may laugh. Now consider the Lama. He is 70 years old and pretty much makes one joke after another. If you watch him he laughs in general very often. This is a person who has few worries. They would be considered "jolly". I perceive I am "jolly" but I perceive many who may read my books are that parent in the super market that is very self conscious.

Self conscious is a symptom of strong emotions. Some may be very concerned about how they look and become depressed if they do not "look" physically proper based on their perspective of what is proper. That is perhaps a rather dangerous state of mind to be in. One might suggest it is a state of mind where one is a slave to what others think about them. Along the line of, "You look a certain way and talk a certain way or you will be an outcast." That is quite a dangerous mindset to have. That mindset is exactly why people who lose their job do very drastic things as a result. That is exactly why people will do drastic things to "fit in" with their peers. People tend to become censors of their own thoughts based on their perceived understood acceptance in their "peer group."

This is for one reason only. Fear of being an outcast or being ostracized. So people will say things so they will not be disliked, hated, not accepted or detested and that means people will say things so they will be popular. So that means there are many people living their life attempting to fit in to this mentally perceived "popularity contest". Life is certainly not a popularity contest.6:25:27 AM

"There is also a psychoanalytical interpretation of Moses' life, put forward by Sigmund Freud in his last book, Moses and Monotheism, in 1937. Freud postulated that Moses was an Egyptian nobleman who adhered to the monotheism of Akhenaten. Following a theory proposed by a contemporary biblical critic, Freud, a committed atheist, believed that Moses was murdered in the

wilderness, producing a collective sense of patricidal guilt that has been at the heart of Judaism ever since. "Judaism had been a religion of the father, Christianity became a religion of the son", he wrote." WIKIPEDIA.COM

This is perhaps a great truth. Of course Moses was just a human being. Of course Moses was perhaps certainly murdered just as Jesus was murdered, just as Mohammed was murdered for the simple reason they were different. It is nonsense to suggest they were murdered for their religious beliefs.

So the ones who label their self as "Jewish" "loved" Moses , were blessed and got another chance with Jesus and "loved" him not because they are "Jewish" but because the left brain sense of time beings are violent as hell and "love" anyone who is different. You may be asking "Oh why do people "love" these wise beings author of many poor books?" The answer is simply **"Left-brain dominated people may find their thought processes vague and difficult to follow, for they are quite opposite in the way they think."** The "sane" kill anything that is different, that is why they are insane.

I am certainly not blaming any "race" of people, it is simply the nature for beings with a sense of time to act out violently and physically violently in general. It is their nature to just "love" everything they do not like because they do not have the brain function to verbally work things out. Do not assume you will ever get me to speak in public. Do not assume you will ever see my picture. Do not assume all the money in the universe would convince to meet with you. I welcome any being to adjust my writings and tone them down so they will please others, but they better be dam sure there is no after life first because if there is, they would be better off tying a stone around their neck and throwing their self into the sea.

It is nonsense to suggest some "evil" people murdered them. It is nonsense to suggest they were murdered by anything but the people they were different from. What this means is:

"People who rely more heavily on the right half of their brain tend to be more imaginative and intuitive.

They see things as a whole and are interested in patterns, shapes and sizes. The right brain is associated with artistic ability like singing, painting, writing poetry, etc. **Left-brain dominated people may find their thought processes vague and difficult to follow, for they are quite opposite in the way they think."**

http://www.indiaparenting.com/raisingchild/data/raisingchild060.shtml

So these beings became extreme right brain dominate and lost their sense of time, and were saying things "Quite the opposite" and "difficult to follow" in relation to ones with Left Brain dominance. So the ones with a strong sense of time and the ones who have a strong sense of hunger butchered Moses, Jesus and Mohammed. Any other suggestion outside of that fact is nonsense. People butcher people who are different than they are. That is a fact of life into infinity. But the clarification of that is this. Extreme right brain dominate people tend to be not so physically violent because they are so extremely cerebral or intelligent or have brain function. So the catch is, they tend to get butchered by the Left brain dominate people because the left brain dominate people or the ones with a strong sense of time, are not intelligent or cerebral so they resort to physical violence. So if you want to figure out who killed these great beings think to yourself if you have a strong sense of time and you have strong hunger or have a strong sense of hunger and you will understand you killed them. Let me clarify that, YOU BUTCHERED THEM. Avoid attempting to question what I understand because you are unable to understand what I understand, by accident.

So this is all in relation to the Salem Witch trials. There were certainly people who knew these "witches" and understood they were not witches but perhaps different. They understood they were just different people, maybe people that were **"quite opposite in the way they think."** and had **"thought processes vague and difficult to follow".** So these "authority" figures determined they must be witches because they are opposite of what we think and they are vague and hard to understand. So the reality is, the "authority " figure namely this Cotton fellow determined if they are not like him they should be killed. So a person who understood these "witches" were not witches but just different would not have spoken up and said anything because they in turn might be deemed "witches". So they were afraid to say anything to the "authority figure" for their own safety. This is in direct relation to Germany during World War 2. Certainly there were Germans who had Jewish friends they liked but were afraid to "not turn them in" because they feared for their own safety. So they did what they did not want to do because they did not want to become an outcast. They gave in to peer pressure. This is not some rare thing. This is the way of the ones with left brain thinking. They huddle in packs because they are unable to think for their self any longer. If you have a strong sense of time I just said you like to hang in packs because you no longer can think for yourself. I am no longer afraid of you with the understanding you killed and butchered many people because they were different than you. So one might suggest you have some infinite paybacks headed your way.

Mohammed was aware of these beings before him that were butchered and this is why we went the physical route. He is wise. Cutting off the head denotes the brain is the problem. There is a distinct disconnect. **"quite opposite in the way they think."** And **"thought processes vague and difficult to follow".** You perceive ones with subconscious dominate minds are insane and they perceive you are insane. The problem is, the ones with subconscious dominate minds are not insane, they are far less delusional and not hallucinating as much as the ones with a strong sense of time. So they are "right"eous or right brained or on the "right hand side" in their cause. They use the intelligent aspect of the mind and they are dealing with people who are essentially mentally retarded in comparison to them. But it is everyone's choice to use the intelligent aspect of the mind and achieve it with mental conditioning techniques or remain retarded. The problem with that is, a law called Baker Act. This denotes when a person I deemed a threat to their self or others they get locked up. So now that I have woken up, I deem anyone with a strong sense of time and a strong sense of hunger a threat to their self and to others and they should be locked up. There is no argument they are a threat to their self and to others because they have far too many hallucinations and delusions which is proven by the fact they have a strong sense of time and a strong sense of hunger and they pee like a frog when they get scared or nervous. There is no argument. There is no need for experiments, that is the factual truth and one of the greatest truths in the universe. I woke up to that truth by accident but it none the less is a great truth. I am no longer ignorant to that great truth. Does that great truth eat you alive? Perhaps you have to go pee like a frog now. Maybe you should take some drugs so you so won't be so stressed out, since you are unable to argue with that great truth no matter how hard you try. Do you still perceive I am a loser because I can't spell cat properly? Are you a little upset that I figured it all out and you will never figure it all out on your own, with your safety and security and isolation and narrow-mindedness? You a little upset a 30 time suicide loser is far beyond your ability to understand? All you can say to yourself is "This guy is totally insane even though he writes books faster than the speed of light and explains stuff no human being has ever explained in the history of mankind."

Don't you get upset, because you will piss all over yourself like a little frog pisses when it is picked up. I do not perceive your college degree is worth the paper it is printed on at this stage of reality I am certain you wish it was.

This concept of infidel denotes ones with a strong sense of time or ones who have strong sense of hunger, period. He cut their heads off because he was aware they butcher anyone that is different than they are in relation to **"quite opposite in the way they think."** And **"thought processes vague and difficult to follow".** So do not tell me about your morals and your laws. I prefer to follow his route because I understand the ones with no sense of time are up against about 6 billion idiots who resort to physical violence as a first resort in dealing with anyone that is different than them, or thinks different than them. So these left brainers have slight brain function and thus scare the hell out of me and thus I shoot on sight. I do not hesitate I seal fate. I will not be hung on the cross of the insane left brainers without taking all of them with me in the process. Ones who speak of right and wrong are fools. Right and wrong in my book are ones with sense of time, are the devil, and evil, and Satan and deserve no quarter, period. They shall get no quarter. I am not capable of these things called mercy and compassion considering what I understand since the accident. I woke up to the fact I live in an insane asylum. If you want a fight I am right here. I am not running. I am not hiding. I am not afraid of an insane being because I will outsmart them and strangle them with their own weapon.

 My purpose is obliteration not cooperation. Perhaps we have come to an understanding. I just assume everyone has a strong sense of time and hunger, that way I can just "swing my sword freely" and without hesitation. Do you perceive I stutter? I won't be preaching peace and love this time around. You are going to need a bigger boat. You do not even have the foggiest idea what this accident means I am. I am not going to insult myself by telling you.

This song sums up every sentence I will ever write for the rest of eternity. Do not listen to it because it is a curse upon you.

http://www.youtube.com/watch?v=MEfmZOhTJvk

I don't make friends with what I own. It won't hurt as bad as long as you keep telling yourself everything is going to be ok. You are equals among those who are like you, but it goes no further than that.

I will go ahead and translate some quotes so you will think everything I say is just subconscious conditioning comments. The ease in which I can manipulate you is laughable.

 Ignorance is truly bliss but it will cost you everything. Perhaps you have already figured out I am raising my army. Perhaps if you are not for me I will direct them to understand you are against me. Punch that into your calculator of safety. I am not going anywhere but your perhaps will be, much sooner than you think. I will sum this up swiftly.

Moses spoke of an adversary. That adversary is the left brainers or the ones with a strong sense of time and strong sense of hunger and thus physical based or ones who pray to the golden calf.

Jesus spoke of the darkness. That darkness is the left brainers or the ones with a strong sense of time and hunger.

Mohammed spoke of the infidels. The infidels are the ones with a strong sense of time or strong sense of hunger.

Buddha spoke of the sane. The Sane are the ones with a strong sense of time and hunger.

Now you understand why you "loved" them all because you are darkness the adversary the devil and the sane. They are better off abolished because they simply know not what they do. It is just the way it is. This is just a fantastic world.

I told you subconscious is a bit haughty. Imagine if Washington believed in peace, love, happiness and safety.

My motto is Slaughter everything with my words and then condition away from embarrassment.

Perhaps you are starting to grasp I am not exactly at a point of being compassionate at this moment in reality since the accident. One might suggest my patience is infinitely thin considering what I understand about you. I allowed you to walk over me once, that is why I will not be passing over you. If you have the capability of fear, right about now you should be infinitely afraid. Do not ask me why, I just type what my fingers suggest.

The thing about relativity is, you perceive I have to tolerate you and I perceive I do not, and we are both right. One might suggest if you want to understand everything, I understand you are going to have to accept some mental punishment because I understand what I understand by suffering far more mental punishment. Ignorance is free; wisdom costs.

Now back to reality. I literally fight battles in my mind 24 hours a day since the accident. That is a fact. It is harsh on a person in "Nirvana" but it is strictly cerebral. The last I checked I sit in my room and write books and have no desire to leave the house let alone take some physical action. It's all in my mind to the extreme. But that leaves some things to ponder.

If we are in fact lemur monkeys, then I am just a monkey that accidentally went extreme right brain or subconscious dominate and have much to talk about now. If we are in fact spiritual beings and there is a spiritual aspect to reality, then I am the second coming and it is all going to be over with soon. I do not know. I tend to perceive I am a lemur monkey but I know nothing for a fact. That is simply a symptom of how extreme of a subconscious state I am in. My opinions change like the wind. That is a fact. I do not encourage any physical violence and that is my weakness. That is a flaw. One has to be able to kick some ass or they will be walked over. That is fact. So this whole situation I find myself in is a great mystery. I do not know exactly what this accident means but I have spoken to enough beings in Nirvana to understand they are having second doubts about many things in relation to the existence of Unnamable. It is perhaps not so cut and dry for them after all. I am in a bubble so do not assume I can tell exactly why this happened to me. All I am aware of is, I am pumping out books because my bleeding fingers suggest I should. I perceive I am just a messenger going with the flow and I am unable to clarify that. I attempt to stick with the subconscious story because the alternative story is perhaps not the best news for ones with a sense of time. I understand I have no fear one way or the other, so I invite the chips to fall where they may. I speak with enough beings in nirvana to understand I tend to correct their misunderstandings and they tend to pick their mouth up off the floor while trying to figure out who the hell I am. They are certainly convinced I must be a learned monk of the highest order and when I suggest I am just a failed suicide they get rather nervous. I am open minded about the whole affair and I have no other choice. One person always get's it. I write infinite books because I understand one always will understand them. A great truth is we are perfect, but many do not know it, and they often show it.

I will attempt to clarify some opposites in relation to left brain and right brain or conscious dominate and subconscious dominate people.

LEFT BRAIN – Conscious Emotional – "Sane" – Infidel – Darkness – Vipers -Adversary Characteristics

Strong sense of time

Strong sense of hunger

Strong sense of daily aches and pains or fatigue

Strong sense of taste and smell.

Ability to be frightened by the dark or "scary" situations easily

Rise in blood pressure when nervous and ability to be nervous

Has very rigid schedules and everything is planned out to the minute

Very control orientated

Does not get along well with others who do not see their point of view or agree with their beliefs

Very concerned with not looking foolish or being embarrassed

Very dedicated to keeping their beliefs stagnate and never changing their opinion or making any contradictory statements.

Scared and frightened about everything including their own thoughts

Very solid short term memory and very weak long term memory

Inability to concentrate for more than an hour at a time

Easily distracted; very poor concentration span

Very entertainment orientated; always looking for fun and pleasure and relaxation

Clings to safety and known situations and fears unknown situations or new situations

Acts out their anger and frustration on the physical stage; physically hurtful to their self and others

Has difficulty admitting they are wrong

Mindfully focused on past events or future expectations

Afraid of spiders or snakes or cemeteries at night

Afraid of being an outcast, afraid to be all alone, afraid to be rejected by their peers

Ability to hold long term grudges

Inability to work things out with words and resorts to physical violence

Inability to admit they are insane

Very materialistically focused

Now I will clarify all of these because I understand who I am dealing with.

Strong sense of time: Always in a rush. Stressed out and saying " There is not enough time in the day." Or "I do not have time." Someone who cannot stay in place for more than a few minutes. Someone who is restless and nervous, and rushed, and has no patience at all in contrast to one with slight sense of time. Many recreational drugs such as pot smoking or drinking makes ones sense of time diminish. This is because these drugs reduce the emotions and one becomes subconscious dominate or right brain dominate to a degree while the drugs lasts. This also happens when one is in love. They can spend a long time with one they love and time does not seem to past as fast. This is a sense of wonder or amazement that silences the sense of time but this is short lived and then they will revert back to strong sense of time after the event or the drug wears off. This is also true with most recreational drugs and pain medicines and psychological prescription drugs; the person reverts to subconscious dominate mind and they feel "free" or "happy" and then when the drugs wears off they "come down" back to emotional conscious state of mind/ left brain so they need more drugs to get back to that "free" state of mind or subconscious state of mind. This leads to drug abuse. So the desire to feel the subconscious aspect is proper but they can never stay at that state with drugs because it is only temporary, so emotional conditioning is required to achieve "nirvana" / subconscious dominate state of mind permanently.

Someone who just rushes to get somewhere and then rushes to go somewhere else are emotional wrecks. Strong sense of hunger: Someone who gets weak physically and mentally when they haven't eaten in 12 hours. Anyone who eats more than 2 meals a day. Anyone who has strong cravings for any type of food. Anyone who dislikes some food and loves other food.

Strong sense of daily aches and pains or fatigue: Anyone who needs to stretch after a few hours of sitting in one place. Anyone who gets tired from concentrating for more than a few hours.

Strong sense of taste and smell: Anyone with the ability to have strong after taste. Ones who drink strong liquor after a the first few shots their taste in greatly decreased. This is because the alcohol makes them go to a subconscious state of mind or silences the emotions and thus the sense of taste is decreased as well as the sense of time. This is right brain characteristics.

I will attempt to allow you to put yourself in my frame of mind for a moment so you can attempt to understand the rage in my words. Imagine that every day you wake up and you see someone kicking a little puppy and beating it mercilessly and you are unable to stop it and you are unable to call someone who can stop it. Then multiply that by a billion and make it a billion puppies being beaten like that with the understanding you cannot stop it , you cannot say anything to stop it and you cannot do anything to stop it. Now imagine how you would feel as far as anger, then you have a slight understanding of how I feel on a daily basis. That is what you will feel if you go subconscious dominate to an extreme. So you should think very carefully before you decide to go subconscious dominate using the emotional conditioning techniques because it is not a matter of whether they work or whether you can do it, it is a matter of you cannot go back once you achieve it, and if you cannot take much mental anguish you will destroy yourself swiftly.

Fear:

I recall I made a pact in my second book I was going to tell the truth as I perceive it and allow the chips to fall where they may. I do not perceive people need to have their hand held. If a person cannot handle the truth, that is their emotional problem, and none of my concern.

Ponder this comment:

"It should be understood that the Buddha did not preach all that he knew. On one occasion while the Buddha was passing through a forest he took a handful of leaves and said: "O bhikkhus, what I have taught is comparable to the leaves in my hand. What I have not taught is comparable to the amount of leaves in the forest."

21

One might suggest that Buddha was suggesting he did not know everything. So this comment would be considered humble. The reality is, Buddha said, what I can teach you is comparable to the leaves in the forest so do not get haughty and think what I have taught you is much. This is because Buddha reached extreme subconscious dominate state the hard way or the proper way. He reached it the only way any of the great beings reached it. It was earned accidentally by facing death when there was no need to face death. He nearly starved to death and he did not have to. He did not have to put himself in a position of dying and he could very well have died but he got lucky and was "found by a little girl just in time." From that point on he achieved extreme subconscious but it took a while to kick in.

I recall it took about 6 months perhaps before I got the "ah ha" sensation after the final suicide attempt. You cannot do that. You cannot attempt that because you perhaps will accomplish suicide. It is just too risky. You have to want to die when there is no reason to die and then you have to get lucky in your attempt to die and fail at it but do it in earnest so your mind believes you're serious about it. That is the only possible way to go to the extreme of subconscious dominate and that is exactly why Buddha said, the middle way, because he did not want there to be many people going around trying to kill their self and hoping they would fail but they would probably not fail, they would die. He expressly suggested physical self harm was not the path. That is right. You are not going to reach extreme subconscious dominate but you can easily reach no sense of time and thus subconscious dominate state of mind.

Buddha was the teacher, Jesus was the teacher, Moses was the teacher, Mohammed was the teacher. They taught so they were not teachable. People sought out them for knowledge and wisdom it was not the other way around. They had "disciples" who wanted to learn more from them. So these beings where the originals. They were the Alphas. Everything radiated out from them. Without them there are no "religions".

I am not so certain you should want to be subconscious dominate. I can make the argument the world will be less physically violent and there will be far fewer wars and murders but I can also make the case the mental torment one will suffer because of the extreme understanding or clarity will make up for that. You can assume Lama has a peaceful life and all fine and dandy but he simply puts on a good show in front of the cameras. It is mentally difficult for a human being to be aware of so much. It is mentally painful. Every time I look at the news and see people bragging about how many "enemies" they killed it rips me apart and I hate the universe. I am not ashamed to admit or to submit that is reality for me now. I cannot escape from that understanding because I am no longer physically able to harm myself in a deliberate fashion outside of smoking cigarettes which I understand I may never be able to quit because I have no desire to quit and I have no concept of them harming me because I can make a very good case that the cigarette might be my only way to get away from this clarity. I mean if I get cancer and die that is one solution to get away from this clarity. I was smoking when this accident happened and now I am stuck with it. I am certain I could just stop smoking and not have any bad side effects but I don't because then I understand I will live longer. That is a symptom of how much mental suffering this extreme clarity causes me, personally. It just hurts. I cannot turn it off. I cannot drink lots of drugs and make it dissipate. I cannot take psychological drugs and make it go away. I am stuck here. I am not about to start telling people they should come here to this place I am at. I would be far more evil if I suggested one should come here to be a better person. I am on the fence about that. I submit I simply do not know if this is better or worse. I am fighting the same battles but I tend to get my ass kicked much more in the world of cerebral thinking than I did in the craving and desire world of physical thinking. I also submit perhaps I will progress from this dark spot I am in, but I am aware the more time that passes the greater the clarity and the more mental suffering is experienced.

I recall in my first book I have no mental suffering and now I am at a point it seems to be all mental suffering. I can hardly tell what is wisdom and what is anguish. I perceive I am all rage at this stage since the accident. I just keep typing into infinity and harming myself mentally with each keystroke. That is where I am at.

I forget what it is like to look at a religion and say "that is evil because it is not my religion." I forget what it is like to hate people my country suggests are the enemy. So I hate myself and I ruin all my books and I cuss and fight and hate myself because I messed up in my last suicide attempt because I cannot do anything right. This is exactly why Buddha suggested the middle way. He did not want anyone to go to the extreme he went to because it perhaps is not mentally as peaceful as it appears, in fact it is mentally as close to gnashing of teeth as one can get.

Perhaps my books are a warning to not seek too much clarity. Perhaps my books are a warning to ones who contemplate suicide that they might mess up and end up in far more anguish than any afterlife situation can afford them. Of course I submit I am just having an off day. Something is troubling me and I am aware of it, but I am unable to pinpoint exactly what it is. Perhaps a combination of things and perhaps it is because the mental progression is making me go further and further into this state of mind and I am having some unwanted mental reactions in my attempts to slow the progression down. I attempt to go into silence and I am unable to. I attempt to stop writing and I end up writing more. I ponder what kind of drugs or medication I could take to stop this, and then I swing back to the reality I am just mentally adjusting and have moments of doubt just like I did early on. I recall the whole reason I went to the neurologist at the 2 month stage was because I had one of these moments of doubt and decided to see if I could find out why I was like this and that didn't exactly work out as I planned. I perceive I am still in doubt about this. I am six books into this writing and I am still attempting to suggest I am just fine and dandy mentally speaking but in reality I am in such an extreme mental progression still I am being ripped apart every single day and I am helpless to stop it or slow it down even for a moment.

6/3/2009 5:02:17 AM

Dogs bark madly when they detect an unknown presence.

"President ….. reiterated that Iran may have some right to nuclear energy". Our Leader should be cautious in his actions because there are certain zealots who are not pleased with him going against their thoughts and these zealots tend to perceive their way is the only way. These zealots will physically harm others if they feel one's do not fit into their narrow minded view of reality. These zealots will physically harm others for a grain of sand they perceive the universe made for them, and them alone. These zealots are mindfully trapped in an isolation chamber and are unable to break free so they are vipers and their venom acts swiftly. The zealots are unable to see anything in the keyhole but their self. Only a wise being accepts you when your opinion is against their own opinion. A lion remembers the prey that gave a good chase. Your enemy motivates you to breathe and ponder. Your enemy gives you something to talk about with your friends. If you speak about your enemy it is because you respect them; if you speak often about them it is because you are in love with them. Some love their enemy more than they love their self. Some will expend more energy to harm their perceived enemy than to assist their own children. One who has enemies spend their life plotting against them and are thus controlled by that enemy. When one understands they are their only enemy, they will have a lifetime of plots to consider, to defeat him. Love you enemy like yourself because your self is your only enemy. One is very unsafe when they perceive they are safe; one is very safe when they understand they will never be safe. Once you face the final illusion you will no longer be fooled by all of the illusions that lead up to it. I am pleased with that last one. You are allowed to quote that last one. I do not perceive any adversaries therefore I have defeated them all. Your greatest enemy is yourself and your worst enemy is your inability to understand that. The enemies in your mind mock your physical attacks on them. I am not graceful but I make up for it inability to understand what grace is. It is humbling to understand the universe does not acknowledge you. All physical wars are the result of a craving or desire; all mental wars are the result of a question or pondering. One who is truly free understands they are never allowed to tell another person what to do ever, because once they do they become a tyrant.

I will give a fair warning to everyone on the planet. I decided to write infinite books. I have to write about something. If you do not desire I write about you avoid ever getting in the headlines because I will write about you and discuss what I perceive is happening based on the headlines and I will not hesitate to do so.

Air-raid sirens sound across Israel as drill reaches peak...

This is what is known in one respect as a cry for help in psychology. On another level it is a way to condition their population to face the reality the government has already made up its mind to go to war.

On another level it is a way to let the ones know who it has decided to attack to get ready to be attacked. So it is rather delusional to announce to the world one is getting ready to attack because the one they attack will be able to prepare properly. The deeper meaning is, there is a little guy who is trying to make an impact in an ocean where they understand they are not very important. I perceive this country will certainly launch an attack on their perceived adversary. This is because they certainly have a death wish. They wish to kill their self. A country that attacks another country usually ends up killing their own countrymen. And the deeper meaning of that is, a country that sacrifices their own youth for tyrannical control goals is in fact a child abuser. The "elders" will not be fighting this war because they are too busy inciting the war. It is a very harsh realization to consider the adults lead the youth to their death and then the adults suggest it is righteous. The dead youth will not perceive it is very righteous but they are in a position of being looked at as an outcast if they do not submit to the direction of their elders. This is all in relation to the fact, one is not free if they steer others to do their bidding, they are simply a tyrant. This is a great truth on many levels. Traditionally there are not many youth manipulating adults because there is no comments about the adults should respect the youth. There is a bias where someone has determined the youth should respect the adults but the adults do not have to respect the youth, so the youth are being looked at as less than equal to the adults. The youth are expendable in contrast to the adults but the misunderstanding about that is, the youth are the future and the adults are on their way out. So the great truth is the youth are as valuable as the adults but the adults do not want to face that reality so the adults suggest the youth should fight their delusional wars for them. So the youth are reduced to cannon fodder and nothing more. Psychologically that is a symptom of mental illness in the adults. That is along the lines of a mother rabbit eating her babies. The adults subconscious understands the youth are there to replace them and the adults are uneasy with that reality. The youth are the first signs the adults are getting older and that suggests the adults time is nearly up. That is perhaps unsettling to some.

To look at the deeper psychology of the war that will occur is to face some facts that are perhaps unseen. This country has already decided to attack Iran. They have already decided to go it alone. They are already past the point of discussion of the situation because they "know". Once they "know" they give up on discussion. One can make an argument that Iran may perhaps have some proxy enticement towards Israel. That is a bias observation because every country has some form of proxy motivations towards other countries. That is simply the nature of labels that borders encourage. Borders encourage an "us against them" mentality. So the psychology involved in this has far less to do with religion and far more to do with projecting dominance. One who needs to project dominance understands subconsciously they are not dominate. It has gone to their head so to speak. They are a little fish in a big ocean and they would be perhaps wise to not attack the ocean because the ocean will swallow them up.

From Israel's point of view Iran is evil. From Iran's point of view Israel is evil. In reality neither country is evil because both countries simply want to live. Living is a struggle in itself. There is no need to create more struggle by physically attacking others. Iran has not invaded Israel. Iran has a right to do whatever they want on their own land. No other country has a right to even say anything about what another country does on their own land unless that country is a control freak. Everyone from a personal to a country scale should mind their own business and if they are attacked they deal with it but they do not anticipate attacks because they lead's to paranoia and insanity. Now Israel is going to sacrifice its own children to attack a country that has not attacked them, so they are the aggressor, and the big fish in the ocean do not like little fish that assume they are big fish.

This is complex and a bit deeper into the psychology of the situation. Russia is a big fish. Russia assists Iran with many weapons and the very nuclear facilities that Israel wants to bomb. So if Israel bombs those facilities they will have to swim through the anti-air missiles Russia has provided Iran. Russia is not evil they are in a working relationship with another country for peaceful purposes and do not wish their friend Iran to be harmed. That is proper. It is good if people work together. So now Israel will not be attacking Iran, Israel will be attacking indirectly of a big fish called Russia. This is why Israel has a death wish habit. Israel has been rebuked by America and America is a big fish. Israel has assumed it is a big fish. That is very dangerous because human beings are not bound by laws that are universally convenient. Translated that means, anything goes. One might prefer to assume there are norms and expectations that can be predicated but that is an illusion believed by ones who subscribe to safety and security.

Iran is a small fish and since Iran is Persian they are use to being attacked. They do not attack they are attacked. A small fish does not base its survival on attacking others they base their situation on the assumption they will be attacked. Now Israel is a small fish and it is basing it assumption on a big fish mentality, it is attacking. I understand perfectly the world sentiment will simply be if Israel attacks Iran the world will look at Israel as a terrorist. That is reality. People do not like bullies. Until a person does something physically they have done nothing. One can find many illusions that they can convince their self one has attacked them but it works both ways. I can look outside and see my neighbor grooming his yard and making it look pretty and I may perceive that is an attack on how poor my yard looks because now my yard looks very poor in contrast to his pretty yard and so I could suggest he indirectly insulted me and that is warrant for me to attack him. That is a symptom of the mind that is under the influence of fear and thus paranoia. It is simply abnormal to harm yourself or your youth to attack a country that has not attacked you. Shooting ones foot to save the good foot. Every country is potentially a target of every other country. That is universal. That is inescapable. That is why fear is destructive because before one knows it all they see are enemies all around them and people do some very strange things when they are afraid because the emotions make one lose clarity and proper thinking ability. If one treats others with disrespect over a period of time they invite their own doom. The deep seeded psychological situation in the "Israel and Iran" event is they both love each other. The generals on each side breathe and eat pondering how they will defeat their perceived enemy. The political leaders breathe and eat pondering what their next comments will be about their perceived enemy. They are mentally dominated by thoughts about their perceived enemy so they are in love with their hate for their perceived enemy. They are lovers that love to harm each other. That can be translated into a relationship where the male beats the wife and then the wife forgives him and this goes on and on for years. It is known as a love hate relationship. One cannot love something without having hate feelings also. One cannot hate something without having love feelings about it also. When a soldier who fights a conflict comes back and says "I have no regrets about the enemies I killed, they were so evil." They are in reality saying "I love to kill that enemy." They literally mentally love that enemy because that enemy puts them in a situation they can kill that enemy. Some people love control so much they will kill their self for it. That is mentally abnormal. A husband gets divorced and goes back to his wife's home and kills her because his love was scorned. There are General's who studied their whole life in the ways of war and they will say anything to extend a war because without a war they have no purpose. There are Weapon companies which want nothing more than there to be infinite wars because they base their whole existence on creating weapons and if there is no war there is no reason for weapons and so these people have no purpose. This psychology can be taken to the internet. Anti –Virus companies live and perhaps even create some of the virus because if there were no virus that infect peoples systems these anti-Virus companies would have no purpose. These companies LOVE to announce there is a dangerous virus just released and "our software can heal it." This is all a symptom of a mind that is abnormal. One should not be pleased to make money or have purpose based on others suffering. This is the extreme depths of psychology. One should not be pleased to make money off the suffering of others. Now we are in the realms of insanity and irresponsibility.

It is abnormal to "go down the road" of making money off of others suffering. The reason it is abnormal is because once that road is taken. there is no limits to how far one will go. One mindfully will become a robber and a thief and monologue to their self around others how wise they are for taking advantage of others. They will suggest they got the better end of that transaction when in reality they are commenting about what a great thief and abuser they are. One is not able to obtain enough money; one is only able to attempt to avoid becoming a slave to it. A confidence artist is one who persuades a customer the items they sell are the best possible price in the universe so they are liars and thus thief's and they will explain they have to make a living. So a person gives up on alternatives to making a living and settles for being a thief. The most clever thieves will push items and suggest they are good items or needed items. They are under the impression that it is okay to take advantage of others as long as they get some money out of it. Money is the thief's motivation and lies are their tool to get it.

 Where does the thief mentality end and a person making an honest living begin?

That is a deep psychological issue. A stock broker will tell a customer it is a good stock to buy even if it is not. The stock broker may perceive it is a good stock to buy and not be aware they are lying because the nature of the stock market is a gamble. So that stock broker is saying relative to the fact I am unable to predict this stocks movements this is a great investment. The stock broker has only one thing in mind, sell stocks to make a living and nothing else matters. If a person is told a psychological drug works good and that person has enough "data" and credentials crammed in front of their name, millions of psychologists will assume they are right. Next thing you know the psychologists are prescribing a drug to everyone they see because their peers are doing the same thing. A few months later a new drug comes out and that initial person says "It is a better drug." The bottom line is all of these people are doing what they do, to be accepted in their peer group and more dangerous than that, to make money.

Soldiers get paid money to kill people. Pharmaceutical companies get paid money to kill people. Religious people get paid money to incite hatred and kill people. Leaders get paid money to kill people. Secrecy groups get paid money to kill people. Parents get paid money to neglect their children.

Parents say I do not have time to raise my child because I have to work. Psychologists say I cannot see my patient for more than an hour because I have to make money. Generals say I do not have time to talk to my perceived enemy because I have to kill him and that what I get paid to do. They are all killing for money.

Perhaps a psychologist will contact me and explain to me how no patients they treated for depression ever took the medicine they prescribed to them and killed their self. Perhaps that psychologist will suggest it is the patents fault. Perhaps that psychologist is unable to submit they kill far more people than they ever help. Perhaps they cannot imagine that because if they understood that was reality they would kill their self. Perhaps ignorance is best since the truth tends to rip one apart. The delusions and hallucinations in the mind are far less harmful than the understandings and truths. One does not want to accept the fact they perhaps killed many people indirectly and are doing it on a daily basis. A serial killer does not perceive they are a killer they perceive they are on a righteous mission and are justified. Perhaps one should punch that into their calculator of darkness. If you have ever paid one penny in taxes and your country is engaged in a foreign war on foreign land for delusional purposes, you are in fact a butcher of women and children so you should take every drug you can get your hands on to attempt to block that understanding out of you mind. You can yell into infinity you would never hurt anyone but if your country is killing people in another land when your country is not even invaded you are an indirect butcher of children. That is ok. You are a butcher of children to put money in the power mongers pockets and you probably encourage your own children to join the war and die to put money in the power mongers pocket. That is okay. Just understand that is what you do and what you are and attempt to live with yourself. You are simply a butcher of children and I find no fault in that because I understand a butcher is only able to butcher. I understand you get more satisfaction out of butchering your own child than others children. That is because every parents secretly hates their child because they wish they had another chance at life and that child reminds them they do not have another chance at life. You do not have to explain to me why you are not a butcher because I understand you are butcher. I understand you are a butcher. That means it is not negotiable. You are a butcher of children on so many levels I am only able to suggest you are a butcher. That is okay because I am certain you do it for money and the acceptance of your peers. We all need to be acceptable by our peers even if we have to butcher children to do it. It is okay to butcher our future as long as it is for money for the power mongers. Do not look at me, you have no right and you never will ever, ever, have a right to even look at me for one split second! I will go play my unnamable dam video game so I do not have to look at you because I will eat you for no reason. I will take your understanding of morals and wring your unnamable dam neck with them. Do you perceive I stutter? You bring every unnamable dam army with you when you come and I will blink you out of existence and I pray to unnamable you test me.

I submit perhaps my emotions are not under control at this time. Thank You. I will go back to wise quotes so I do not have to remind myself I allow you to breathe because I am an infinite sadist. 8:32:03 AM

"A man who has not passed through the inferno of his passions has never overcome them." Carl Jung

If one never gets angry they no longer have brain function. Anger is relative to understanding; not acting on that anger in a physical way is relative to wisdom. Anger is a gift to the wise for their efforts. When a mentally weak person understands they are unable to direct anyone but their self they usually implode.

"A particularly beautiful woman is a source of terror. As a rule, a beautiful woman is a terrible disappointment." Carl Jung

All women are beautiful but few men have the wisdom to see that. Men fight among their self because women defeated them swiftly.

Suicide is a sign of infinite humility and meekness. One denies their own self when they do not have to. That is what meek is. Do you perceive I am crazy or beyond your understanding?

The psychology about women is a man with left brain dominance has ideals of isolation in relation to "they like certain kinds of women." They like some women and do not like others. One in extreme right brain see's all women with awe and amazement simply because they are different. So some cultures treat women poorly because the males cannot control the women. This is the same psychology when a man kills a women or hurts a women who has scorned his love. Love is a form of control in relation to "if you love someone set them free." If a male loves a women too much and that women scorns their advances a man may harm that women or harm their self because that male understands they cannot control that women. That is a symptom that a male subconsciously understands the females are not like they are. Opposites attract. This is complex because likes attract also. Both are valid but apply to different situations. Even in a lesbian couple situation one is the "male" and one is the "female" in characteristics. So in reality a lesbian couple in not an abnormality. There are relationships where the male is dominate and the female is submissive and also relationships where the male is submissive and the female is dominate. There are no relationships where both are submissive or both are dominate because that would defeat the purpose of the relationship. This is in relation to the give and take concept. I will attempt to sum up my mental state in regards to women. In this extreme clarity or subconscious extreme the rage a male naturally has is converted to cerebral rage when in general a males rage is typically physical rage. As in a male goes to a bar looking for a fight. So when I see women even a picture on the internet , even a picture of their leg or face or anything, not porno, just a picture I melt because they are the opposite extreme of where I am at mentally. They are submission and I am rage. So they can destroy me if I go down that path. I would be unable to have enough women because I am attracted to all of them. There is no women that I would be able to mentally say is not infinitely submissive in contrast to this mental rage I have, so they are all perfect because they are perfect opposites of me. So my mindset is to sit in my room and write infinite books because anything outside of that will destroy me. I cannot go down the road of a vacation or pleasure or comfort because it will destroy me. I will go to the extreme. I cannot go to the monks as they suggest because their temples of gold remind me of why I attempted to kill myself. I cannot go to a place of comfort or luxury because that reminds me of why I tried to kill myself for 10 plus years. I decided to write infinite book two months after the accident because as I understand now, that is my only chance to not destroy myself with "worldly" pleasures and luxuries. My mind will not allow me to ever leave this room or get out of my contract to write infinite books. It will trick me and suggest everyone is evil or everyone is threat so it is best you stay in your room and write books about those threats. I am not afraid of anyone or anything but I am in a mindset to have battles mentally to give me things to write about because I decided to write infinite books, period, until I die. That is the reality that is on my plate. Everything in the universe pales in contrast to my decision to write infinite books and I submit my books are horrible and just down right vain, and stupid, and just go around in circles. I am perhaps the worst author in the universe of authors but that is not relevant at all. The only thing that is relevant is that I write infinite books. I do not even think about if my books sell and I give them away on download sites so it is not even about money. It is writing infinite books without any understood purpose. I do not even know what I write about. I have no true end goal. I have no true end reason to write infinite books, somehow I just decided to. I perceive when I saw the neurologist he said some things and then said "but I wouldn't write any books about it." And in my extreme subconscious state it heard "write infinite books." But that is perhaps an illusion because I perceive I was at a stage of feeling isolated on some of the forums and chat rooms I was talking in. They never had infinite people in them. So I felt mentally isolated. So I determined writing a book would mean every person from here on out would have a chance to read them because they would forever be in the collective of information so to speak. But that is far too relative to purpose. If my goal was to write proper books I would at least edit them. I would at least take out all the rage comments. I would at least have common sense to make sure there were no spelling errors. So then I am reduced back to, I write infinite books for no purpose or my purpose is to write infinite books that have no purpose.

I do not perceive anyone can reach extreme subconscious dominate or extreme right brain dominate unless they do it the hard way and the hard way means it has to be a failed suicide attempt that came extremely close to being successful. So it has to be an accident. So no one can do that intentionally because they may go too far and then die. So there are simply degree's one can reach diminished sense of time and diminished cravings and desires but there is no one who is going to reach the extreme unless they do it the hard way or by accident. That is just the way it is. One is not arrogant if they brag about what a loser they are.

I spoke to the female monk and she suggested **"SerendipityJane Someone must have harmed you first and taken your self-confidence away - it's a crime nobody was charged for."**

And this is exactly it. So I write books to exact my vengeance. I write infinite books to remind them I am not a loser they said I am. So I am doing exactly what they did to me. I am saying "You are a loser and I am not a loser", so I am destroying myself because I cannot forgive them for what they did to me. But I am okay with that. I have no morals and I have no class. I swallowed my morals and class with a handful of pills. The truth is, it is too late for me. My fate is sealed mentally. My mindset is sealed. No being is going to be able to persuade me I should forgive because I am unable to understand what that is. I no longer detect wisdom or rage it all looks the same to me. When I type sentences and tears start flowing from my eyes I am unable to tell if that is tears of joy or tears of wisdom or tears of rage or tears of hate or tears of understanding. It simply fades so fast that I cannot grasp what it is. The tears flow and less than a moment later they stop and then a moment later they start again and then they stop. One comment a psychologist will suggest how do you feel? Well one has to have that feeling long enough to understand how they feel. If one goes from humor to sadness to concentration to misery to anger to rage to clarity in one minute how do they explain exactly what they feel? The answer is nothingness or everythingness or infinite shades but no set shade for more than a moment.

"All the works of man have their origin in creative fantasy. What right have we then to depreciate imagination."
Carl Jung

Let freedom of mind reign and that goes hand in hand with freedom of speech.

The truth is, no being has the right to pass a law that says that person cannot say a word because then they indirectly pass a law that says that person cannot have a thought. When a person suggests in any way another person is not allowed to say something, no matter what it is, that initial person has determined they are God of all creation and are intelligent enough to decide what is proper to say and what is not proper to say. When a person says "Do not say that." They are saying "I am all knowing" and thus they are insane from their delusions. They are essentially attempting to force their narrow-mindedness on others and in turn create narrow-mindedness in the one they scold, so they are a threat to their own mental state of mind and are also a threat to others mental state of mind. The bottom line is no person knows a dam thing in relation to what is proper to say and what is improper to say, period, or they suggest they are God of all. I do not know anything but I understand everything about nothing.

"Beauty is the gift of God." – Aristotle

When one has the man upstairs unlocked(subconscious/right brain) they see beauty in everything because they can look at anything and find wisdom or purpose in it. Beauty is being wise enough to understand nothing is evil or good but simply there to ponder in order to come to further understandings. This is also known as seeing everything as one thing, that one thing is "to ponder to come to further understandings."

One might suggest there is a murderer in prison and he is evil. Then I will suggest that murderer in prison is perhaps under the influence of the left brain or conscious emotional aspect of the mind and has allowed his desires and cravings for control over perhaps money or control over others to enter the physical world and that is what caused him to murder someone. A thief in prison is a person who has taken others money or valuables because they were unable to conform to the "norms" expected ways to gain money to have food to eat. If this thief and murderer were not in prison I would not have been able write about them in my books and so they are in prison for a reason, and that reason is, so I am able to ponder them and come to further understandings. If people do not do anything then I will not have anything to write about, so please act natural.

"As far as we can discern, the sole purpose of human existence is to kindle a light in the darkness of mere being. " Carl Jung

This is a great truth. A human being is not ever going to be some light of the world, but they can at times show flickers of light from the darkness within their thoughts. Human perfection is relative to the fact they can adapt to any situation. We adapted from a lemur monkey to a lemur monkey who does not think we are a lemur monkey.

Foreign Secretary D M said: "Hostage-taking and murder can never be justified whatever the cause."

Oh look someone said something and it is printed in the news. Let me tell you something "Mr. I live in England." Your country does not allow people to speak freely or have absolute freedom of speech so you hold all of them mentally hostage and in turn they are unable to live their purpose because you harm them if they speak freely and so you mentally murder them. Perhaps you should go back to school and stay away from saying words in public because a being with brain function may come across your delusional words and quote them in his infinite books and make you look like an ass.

Hostage taking and murder is relative to the observer.

"Children are educated by what the grown-up is and not by his talk." Carl Jung

Suffer the children because the adults know not what they do. Of course to clarify that, children are naturally subconscious dominate and adults are naturally conscious emotional dominate because their parents conditioned them to be conscious emotional dominate with all of their "rules and Laws" and "this is how it will be done under my roof" insanity. I look at a supernova at this stage in humanity as a blessing.

"Even a happy life cannot be without a measure of darkness, and the word happy would lose its meaning if it were not balanced by sadness. It is far better take things as they come along with patience and equanimity."
Carl Jung

Yes this is in direct relation to the reality, emotions give off contrast. So the right brain see's everything as one thing or the right brain/subconscious aspect finds patterns that make everything appear as one thing. So good is only relative to ones with left brain /conscious emotional aspect of the mind. They tend to rely on good and then they know what is bad. The subconscious dominate people tend to see good and bad as the same thing because the ability to find patterns makes them perceive there is only things, not good or bad things. So Jung was found dead in his bed with a copy of Buddha's teachings at his bed side because Jung was subconscious dominate and was attempting to understand more from the Master which was Buddha and there were several other masters who were misunderstood by the "ones who know" . He was Buddha of the age which means he is the teacher of the age in relation to where he arrived. Now the new Buddha of the age has arrived and I am clarifying all the misunderstanding from the last age. There is no purpose to it, it simply is. It simply is the way it is. I prefer to be back in the herd at times but then I understand what I want is not relevant.

"Every form of addiction is bad, no matter whether the narcotic be alcohol or morphine or idealism."
Carl Jung

This is interesting because he said bad; but it was also an inside joke. Addiction is another way to say desire or cravings. One person may wish to control others by forcing their religion or political views down that person's throat. That is what the idealism comment is referring to. So the great truth is one is not allowed to force their beliefs down anyone's throat ever, no matter what they think. One is not allowed to tell another person they are not allowed to do drugs, or say certain things because when they do they become the most arrogant fool in history because they are saying "I know what is best for everyone." I have news for anyone who perceives they know what is best, You will never, ever , ever, ever, know what is best for anyone but yourself, period. Many control freaks in this world go around assuming they are God because they subconsciously understand they are nothing.

"Everything that irritates us about others can lead us to an understanding of ourselves."
Carl Jung

The insane and the sane enable me to come up with infinite jokes to write in my infinite books. This comment is relative to this oneness aspect the subconscious or right brain dominate person is in. When one hates someone they subconsciously love that person or crave to be like that person.

This is rather complex but it is easily explainable. Consider this definition of right brain characteristics.

"Left-brain dominated people may find their thought processes vague and difficult to follow, for they are quite opposite in the way they think."

This word opposite is exactly what the subconscious is. It is the opposite of the left brain conscious emotional aspect. So then one can understand this Jesus being who spoke of the Anti-Christ was referring to left brain people because they were anti or opposite of how Jesus was mindfully. So in case you are not pissed off enough, if you have a strong sense of time and have a strong sense of hunger you are the anti Christ Jesus spoke about. I perceive what he said was very accurate and proven by the description of right brain characteristics to a T. He said ANTI which is opposite. **"are quite opposite in the way they think."**

This is the disconnect again. The ones with silenced sense of time are opposite to ones with strong sense of time so they are polar opposites or anti in relation to each other. They simply are not supposed to see eye to eye. The clarification needed with that is. One who is subconscious dominate is using the intelligent aspect of the mind so they will easily convince ones with the conscious or left brain aspect of the mind to do their bidding or will appear wise to the left brainers. Simply put, one has 100% of their mental faculties and one has 10%, so the only way the 10%ers have a chance in hell is to resort to physical violence against the 100%ers. It is akin to a conscious being in an argument with a being in a coma. Who do you think is going to win?

"Follow that will and that way which experience confirms to be your own."
Carl Jung

This is in relation to thinking for yourself and avoid the herd mentality. The herd mentality can lead one to doing things to be accepted in the herd that they would not do if they were alone. Peer pressure. It is everywhere in everything and the only solution is to be mindful of that fact and attempt to detect it and avoid it. We are surrounded by people but one can take what they say to them with a grain of salt. This is why the devil's advocate mindset is important. Do not agree often with people. If they do not like that then they are not worth listening to because their mind is locked and isolated. Argue with your own beliefs and argue with others beliefs. This is what keeps the subconscious happy. The subconscious is far too cerebral to fall to agreements. This is not physical fights and wars this is cerebral and mental fights and wars. Go into a religious chat room and tell them you doubt their beliefs and you will be banned. It simply does not matter what the religion is. What is happening is people who rest on their beliefs are mentally narrow minded and thus their subconscious aspect is frozen. They are quite certain you must be the devil if you do not believe what they believe because they cannot submit they are wrong. Submitting one is wrong is very hard to do if one has an emotional left brain dominate mind. When one is subconscious dominate it is nearly impossible to ever submit one is right. I mean in all reality I am unable to know what is right in this subconscious extreme state of mind. That is strictly cerebrally speaking. I am harmless physically speak but I am a leviathan mentally speaking. I am Heimdall after all. I can hear the grass grow. I am the messenger between the gods "insane" and humans "sane". It simply does not matter if you laugh at that because subconsciously you understand I certainly am. I am uncertain if others will perceive what I speak about is right but I am certain everything I speak about is perfectly accurate. If you perceive I make a contradiction it is because you have not read my infinite books yet and I spread out everything I say over infinite books because that is how much I have to explain to clarify the misunderstandings created by the "Buddha's of the last age." I am fixing things and it will take infinite books to fix the things that are broken.

"Great talents are the most lovely and often the most dangerous fruits on the tree of humanity. They hang upon the most slender twigs that are easily snapped off."
Carl Jung

Yes Carl is aware the ones who "know" end up slaughtering the ones who matter. That is the nature of the "sane" they kill anything that is different. They just do. They are the vipers and they are the darkness and they are the devil. So simply bring it and we will see if you are as tough as you think you are, because there is one being who understands you slaughtered a lot of beings I happen to respect now, and you may perceive your attacking me but I assure you I am seeking retribution on you. I will invite you in to my table so I can slaughter you like you slaughtered them. Perhaps we have come to an understanding. I do not hide from things that pose no threat to me. I already looked death in the eyes and it ran away. Do you perceive I fear anything you can do to me? Last I checked I have freedom to kill anyone who poses a threat to my safety and that is about the most open ended invitation in the universe. Carl is really funny. I do not perceive he is smart I perceive he is quite a comedian.

"If one does not understand a person, one tends to regard him as a fool."
Carl Jung

This is relative to "kill anything that is different." You simply should think am a fool because I understand you are fool. That is a symptom of how extreme mentally I am into this subconscious state. Do you think I am physically violent? You are wrong. Do you think I am crazy? You are wrong. Do you think I am a fool? You are wrong. Simply put **"Left-brain dominated people may find their thought processes vague and difficult to follow"** , What "may find their thought processes difficult to follow" is simply saying, I am unnamable dam light years beyond your mental ability to grasp and because your emotions and ego is so strong you will just dismiss me as a fool or crazy or insane but in reality you are not even on the same planet as far as cerebral clarity is concerned. I had an accident and became like this, so it does not even matter if you are comfortable with that reality, because you still assume you are relevant to anything at this stage of humanity. You are no longer relevant and your opinions are no longer relevant. You had your chance to produce and you blew it. Now the master has arrived and is taking over the house. Do you think I am arrogant or do you think I am telling great truths? I perceive I am telling great truths.

"If there is anything that we wish to change in the child, we should first examine it and see whether it is not something that could better be changed in ourselves."
Carl Jung

See Carl was full of rage also but he was afraid to say exactly what he wanted to say. I will clarify what Carl was attempting to say. You leave the children out of your unnamable dam insane money making pharmaceutical delusions or you will pay with your unnamable dam soul. You better pray to unnamable there is no after life if you keep pumping children with your drugs to make them like you are. You are not dealing with a human being, you are dealing with an unknown presence, and you would be wise to not assume I am kidding. The children are subconscious dominate when they are born and you perceive they are "messed up" because you are brain dead. So you pump them with drugs so they will be brain dead like you are. What do think I am going to do to you for doing that? Use your imagination.

You need to stay away from Carl he is evil. Many parents try to raise their children in their image and the problem with that is, if the parent was an image worthy of that child, that parent would be wise enough to understand they are not allowed to force a child to be like they are. Perhaps the sane will never, ever, ever understand that.

"It is a fact that cannot be denied: the wickedness of others becomes our own wickedness because it kindles something evil in our own hearts."
Carl Jung

All are ruthless but the wise do not allow that darkness to enter into physical harm on others. Anton Lavey the founder of the Church of Satan said it properly. "An it harm none do what thou will." I think if even 1/1000th of the world could accomplish this it would be a great world. This means it is okay to verbally argue and even be arrogant but don't bring it to a level of hitting people or killing people because then you go into the realms of insanity. If you hit or kill someone you are insane, no question about it. It is all mindset. People who hit or kill other people cannot form the proper words to express their anger and they just kill in the physical world to express the anger in their thoughts. We are all wicked and some are wicked and physically harmful to others. You can yell and cuss if you are mad that is why you have vocal cords. The masters can say a humble comment that is far more piercing than the sharpest sword. If you are upset with someone do not resort to physical means, come up with a mental plan or a well phrased word or sentence to exact your revenge. You have to get revenge because if you didn't you would go mad.

Simple test: Ask a friend to slap you in the face lightly about 100 times and call you insults as they do it. You won't be able to handle that you will well up with rage and want to knock their head off. That is right. That is the way of the left brainers. They get emotional swiftly and for long periods of time. My grudge is for infinity but I use it as a mental tool to keep writing. That is fine, that is proper. I am really not in a mental state to be anger or vengeful for very long or I could not write these books this swiftly. I would be "consumed with rage" and my mind would not function. This is the opposite aspect again with subconscious dominate people. I perceive I am full of rage but that drives me to write swiftly so that is a blessing. A left brainer with rage will let that seed of rage fester in their mind until all they can think of is how to exact revenge in a physical fashion. They have given up on the mental power they possess and resort to physical violence. From my perspective I am justified in my rage but my rage is my motivator. I am not pleased; if I was pleased I would not have anything to write about I would sit and waste my life doing nothing. So I have turned my hate of myself and my hate of the world and then I translate that hate of the world and myself into words in a book instead of slashing my wrists and taking a handful of pills every few months. Nothing else has changed except I went from physical attacks to verbal attacks to keep the wickedness in check. That is what Carl is explaining. I see your wickedness and it makes me have wickedness. If you were not wicked I would not be wicked, and if I was not wicked you would not be wicked. So that is proof you are wicked because when you think I am wicked, you are looking at a mirror image of yourself. Perhaps that is beyond your ability to ever understand, you perhaps think you are good and that is the humor of life. You actually think you are capable of being good. I am simply at a level of understanding I am not ever capable of being good but I am capable of turning my wickedness into verbal jousting as opposed to physically harming others. Ones who suggest they are good are the most arrogant self centered delusional beings in history. No one is good because that would denote they are not good because a good person would never admit they are good. That is what being meek is all about. But of course I am Heimdall and I have no morals and no class. I have no concept of what good even is. So I can say I am good, but mentally I do not even know what that is. I cannot tell at this stage of the accident what wickedness is. Maybe I am wicked because I cuss in my books. If you think I am wicked because I cuss that means subconsciously you understand you are wicked when you cuss. What you perceive has nothing to do with me. All of your judgments are about you. I already judged myself with a handful of pills so I am immune to your consultations into infinity. Simply put, your judgments over me no longer have any power because I do not even believe the definitions of the words you speak about me. Perhaps that is a nice way of saying, save your judgments for those who acknowledge your opinions matter and save your judgments for those who do not understand when you speak you are just talking to yourself. The great trick is when you say something verbally to someone you regret, you honestly remind them you were talking to yourself and about yourself. You remind them no matter what you say you are always talking to yourself and about yourself because in reality you are. Never say anything to anyone that makes it appear you are trying to correct them because in reality you will never ever be able to correct anyone but yourself. If you are unable to face that truth then never speak of humility because you simply do not understand the definition of it.

"Knowing your own darkness is the best method for dealing with the darknesses of other people. "
Carl Jung

Carl is truly evil as hell so stay away from him. In fact he is some sort of terroristic threat. According to my spell checker darknesses is not a word so Carl is dumb because he cannot even spell. He actually snuck in a word that is not a word to see if anyone noticed, and apparently no one did. I will explain this quote plain and simple. I understand you clearly because I went to such a dark emotional place you appear as light in contrast to the darkness I have experienced. Simply put, you detect I am evil because I kicked evil's ass. I am far more dark than darkness, you are just darkness. I am mindfully at the level beyond pitch black. There is no name for it. It is unnamable and therefore it can take on the form of anything. Evil is good in contrast to IT, rage is good in contrast to IT. So it is beyond the realms of labels.

Now it is time for a reader judgment on the author quiz.

Do you perceive the author is:

A: Extremely left brain dominate or an emotional wreck.

B: Extremely right brain dominate or extremely subconscious dominate.

C: A lemur monkey on an ego trip.

D: Heimdall

E: Buddha of the Age

F: Nothing at all.

"Knowledge   rests   not   upon   truth   alone,   but   upon   error   also."
Carl Jung

One understands more from making mistakes than getting it right.

I am the only one on my train of thought.

6/4/2009 4:01:53 AM - I will try to write this book again because everything up to this point in the book is foolishness. So the real book will start now.

There are some complex emotional considerations one should face so they are able to detect these emotions. I will type some sentences and when you read them attempt to feel if they excite your emotions. This is simply why I am harsh in my words because you are perhaps so emotional you cannot stand yourself.

You are perfect.

You are a loser and never will amount to anything.

Everyone loves you.

You are an insult to life itself.

You are the best person in the universe.

You are the definition of evil.

You are kind to everyone you meet.

You rape small children.

You certainly should feel some emotions from reading those sentences. This is because your mind is conditioned to believe the definitions of the words. If someone says you're a loser you believe you are a loser. If someone says you're intelligent you believe you are intelligent. The subconscious is simply assuming the role of the words because the mind is not conditioned enough to understand that is what subconscious does. Subconscious is a chameleon. You tell someone they are a failure they will start believing it. You tell someone they are wise they will start believing it. Both are things. You tell someone they are wise and they will become prideful and arrogant. You tell someone they are dumb and they will become suicidal and hate their self. You compliment someone and they will become boastful. You insult someone and they will become hateful. This is simply because subconscious assumes any identity because it has no identity. Subconscious has infinite shades of pale. This is exactly why I write my books as diaries denoted by time stamps. I cannot talk to you. Anything I say to you I understand is improper, so I talk to myself. I understand some may read my personal diaries and it will harm them. They may assume I am intelligent or special or wise or hateful or arrogant or boastful or insane or sane and the truth is they are wrong. I am not mentally anything that is why I understand nothingness. I understand many will become envious and jealous that I am able to suggest what I suggest and they will idolize me because they do not understand I got "tapped". Tapped denotes it was not my doing or it was a mistake I am like this. Some may not be able to mentally handle that and they will determine I have evil or I am a saint or I am something they are not and that will harm them and they may decide to take physical action against me and that will certainly harm them. I am not paranoid because that would suggest I am afraid. I am simply mindful I am in a world of beings who are not prone to clear thoughts and they take their thoughts and translate them into physical violence. Some may suggest that would not happen. Some may suggest it is okay to associate with people in general. That is because they are not thinking clearly. The "sane" tend to butcher what is different. That is what I understand about the sane. I do not fear death because I defeated it but I am in a position I must avoid the general public because I am aware of who they are and what they are. I must hide because I understand I am in an insane asylum. There are many that hide. Some assume the role of a "humble" servant and so they tend to be relegated to the stage of harmlessness and so the sane do not see them as a threat and they leave them alone generally speaking. I am no such monster. This is simply the reality, I am the teacher. There are not going to be any people who are going to teach me. They will make comments and I will agree and then go into a 30 minute class and teach them. They will say anything to me and I will monologue and clarify for them what they just tried to teach me. All these books really are is simply me asking questions and then answering them. There are many examples in religious texts of questions and then they are answered. Some are in the form of parables and some are simply invented questioners and then the answer is given by the "authority" or teacher. I can just as easily ask myself a question and then answer it to get myself to start monologue. I am not picky what question is asked I only seek to answer questions simply because I do not know what the answer is until after the monologue is over. I in fact teach myself as I go. I know nothing for a fact but I can monologue myself into understandings and then I will forget what I learned and that will put me in a situation to seek another question to come to understandings about. I am not concerned with absolutes; I am only concerned with further monologue.

This is why Subconscious is the devil's advocate. It simply cannot agree because that would mean it has to shut up and subconscious never wants to shut up. This is relevant to people who are motor mouths. They go on and on and on about stuff and people who hear them say "What the hell are you talking about?" and they say "I am just thinking out loud." Or "I am just talking to myself." So then there are people with no brain function who will tell these motor mouths to "Shut up, your bugging me." This is why the ones with no brain function are abominations because they seek isolation and are afraid to speak their mind and that is why they have no mind they only have hatred and guilt and self conscious delusions in their mind because they have abused their mind and most likely it is because they were taught by the adults to shut up and keep their mouth shut, because the adults "know not what they do and know not what they say." If you ever tell anyone to shut up or keep their mouth shut, I will go out of my way to look for you, because I have an infinitely long discussion I wish to have with you. Perhaps we have come to an understanding.6:07:29 AM

I will make another further comment in relation to the above. When these beings called "terrorists" make a speech to the world and the world does not counter argue all of the points made in the "terrorists" speech, the "terrorists" win. The "terrorists" are attempting to communicate and every time they do the ones with no brain function say things like "We will not even respond to that statement." That is an indication they have no brain function. That is an indication that being who says that should not even be allowed to make public comments at all, let alone be in a position of power because they simply do not have the brain function to be able to "argue" points when the "terrorists" make comments. The comments are like a haggle. The "terrorists" make comments and wait to hear the counter argument. When there is no counter argument then the "terrorists" win in the eyes of the world. So the "terrorists" can say whatever they want because they understand they are dealing with beings with no brain function. I will counter the "terrorists "recent comments and arguments since there are no being in the universe that are capable of verbal jousting with the "terrorists". I will do what you are unable to do.

"In Swat Valley about one million Muslims were displaced including women, children and old men and now they are homeless," said bin Laden. "This means that Obama has planted new seeds for hatred and revenge against the Americans and the number of seeds is as many as the number of the people who were displaced from Swat valley. Obama has followed the steps of (Bush) who established wars with other nations. American people should prepare themselves for coming wars."

I will remind you Osama the seeds of the tree that your fruits come from encourage you to sacrifice your own offspring for your delusional worldly goals. Osama your fruits are as bitter as the fruits of the Americans. You certainly are in no position to judge the fruits of others because I am aware your fruits are of physical violence and anger and you should perhaps consider the Prophets words and attempt to focus on and avoid wrath as the prophets suggested so you do not look like the jaw bone of an ass on the world stage. Perhaps Osama you have determined your are wiser than

37

the Prophet because you ignore his comments about avoid wrath and thus you spit in his face. Perhaps the Prophet will be interested in meeting you so you can explain why you are above his comments in relation to avoiding physical wrath.

 I will quote the Holy Book since you Osama are obviously unable to understand the words in the holy book.

001.007 The way of those on whom Thou hast bestowed Thy Grace, those whose (portion) is not wrath, and who go not astray.

Al-Qur'an, 001.007 (Al-Fatiha [The Opening])

Osama, this simply states if one has grace they will not have physical wrath towards their fellow man. That means you are inciting physical wrath and encouraging others to do the same by your example. You are ASTRAY and you are leading the children who look up to you ,ASTRAY. This is why it is perhaps wise for you to correct your course because the prophet does not appreciate ones who spit in his face. I assure you Osama because of your fruits, you have no problems in this life in contrast to the infinite problems you are going to face in the next life when you open your eyes and the Prophet is looking into your eyes seeking an explanation for why you lead his children ASTRAY with you encouragement of Physical Wrath upon others.

You perhaps may perceive you have problems in this world Osama, but I understand the problems you have in this world are blessings compared to the infinite problems you are going to face in the next world if you do not correct yourself and start to encourage proper fruits in others.

"Those whose portion is not wrath" means those who are not physically wrathful against others will not go astray. Those who are not physically wrathful against other will have proper fruits for others to see and they will not lead the offspring astray.

Osama never speak of the Holy Book again because you are an abomination to the Holy Book and you only increase the infinite gnashing of teeth you will suffer whenever you mention one word from the Holy Book. I declare you are no longer associated with any religion because your fruits, I have determined, are an abomination to all that is proper. If you have a problem with anything I say, you seek me swiftly so I can sever your venomous head. You will no longer insult and blaspheme the beings I have determined are wise, that is the way it is now Osama, so you go back and ponder your next comment you make on the world stage, because I will be waiting for your next comment so that I can server your head with it. Osama I have already determined you have lead the children ASTRAY and I will not tolerate such actions and so I will humbly remind you, I will be waiting for you on the infinite battlefield and you will understand swiftly you will have no place to hide and I will assist you in understanding what true wrath is. Perhaps you should not assume I have just levied a curse upon you because if you understood I just have levied a curse upon you, you would no longer be able to function. Osama I perceive you could have done much more if you would have decided to write infinite books instead of use the "sword". Better luck next time.

I am certain that will get his attention. I will be waiting for his next comment because I eat for no reason.

This is what verbal jousting is all about. He will certainly hear about this comment eventually and perhaps have a good laugh. One cannot harm anyone with words but perhaps ones can perceive the words can harm them and so the words shall harm them. I recall at one point in my life someone said I was a loser and I was not at the mental level of clarity to be able to understand they were not talking to me, they were talking to their self. Osama is not talking to us he is talking to himself because he is aware he is leading children to their death for his own selfish reasons and because he misunderstood the teachings of Mohammed. There are many misunderstandings in the world. One is wise to be mindful of that and understand no being is really talking to them. The beings are simply talking to their self and reminding their self of what they already understand. Certainly Osama, at the core of his being or on a subconscious level is rather regretful because he understands many young children have died in vain for him. These beings he has "killed", died for him. So Osama has an extreme form of a God complex. It is okay to perceive on is god as long as it remains in the realms of verbal jousting and mental jousting. It is valid based on the religious texts because god made man in his image. This means humans based on the religious texts are a little bit godlike to say the least. Every being has a little bit of god in them because god said I made man in my image. So it is logical to suggest one is godlike or even god because one has the essence of god in them, and this is based on a religious text that suggests "god made man in his image." So if anyone who claims they are religious has a problem with that, they should swiftly stop reading religious texts because they are unable to grasp them at all. They are only harming their self and looking like the jawbone of an ass in the process. Perhaps they are wise to allow the ones who understand the religious texts to speak about them, and that way they can just be reduced to listening and learning. My train of thought has trailed off the tracks.6:50:25 AM

So the lesson is. When someone says something to you, they are begging for an argument or for communication and only one with no brain function would walk away from a verbal challenge. Everyone knows the language but few know how to use it properly. If you do not get your feelings out in words you are going to get your feelings out in physical actions. One must be mindful to be able to detect who can handle a verbal joust and who cannot. One must be mindful to avoid upsetting ones who are insane and are not aware they are insane. If you submit to me you are insane I will understand you certainly are not insane. That is the whole premise of insanity. The insane simply do not understand they are insane so they are dangerous. The sane submit they are insane; it is not about humility as much as it is about reality. You are allowed to quote that last one.

Try this experiment. Go into a room full of people you know and say "I think I am insane." They will instantly start saying things like "You are not insane you are fine." Or "There are more insane people than you trust me." This is because they are insane. They are unable to submit they are insane so they cannot tell you are insane. I submit I am fully insane in every possible way except I do not take my thoughts and translate them in physical harm on others including myself outside of the fact I smoke cigarettes swiftly because I do not want to be here any longer than I have to because I am trapped in limbo, and I simply wish to go home now. I simply have been here for eternity and I want to go home. That is all I want to do. I do not desire to write infinite books any longer. I do not desire to watch beings kill each other any longer. I am unable to take the infinite gnashing of teeth caused by the understandings any longer. I simply wish to go home now. What do you perceive of me now? What judgments will pass upon me now? I must play my video game before I implode.7:08:11 AM

9:21:10 AM - They want a freak show and I want many fish to eat for no reason. They detect my insanity which enables me to shield their eyes from my trap covering the bottomless pit. They are full of shame and envy because they are unable to understand what I know without effort. They hate my freedom. They hate my ability to speak freely without fear. They hate my ultimate freedom because they thrive on isolation and hate. They suggest I should have compassion because they are unaware I am here to devour for no reason. I am not concerned about their difficulties and insane moralistic ponderings. I eat for no reason and I am unable to understand their delusions of purpose. I will convince the holy they are whores and the whores they are saints. I will welcome them to my table and devour them in my stable. I will not be ashamed or show fear in my purpose. I fear not my purpose and my purpose is to not show fear. I will no longer allow the words to scare me. I will devour the emotions if they wish; seed me. I am Heimdall the one who does not blink; I will watch them all go down my sink. They will run in fear when they understand, I devour them all with my right hand. Who are they to question me? I paid the price for which they flee. I do not care; I never blink, I'll watch them all go down my sink. They will wish they never spoke. Heimdall is here to watch them choke. They can doubt with all their might while Heimdall devours them on sight. I eat the dark and eat the light they both insult my perfect sight. I feel no pain for I am numb, they will understand the slumber from which I have come. They will beg like chickens do before that knife shows them who is true. They will pray with all their might as I devour them to my light. They will wish they never spoke when Heimdall applies that final choke. They will pray like morals do but Heimdall doesn't fit that shoe. I am not about to wait, to devour the ones that sealed my fate.

They will beg and I will laugh as they sacrifice their golden calf. You are allowed to ponder your fate, but keep in mind it won't be great. I'm not late that's what you hate. I don't hesitate to seal your fate. You're not so great, you just wait.

EXCLUSIVE: Never before published Hitler photographs...

http://www.life.com/image/first/in-gallery/27022/adolf-hitler-up-close

This world loves Hitler. The ones who brag about how evil Hitler was are so in love with Hitler subconsciously they would kill their self to be like he was for one second. They build monument's to tell everyone how evil Hitler was because subconsciously they love him with all of their might. Without Hitler some of these beings would blow their brains out because they would have no purpose at all in life. You tell me you do not love Hitler and I will convince you, you are delusional beyond all understanding, and I will do it swiftly. I am not in love with Hitler because he wishes he was me.

I do not insult people because I simply do not care for them. They bore me to life. They all wish they were me but I want nothing to do with them, when it comes right down to it. I do not need anyone to give me purpose. I simply tolerate them because I have infinite compassion. Don't ever think otherwise.

Now the ones who openly say they love Hitler are at least slightly in touch with reality. They at least can detect a being who had an impact of history without throwing judgments all over the place. They are at least humble to suggest a being was greater than they are. Do not give me your insane logic that evil is bad and good is holy because you do bot know what evil is and you do not know what holy is, you are delusional and insane. Your holy is my insanity and your evil is my parody.

My strategy to avoid associating with anyone ever is to publish my book in diary format. If any being in the universe suggest I am judgmental I will swiftly remind them they are a voyeur and have no right to invade my privacy and should swiftly pray to their unnamable there is no afterlife because if there is, they insulted the dead by invading my grave site called my diaries.

I recall I discussed this in an earlier diary but just to clarify. Hitler tried to be an art student and the "norms" of society said he was not an artist. Then Hitler decided to kill himself. Anyone who joins the military is suicidal. Ask any soldier in the universe if they are aware they can get killed in the military and they will say "yes I am aware." That means they are suicidal because they signed up for it on their own freewill or worse they were forced into the military. So Hitler joined the military to kill himself. He charged the bunkers in hopes he would die. He wanted to die. But somehow the bullets just kept missing him to the degree he lost fear of death. That is what Hitler's strength was. He lost his fear of death and so he lost his fear of everything. The problem is he did not go far enough mentally to the stage where he was at extreme subconscious which is cerebral state of mind. So he had the haughty arrogant aspect of subconscious dominate that is a fact but he also had vestiges of the physical desires left. So he desired to take over the world and that lead him to act out in physical ways. He had the classic signs of one with subconscious dominate state of mind but he also has parts of the physical aspects of conscious(left brain) emotional mind. That is a dangerous combination. He allowed the power of the subconscious state achieved from facing death to manipulate him in a physical way. It is okay to perceive you are rulers of the universe but avoid bringing that into the physical world in relation to physically harming people. One can do many things in their mind and say many things and that is ok, but once one starts to apply that to physically harm others they are doomed. It is okay for Hitler to suggest he is of the master race because we are lemur monkeys and we say stupid things, there is no harm in that, but once a person starts thinking they are a "special" race or a "chosen" race and starts acting it out by using physical violence on others, they need to be locked up because they are dangerous lemur monkeys. One is allowed to say anything they want vocally but once they bring it into a physically harming others realm they have allowed the delusions in their mind to affect them and they are dangerous.

It is okay to preach how great an anti-depressant drugs is, but the moment you start prescribing it to people, you harm them, you bring your delusions in the physically harming people and you are dangerous. There are no psychological drugs that will help the human mind that is a delusion or a money making assumption. Some people do not make it through, mentally speaking. That is not your business, that is not my business. Just because you prescribe a psychological drug for someone it does mean you are helping them, it means you are making money off of other peoples suffering. Heimdall just told me he does not like ones who make money at the detriment of others. Perhaps you should laugh that off because it does not matter much either way what you think about that comment at this moment in the universe. A judge once told me "If you want to kill yourself there is nothing anyone can do about it." That is great wisdom. Prescribe people who are suicidal sugar pills and tell them it is the greatest drug known to mankind. Prescribe people who are suicidal a bottle of liquor or a bag of pot and tell them to do as much as they need to get better. Sometimes a cigar is just a cigar, to quote Freud. You probably assume Freud was an idiot don't you. You probably think you are much smarter then he was don't you. I will give you a reality check. You will never ever be in his ballpark, I promise you that.

My point being, drugs psychologically cannot help a person work out their mental problems.

I can swing the other way and say, I am glad my psychologist prescribed me thirty 20 milligram pills of Paxil because later I took a handful and when I understood I was very ill, I did not call for help and accepted death, and just went to sleep, and that is what caused the accident and now I write infinite books, and I have no desire to harm myself physically anymore or harm anyone physically anymore.

So then I can say, Thank you psychologist for allowing me the opportunity to kill myself so now I am trapped in limbo and I am doomed to write infinite books about nothing, into infinity, even after I physically die. I will be writing my infinite books of vanity for eternity. Thank You psychologist you have helped me with your wisdom.

So now perhaps you will understand, you know not what you do. Lama suggested "Past is past." What this means is, I cannot take it back. I am permanently stuck in this state of mind. Suing someone for money would not help me. I do not wish to do anything anymore. I have no cravings or desires for life because I am no longer in life, mentally speaking thanks to the pills my psychologist prescribed me so she should make money from prescribing pills that do nothing. You perhaps will tell your friends how crazy I am or how dangerous I am or how weird I am but the honest truth is, subconsciously you're a dog barking at an unknown presence. You are unable to insult me any more than you already have. You are unable to kill me anymore than I already am killed. I am trapped and you want to help me, and that just tells me you think I am a liar. I do not want to be on the world stage I just want to find exit stage left.

I do not know I am dead, I understand I am dead. There is no fatigue in infinity so pumping out books every month means nothing. It does not fatigue me or stress me or worry me because I am in infinity and the worst thing that can happen from me writing my books is I will die and that is a blessing to me. One might suggest I am infinitely unorthodox. So what I understand, everything there is to understand. That means nothing or to quote Vietnam War soldiers "It don't mean nothin." My understandings are not going to rescue me. Whatever you think about me is not going to make one ounce of difference to me. My fate is sealed. It is too late for me now. All I can think is maybe if that psychologist would have said "go get drunk and don't worry so much." Instead of give me those pills, just maybe if they would said that I would have not taken those pills. You do not even understand that. The illusions are thick up here, I mean down here, I mean over here. I think I just ruined another book. I will converse with my video game to get its opinion about it.11:50:32 AM

If people want to be hung like the Shaolin monk hung himself today, they have come to the right place.

'ANY WORLD ORDER THAT ELEVATES ONE NATION OVER ANOTHER WILL FAIL'...

See religious racist zealots hate when someone suggests they are not "better" than everyone else. This is because they are extremely left brain dominate. The left brain makes one perceive they are righteous or good or better, but the subconscious perceives one is the only thing that matters, the difference is, subconscious will not allow one to harm others physically. These religious zealots will physically kill anyone who does not subscribe to their set of delusions. That is the difference. It is okay for these zealots to say they are "chosen" but once they start slaughtering other people based on that delusion, they are dangerous and should not be trusted ever. The zealots will kill you and suggest it is righteous. That is how delusional they are. They are serial killers who convince their self it is okay to kill again. It is okay to be arrogant in your words because that enables others to insult you and then you will have emotions to block, but when one speaks arrogance and then has a sea of corpses outside of their city as a result, they have simply lost their mind and they are dangerous. Ones perceptions are relative to them alone, but when ones brings their perceptions into the form of physically harming others, they are text book definition of delusional being who physically attacks hallucinations caused by their mind. If there is a unnamable and you kill someone in ITS name, you better believe you are going to be in infinite gnashing of teeth for eternity. Expect that, so you will not be so shocked when it is.

I will clarify this.

Moses said "Let my people go." He did not fight a physical war, he waged a war of words to get "his people" released. "His people" are ones who he assisted to reach slight sense of time or no strong hunger and ones who are cerebral and not physical orientated or right brain dominate.

Essentially ones who have no sense of time are "his people". These are ones who do not physically harm others. Ones who are physically orientated/ left brain slaughtered Moses. It is perhaps a shame you have slaughtered so many children because your mind was unable to understand what I understand without effort. Either way your fate is already sealed because of your slaughtering, do not underestimate that.

If you have a strong sense of time, strong hunger and feel fatigue easily, you are factually not his people, you are factually the ones who slaughtered him. Why don't you write infinite books about how that is not possible so I can laugh at your inability to write one book about how that is not possible. One might be asking "Oh author of infinite poor books how can it be that people slaughtered Moses"

"Left-brain dominated people(That have strong sense of time and thus are physically violent and impatient) may find their (Moses's people)thought processes vague (Say things like you are on drugs or you are evil)and difficult to follow(because left brainers have slight brain function so they are quite opposite in the way they think and so the left brainers usually end up slaughtering the extreme right brainers". Example Moses, Jesus, Mohammed. All slaughtered by the left brainers because they were **"quite opposite in the way they think"** in relation to the left brainers who have slight brain function and thus resort to physical violence to solve their problems. The Bible clearly says "Blessed are the peace makers." This is translated as "Blessed are the ones with right brain dominate minds or "on the right hand" as in "right"ous because they are extremely cerebral and not physically violent." Blessed are them for they are gentle like lambs in contrast to those harming others physically. One being suggested "they hear the words but do not understand" that is because, **Left-brain dominated people(have strong sense of time and thus are physically violent and impatient) may find their (Moses' people)thought processes vague (Say things like you are on drugs or you are evil)and difficult to follow(because left brainers have slight brain function), for they are _quite opposite_ in the way they think.**

Quite opposite. They read the words these wise beings suggest and the left brainers perceive the wise beings are "weird, evil, insane, on drugs" and then the left brainers determine they should kill them because they are perceived to be different by left brainers. There is simply nothing to argue about. Face reality and grow up. So now you understand everything about these wise beings, you march your ass outside and start proclaiming you had it all wrong all along. You had it all wrong and you encouraged hate and hostility and murder because you had it all wrong and misunderstood everything these wise beings were saying all along. And then you pray someone has mercy on your soul because I certainly may not. To suggest you are "meek shall inherit the earth" while you go around telling other beings you are "chosen" and they are not, is the most arrogant comment one can ever make. I got news for you, you're a unnamable dam lemur monkey and if you don't like it, bring it, boy. You are chosen for infinite punishment and infinite gnashing of teeth, but I would not be bragging about that, boy.

Being obese and wise is impossible.

This is great wisdom even though I am uncertain who came up with this particular quote . I will quote it out of respect for the infinitely wise person who said it even though I do not know who said it.

"Being obese and wise is impossible."

The whole premise behind loss of cravings and desires and thus diminished desire to eat is based on the fact when one with a strong sense of time, eat so they feel satisfaction. One craves certain foods and when they eat those foods they feel satisfaction. When one is extreme right brain or has slight sense of time, cravings are all but gone so there is no satisfaction after one eats. There simply is no pleasure from eating. There simply is no mental escape from eating certain foods. This is also true with drugs and money and many other physical attachments. One does not eat food they dislike because they would get no satisfaction from it so they eat food they like so they get satisfaction from it. One might suggest if you have a strong craving for a certain food you are certainly left brain dominate and thus have a strong sense of time and have attachments mentally that when not met you become depressed.

Letter to someone about something:

I accidentally became extreme right brained which means I lost my sense of time. Some call this nirvana. This means I am in nothingness. That is complex. But what it means is I have few cravings or desires in relation to satisfaction. "i cant get no satisfaction." lol

I do not sense past or future because my short term memory is nearly gone. I am like mr magoo. I cannot tell I'am writing books fast, and i cannot feel fatigue or mental strain so I can wake up and write for 18 hours and never even get up to stretch or eat and I feel no side effects.

So a left brain person is **quite opposite** .

They sense past and future and have a strong sense of time, and strong desires and cravings and they get satisfaction.

They tend to act in a more physical way and right brain people tend to act in a more cerebral way.

In relation to the comment "Blessed are the peacemakers"

Some ones with no sense of time or ones in nirvana or right brain extreme, tend to fight their battles within, in relation to "the kingdom is within" their minds. The left brains people tend to fight their battles in the physical world. Some seek satisfaction from drugs or money and many other things because they get satisfaction from these things because they are not as cerebral based. I would get no satisfaction from a vacation because I am on a permanent mental vacation so to speak.

So I am very weird in contrast to ones with left brain or ones with a sense of time because

people may find their thought processes vague and difficult to follow

So in this respect I am in another world mentally than those with left brain and because of the way I achieved it, I tend to be weary of anyone who attempts to "control" me so to speak because I am at the extreme of nirvana or right brain.

"Right brains are honored in eastern cultures more than western." **They are seen as less smart because of the manner in which they process information.** Rights don't go from Point A to Point B. **Right brains don't like to listen to directions** (in relation to children who do not like to listen to directions and then adults deem they are troubled children and in relation to freedom because freedom is all about not being controlled.)and don't like to read them

I have no concept of time. I am mentally literally in infinity and that denotes I am unable to appreciate control. Two months after the accident I decided to write infinite books. So far 5 books in 5 months and I am 30k words into the sixth book and I started it 2 days ago. I will write books until I drop and I feel no need to eat so M reminds me to eat. The monks suggest they will allow me to write infinite books and they will stay out of my way but I feel I like to stay here because I am ware many wish to claim me, so to speak. My only focus is to write infinite books until I drop I am not aware of any other purpose at this time.

Thank You

END2:27:21 PM

"don't like to listen to directions" I will sum this aspect up swiftly. I don't follow rules, even my own rules and that translates into, I have no morals and no class. That is why I understand everything and you never will. I have no limits and you are in a cage. So you stay in your little isolation security cage because the big fish has arrived, and he eats for no reason. I will do anything to remain free so you should never assume I wouldn't. I had to kill myself to get free so you should never assume I wouldn't do it again to remain free. I am what is known as a post-suicide and you never met one of those so you should think very carefully before attempting to speak to me."Rights think and learn in visual, kinesthetic and audio images. They don't memorize well"

What this comment about "they do not memorize well" means is, when you have a test based on memory as in memorize how to spell these words or memorize how to do this math problem, you are in fact conditioning these right brain beings into left brain.

You are failing them because they are lacking in memory because they have real wisdom. That is the trade off. You can be physically based and desire and craving based or you can be cerebral based and wise and non violent. So essentially spelling tests are turning any child who is naturally right brain dominate into a left brain physical based physical violence based beings.

All children are right brain dominate when born because if they had a sense of time they would rip the mother apart while in the womb. They would be claustrophobic and paranoid and impatient. So "suffer the children to come unto me" means Jesus was aware what "you" do to them. And he said "you know not you do." You are turning perfect mindful beings into violent physically based monsters every time you give them a spelling test and fail them when their memory isn't working properly because they are wise or right brain dominate. So why don't you just think about that for the rest of eternity and think about how many children you ruined with your "tests of wisdom". Why don't you write infinite books about how nothing I say can be true, boy.

Extreme Right brain dom = subconscious dom = slight sense of time = Nirvana = very cerebral

I am infinitely mad because I already understand you will keep giving small children spelling tests and then tell them they are failures when they cannot remember the words. So never assume you are safe from me, the last thing in the universe you are, is safe from me. You are infinitely far from safe.

I think I just ruined my book. I blame it on the rain, I mean the hurricane, I mean the super nova. I am a lemur monkey, what the hell do you expect. I really thought you were some sort of sloth as in "slow" mentally speaking but I cannot argue with lemur monkey, they are kind of "slow" also. I should be compassionate considering you are in fact a lemur monkey but women are not lemur monkeys they are some sort of, I am not certain, some eye beam kind of creature.

Infinity has no favorites and takes no sides.

There is no fast or slow in infinity there just is.

Okay back to reality.

"Man needs difficulties; they are necessary for health." Carl Jung

Mental struggles make us humble, physical wars make us barbaric.

The great truth is, you may have strong emotions and they cause a sense of time and they cause labels. This locks the mind up and makes it take everything personal. I had an accident and got thrown into infinity. I lost all labels and all time stamps and I cannot find solid ground at all. They asked Lama what is reality, and I laughed so hard because he said. North, south, east, west, up and down. You perhaps do not even find the humor in that. What he was saying is, he is the center of reality and reality is infinity. That is true for everyone. A general once said something to the effect ,"When things go wrong with your command start searching for the reason starting in concentric circles around your own two feet." That is exactly right. The universe starts at you and moves outward. You cannot figure out where you are by looking outward you can only figure out where you are at by looking at yourself or inward. Your problems are usually found in the same spot your own two feet are in. Lama said north , south, east, west ,up and down and he was hesitant. It is as if we wasn't really sure. So this whole right brain dominate subconscious dominate extreme turns one into an absent minded professor. I can verbally joust with Lama as I did in my last book because he will not get upset he will laugh and say "this guy is more insane than I am." We as in the subconscious dominate to an extreme are insane but we are not physically insane as in we do not mean harm, we are jokes. We are jokes to ourselves and jokes to you. You simply are not going to be able to get a straight answer out of me because I am far too philosophical. You may perceive I am very hostile but in reality I am not use to this state of mind. The understanding or clarity harms me greatly for moments and then I snap back and crack jokes and I do that many times a day. I cannot fix it and I cannot stop it. It simply does not matter anyway. Whatever happens is probably for the best. I can slightly say one great truth. I used to be very physically harmful to myself and now I write many books and never think about harming myself. So I rest in the fact I am better off now. Nothing else is relevant because I was getting very close to offing myself in my many years of depression so if something happens to me I am on borrowed time anyway. That is about as close to a solid understanding as I am capable of. I tell my neurologist it was a good accident. I am not physically violent towards myself now. That to me is progress. That may be as far as I will ever get. I made some progress in my life so that to me is something. It is all really an inside joke to me at this stage. I try my hardest to get mad in my books but I tend to fail and come across as wishy washy.

I just overheard the news and this M person said "Fact, they did it, they are the bad guys." And I fell out of my chair. Then he said "They are sophisticated people." Perhaps he missed the lemur monkey show. Rocks are very sophisticated rocks. The rocks sophistication is extremely sophisticated, sophisticationally speaking, so to speak.

This is a comment by Buddha.

"A wise man, recognizing that the world is but an illusion, does not act as if it were real, so he escapes the suffering."

This needs clarification. A wise man denotes one who is extreme right brain or subconscious dominate. The world is not an illusion but words from others are not directed at you. This means do not take anything anyone says to you seriously. Do not believe the definitions of words because words are simply grunts from people who are talking to their self. If someone wants to physically harm you they will find a way so you cannot defend against that completely, you can just isolate yourself in a hole of fear. But if they want to, they will find your there also. Now words are another game. They are illusions. If someone praises you with words that is an illusion, if someone insults you with words that is an illusion. The best way to respond to either is to say thank you or perhaps. So do not act as if it were real , means, If someone insults them, they do not resort to physical violence but that is only certain if one is a wise man or one is extreme right brain or subconscious dominate.

I am not saying you should be subconscious dominate. I am not saying that at all because I got robbed of my ability to feel satisfaction. I am trapped in writing infinite books. I am unable to taste food. I am unable to remember what my books are about. I am unable to tell how much time has passed. I am stuck in some sort of weird mental state and I am unable to escape it so I would be a fool to say you should definitely do this. I do not perceive we are all supposed to be like this. I perceive there has to be both to have either. If everyone is subconscious dominate then no one is, because there is no contrast. Perhaps this is what the middle way is. Everything is for a reason. Perhaps "everyone should reach no sense of time to be less physically orientated" is in fact a delusion. I miss satisfaction. I miss having a big meal and saying "That was delicious and I am satisfied." So this accident may be a good lesson about why not to go too far into the subconscious extreme. Maybe try to be a little less emotional but do not think you are righteous because I understand I am at the extreme and it is no picnic. I am certainly better off this way but that is relative to the fact I was extremely suicidal before. It is perhaps foolishness to assume you are wise to "meek shall inherit the earth" and "Turn the other cheek" and Submit" and "avoid anger to avoid suffering". Taken to its extreme it is a mental battle every single day. The entire physical spectrum is gone. No desire, no cravings you are a machine in the now. That is the extreme. So I am aware why I do not preach this method because I am at the extreme and I am not foolish enough to suggest you are unwise to not seek this extreme. You are perhaps very wise to not seek this extreme. I messed up so I am doomed. That's an honest statement. I find no fault with those who hold onto emotions and sense of time, I am harsh with them because I hate the fact I am no longer among them. I miss it and it has only been seven months. I try to be angry because I miss it. I try to be haughty because I miss it. I try to feel something but I cannot. I feel nothing. I am in a machine state. I am a machine and I can emulate emotions but in reality I feel absolutely nothing emotionally. I will sit here in my little stupid chair and write into infinity and I perhaps will never blink and I perhaps will never get tired and I perhaps will never feel happiness or sadness I will just attempt to emulate those emotions because I can no longer have those emotions. So I am biased. I am uncertain if others who reach this no sense of time are at this extreme. Perhaps they are not. Perhaps they are at a stage they are happy and joyful. Perhaps they still have a sense of taste. Perhaps they still have a sense of satisfaction. I certainly do not, so I am only able to explain how it is from my perspective. So you see I am perhaps attempting to tell you to avoid this. Perhaps it is best to be able to feel. Perhaps it is best to be able to get sad and happy and satisfaction. Perhaps it is best to suffer a little bit. Perhaps it is best to stay in an emotional state. I perceive I am overloading. I perceive I am on the verge of losing my mind totally. I have to ponder sedatives now. I have to ponder ways to calm down. I have to ponder ways to dumb myself down because the progression is too fast.

So you see, I am experiencing what happens when you "those who try to save their self will lose their self, those who lose their self will find their self." I lost myself and found the machine which is subconscious. No morals and no concept of time and no feelings and no class. There is simply no such thing as going back. Every day I try to attack and feel emotions in my books. I try to fight with all of my might to go back and it is all in vain. I went from concern I would go back and in 5 months I am now at a stage of trying to find things that might make me go back.

This is exactly why there are monks who teach people to deal with this state of mind. These monks spend their whole life learning how to teach people to deal with this alternate state of mind. It is far beyond the range of "take this pill three times a day". I have taken all the pills and all the drugs and I am certain they are no match for this thing. They are jokes in contrast to this machine state of mind. So perhaps that is a wakeup call for you in case you assume I am suggesting you become like this. I am not suggesting it this moment in time. Perhaps it is a curse we can talk to each other and tell each other how to reach this state of mind. I honestly do not think these early wise beings wanted it to be a "do this or you are evil" kind of thing. From what I understand they had one hell of a mental ride and if I understand them well enough, they were suffering mentally quite a bit. I do not mean they were weak I mean this state of mind is very harsh on a person. I submit I may not be use to it yet, but I am aware I keep going further into it. I keep getting more and more machine state. I keep typing more and more and more and more. I cannot even break free to play the video game. I cannot even break free to eat. I cannot even break free to pause. The entire physical emotional world is dying in my mind. I perceive I am a machine waiting for input so I can respond. So my only defense is to keep yelling and screaming to emulate rage because I am mindful that will not be possible much longer. I am trying to hold onto my old self and I cannot.6:12:08 PM

4:49:33 AM

"Time is a component of the measuring system used to sequence events, to compare the durations of events and the intervals between them, and to quantify the motions of objects. Time has been a major subject of religion, philosophy, and science, but defining it in a non-controversial manner applicable to all fields of study has consistently eluded the greatest scholars." WIKIPEDIA.COM

"used to sequence events" = left brain acknowledges time , right brain has no sequence so it only see's infinity. Left Brain perceives past, present and future and right brain see's past present and future as one thing. So time is relative or varies to perception which is controlled by the gamma waves in the brain. There is perhaps "absolute time" but that is something that is beyond observation. I will clarify this in the next book.

"A gamma wave is a pattern of brain waves. Brain waves are associated with perception, consciousness and have been used in the study of concentration on a particular object or activity."

"Gamma waves are involved in higher mental activity"

Higher mental activity relates to extreme concentration or heightened awareness. So the heightened awareness one achieves with extreme right brain, wakes one up to the fact there is "no time." Event sequences are not a function of time but simply things happening in an infinite vacuum. An atom never dies if left alone in a vacuum so an atom is infinite. "It depends on which isotope of which element you are talking about. Carbon's isotope C-12 lasts forever because it is a stable, non-radioactive element."

http://wiki.answers.com/Q/How_long_does_an_atom_live

So a carbon atom defies time itself. If time was a true field it would decay all atoms, but a carbon isotope lasts forever. Maybe that is not true, maybe it just seems like it lasts forever.

This is some pattern matching so take it with a grain of salt.

Atomic			Number			6
Atomic		Mass		Average:		12.011
Melting	Point:	3823	K	(3550°C	or	6422°F)
Boiling	Point:	4098	K	(3825°C	or	6917°F)
Density:						2.267g/cu.cm.
Velocity	of		sound	[/m	s-1]:	18350
Hardness		Scale		Mohs:		0.5
Stable Isomers (2)						

Six electrons. In relation to the beast.

Atomic mass in relation to the number of disciples.

Carbon is in the food you eat, the clothes you wear, the cosmetics you use and the gasoline that fuels your car. Six denotes physical, earthly.

So the carbon atom (C-12 lasts forever) defies or proves there is no time because if it lasts forever, then there could not have been a big bang. Big bang denotes a beginning yet Carbon denotes forever. So there are many things happening that give off the illusion of time but Carbon proves there is only forever because if there was time, carbon would be decayed by actual time.

Carbon-12 is the most abundant of the two stable isotopes of the element carbon, accounting for 98.89% of carbon; it contains **6 protons, 6 neutrons, and 6 electrons.**

666 is the proof there is no time. Carbon-12 represents and proves infinity of forever. It is a stable isotope. It is the most abundant. This suggests infinity or forever is the main stay and everything else that appears to suggest limits or decay are side issues. The main stay is infinity or no decay. Its only possible to have no decay in a True Vacuum. A true Vacuum eliminates the possibility of decay. So the beast(666)= Carbon -12, would suggest proof this is infinity and not a sequential string of events.

"The known atomic number 7 has 1 sense: Nitrogen a common nonmetallic element that is **normally a colorless odorless tasteless inert diatomic gas; constitutes 78 percent of the atmosphere by volume; a constituent of all living tissues = nothingness = without form = unnamable**

The element seemed so inert that Lavoisier named it azote, meaning "without life". Without life = unnamable = void = no past present or future = inanimate = no sense of taste, no sense of smell, no color = black void ="Gen 1:2 And the earth(universe) was **without form, and void;** and **darkness** was upon the face of the deep."

Without form = vacuum ; void = vacuum ; darkness = colorless; deep = infinity = true vacuum = no time = carbon 12 that lasts forever. Carbon 12 lasts forever so it is impossible there is time because forever and limited cannot both be true at once. So the universe is all a true vacuum and there are things in the true vacuum that give off the impression time or sequenced events are happening but Carbon 12, denoted contains **6 protons, 6 neutrons, and 6 electrons** and being the most abundant isotope suggests there is no time, just forever or infinity.

Isotope = Hence Todd suggested the Greek term for "at the same place" as a suitable name. At the same place denotes "I am the alpha and omega the beginning and the end." This denotes everything is one thing. The past is the future and the future is the past, in a true vacuum. This is explained with IS. Everything IS, not going to be or was, everything IS or "at the same place". I will go play my video game since I understand there is no argument for what I just accomplished. Enjoy your vacuum but don't knock yourself out. It simply does not matter if I explain it properly to you or not. I understand it, and it is perhaps best if you do not understand it. Ignorance is truly an acquired taste. What I just explained kind of kills the whole "can't wait to see what happens" fun. I think it is best people stay in ignorance because once they understand it is all a true vacuum what is the point. Why do you want to know the truth? Perhaps a better way to put it is, you cannot handle the truth if you have emotions of feelings or sentimentality. The truth will set you free but that is not such a good thing. Ignorance keeps one on the tread mill. It is factually beyond a doubt this "reality" is nothing but a true vacuum but that is not a good thing to boast about because then one has to face the fact nothing is really truly happening at all. That is too harsh for a mind to understand if that mind is not awake. It is a rather bitter pill to swallow. Only a mind in a machine state that is not affected by emotions or sentiments can look at the true vacuum reality and accept it and go on. A mind with too many emotions and desires for purpose would perhaps snap. One's mind would have to accept the fact all of its attachments in life are illusions and this would be to strong of a reality for an emotional mind to accept, so that mind would attack that understanding because it would be unable to face the reality it has been doing many things to hold on to these attachments and it has all been for nothing. That understanding would require extreme humility and one would have to be very meek to grasp, all of their battles in life have been for naught. I just destroyed your perceived universe so your only defense would be to suggest I am insane, and I will submit I am insane, for your benefit. I will submit I am insane so that you can have purpose. You will have no purpose if I submit I tell the truth.5:41:00 AM

I understand why I never edit my books and leave the anger in my books because I have been aware from the start, there is nothing happening. Some may perceive anger in my words or rage but that is because they perceive illusions that are simply not happening in reality. I understand I write book swiftly because I am acting natural. I am not trying to be good or be bad, I am just being what I am. I am not trying to satisfy any delusional craving for satisfaction or acceptance. I understand now. I understand why I do not wish to push my beliefs or my understandings on anyone. I understand it would perhaps be far too harsh for ones not in a machine state to handle. It perhaps would harm them mentally because it would shatter their purpose. I have no purpose but I do have the emotional capacity to be harmed by that understanding.

I ponder if the supreme being is not outside of the vacuum "of space". The morals that unnamable and evil suggest would perhaps not be possible relative to a supreme being in infinity because morals would denote labels and labels would be contrast and contrast is not possible in infinity because everything would be one thing. So these morals or values are perhaps a solution to attempt to keep everyone mindfully fearful and this is a valid solution because without a certain fear factor there may be total chaos in humanity.

Like a child in the womb this supreme being would not be able to have emotions because they would drive it mad in infinity. If every time it saw a person do a harmful thing it would rip itself apart.

So it would only be viable in a machine state of mind. It would take things as they come and have no expectation for the future and have altered memory the past. It would have to function in real time and also be passive about anything that happens or not able to judge. It would have to be without judgment because judgments would lead it to destroy itself. There would be too many judgments to pass so it would destroy itself attempting to keep up in infinity so it would become emotionless. It would be passive. It would be like a computer or a machine. A computer does not get worried if you get a bunch of popup ad viruses. If one yells at their computer the computer has no response. If one is happy with the computer the computer has no response. It is in a state of now. It waits for input and then reacts to that input but that no expectations when the next input will happen. So these computers may very well be mans indirect creation of the machine state of mind or the subconscious or extreme right brain state of mind. So this is perhaps what happened to me.

I played the video game which is a computer game , and the computer is a humans invention indirectly or subconsciously modeled after the subconscious machine aspect of the mind. So after playing the machine for an extreme amount of time I woke up to the machine and became like the machine. This would fall in line with the subconscious assumes the identity of anything it comes in contact with. So after an extreme amount of playing the game and considering the game was very difficult because it was for real money, I assumed the identity or mental state of a machine or pure logical thought , to defeat the machine, and in doing so I became a machine. I have many characteristics of a machine. No sense of time, few emotional attachments, no worry, no real concept of past or future, not a very strong short term memory but my "RAM" random access memory is quite strong.

So to put it in an logic equation:

Man makes computer = computer is in the image of subconscious or machine logic state = person plays on machine and becomes extreme subconscious or extreme logic state.

In a computer file system there is random access files and sequential files.

So the sequential files are the slower or less powerful method of retrieving data and the random access files are the more powerful way of retrieving data.

Left brain is sequential based and thus the less powerful aspect and that sequential aspect means one has a good short term memory but they also have emotions and contrast and thus a strong sense of time.

Right brain is the powerhouse, and it has random access, but it has poor short term memory but powerful concentration and the ability to detect patterns.

So left brain is conscious emotional and right brain is subconscious lack of emotions or the machine state.

So this means computers are an invention by man that resembles the subconscious or right brain and in turn people will slowly start to become subconscious dominate and right brain dominate or reach the machine state of mind. So man has invented something that will ensure mankind will become this machine state of mind, and man has invented the computer perhaps subconsciously or indirectly to achieve that.

So a person finds the computer "fun" and exciting which is an emotional left brain symptom but then they stay on the computer and slowly it transforms their mind to right brain or machine state or subconscious dominate. This is perhaps obvious to some.

So all of the main religions attempt to suggest ways to reach the subconscious state of mind which is the machine state or the no sense of time state of mind or the state of mind without judgments in relation to good or bad, or the infinity state of mind, and they are all obsolete now because computers will do the exact same thing and it is not a question of if computers will do it, computers will do it because they are far to "attractive" or "fun".

So mankind has created a machine that is better than he is , in relation to a computer can do far more calculations in a second than a human can, and now humans are assuming the identity of the machines because that is what subconscious does. Subconscious finds something an attaches or assumes its identity. So we have indirectly turned ourselves into the "Borg" or machines by creating machines greater than us. There is no possible way to avoid that now. Computers are to "popular. They are everywhere and everyone loves them to one degree or another. We will be assimilated by our own creation.

This would explain the world financial collapse. A machine state of mind means money is only needed to buy food and some other mild things. Money serves no purpose outside of basic needs because money is a desire or craving based material thing. One does not need a big house because one who is becoming like a machine mentally no longer gets gratification from having big material objects because the emotions such as greed and lust or pride are being silenced as a result of using computers. People who use computers are becoming more interested in cerebral thoughts and less interested in monetary or physical aspects because the subconscious is more cerebral. So the revolution is that we made computers and they are turning us into machines. So computers are an invention that will have an unintended consequence on society. Computer are going to turn us away from emotions and judgments and thus hate and wars and turn us into an extremely cerebral docile species.

One simple example of looking at how computers are in fact emotional conditioning tools is to look at the events that happen when a person gets a virus on their computer. Some people get a pop up ad virus and freak out and get very angry and usually end up calling a "wise man" who can come and get the virus off their system. Then there are ones who get a virus and do not panic and think what they should do. They may research the virus and find the best solution or software to clean that virus so, they avoided panic or avoided getting emotional and instead, think the problem through and thus come to an understanding and learned from that "suffering" or that virus. So they did not lose their head when all around them was madness. So they avoided emotions or fear or panic and thus thought their way out of the problem. So the point would be summed up as. Life throws problems at people and some people get emotional and panic and are defeated by the problems and some people keep their cool and think through the problem. It is perhaps much deeper than that because the internet puts so much knowledge at ones finger tips, one is almost unable not find a solution to their problem. I recall a joke I read and it shows a patient in a doctor's office and the patient said "I have already diagnosed myself online but I am here for a second opinion." So the society is based on specialists. For example a stock broker is a stock specialist but now with the internet one can do their own research so they are putting the stock broker out of business. A doctor is essentially in general reduced to a person who has the ability to prescribe test such as CT pr MRI scans. They essentially do not know anything a person cannot find out about on the internet. The amount of information on the internet makes any specialist pale in comparison and since the internet is still in its infancy the "specialists" will only become more out of date as time goes on.

Education itself it extinct because there is no school that can ever compare to the amount of information one can find on the internet at the click of a mouse. A school is simply a teacher teaching a subject to a student. That student can sit at home and find much better quality information from far more perspectives than that teacher can ever provide. One can go into a chat room and speak their mind and they will be taught all they ever need to know about sociology and psychology.

"The Internet was originally developed by DARPA, the Defense Advanced Research Projects Agency, as a means to share information on defense research between involved universities and defense research facilities."

http://wiki.answers.com/Q/Who_invented_the_Internet

The DARPA is a branch of the DOD or Department of Defense. The internet is what is known as a social engineering experiment created by the "higher ups". The end results of the "experiment" were already understood and so the internet is simply a drug that was given to society with the understanding it would have certain effects or outcomes on society.

Stalin suggested "Religion is the opiate of the masses" I am suggesting the internet is the new opiate.

It is rather a complex concept to consider because this means the internet is a Trojan Horse. It is well disguised as light. But that is also a misunderstanding. One can argue if the internet makes one more docile and makes on more subconscious dominate or cerebral and less prone to physical violence it is a good thing. Perhaps that is a bad thing. Either way it is a bit too late to change it now. China blocks its people from viewing certain web sites because knowledge is power.

Now consider this concept. The DOD creates this Trojan horse that is masked as knowledge and appears to be a great tool for the masses. The DOD understands no country would be able to resist such a tasty treat as an information highway. Who on earth would suggest knowledge and loss of ignorance as a result, is bad? The reality is, as one gets less ignorant, ones become "wiser" and thus becomes more docile, and therefore less "combative". So the masses become sedated. The "opiate of the masses" is the internet.

Washington in his final years retreated to his farm and focused on growing food. In doing this he was out in the rain and this caused him illness which eventually killed him. So Washington was a farmer and then undertook this "revolution" to allow everyone to be considered free and it was quite a struggle and after it was over he went back to farming. Just before he died he pondered that he was a farmer and he fought this huge revolution and then he was free to farm and he understood before the revolution he was free to farm, so the revolution was extreme vanity because his last words were "Tis well." In relation to "just as well." He went through all of that effort to be able to be free to farm when he was free to farm anyway. He went full circle and realized he did nothing but go to a great amount of effort to do what he was allowed to do anyway.

Consider these people in the Amazon who have no contact with civilization. They are hunters and gatherers. They have no crops. They have no set place to live. That wander from area to area where the hunting and gathering is good. They have a wide variety of things they eat on a day to day basis based on what they gathered that day. They are not doing anything but living in the moment. They have no expectations of the future in relation to a "retirement fund" or a "retirement house" or vacations or goals to reach for the future. These people have no laws or rules because they are bound by the law of nature which is survival of the fittest. They have no laws because no person in their group is going to "rip" them off or steal from them because they have nothing to steal. They exist on a day to day basis. They have certain plants that they use for recreation or as recreational drugs and it is not because they are ignorant or foolish but because the drugs are there. They have discovered a way to enhance their situation or make it alerted which is a form of release. This is in relation to Freud who suggested "Sometimes a cigar is just a cigar." Maybe sometimes a drug is not evil and is not good, it just is. Maybe people who do drugs are not evil or good they just do the drugs because they can do the drugs.

The concept that drugs harm the mind or the person is perhaps misguided because ignorance is bliss or spiritual joy. If society seeks absolute tolerance society will lose spiritual joy. This is perhaps complex but, if everyone gets along and no one argues or fights then we becomes one collective and therefore we lose the capacity for emotions. So this group called the Taliban are perceived to be against technology and against education. So one might suggest they are for ignorance or are against too much understanding or knowledge because too much understanding or knowledge means one will eventually lose bliss or spiritual joy or become a machine. Society in general wants to know all the answers but after they find the last answer what is left? There will simply no longer be wonder and awe. There will no longer be conflict. There will no longer be battles to fight. This is relative to the characteristics of a true vacuum in relation to, much ado about nothing. There is much effort required to chase ones tail.

The serpent that is eating his own tail is trying very hard to be relevant, but accomplishing nothing. So there are many people attempting to eat their own tail because subconsciously they are aware there is nothing else to do but to try to be relevant, in a true vacuum.

So the opposite point of view of education is important and progress is important means everyone will eventually lose their bliss and spiritual joy because no matter what anyone thinks, if we continue to become more educated and less ignorant we are going to discover we have no purpose, and then chaos will rule.

So the DOD invented the internet as a form of sedating the masses and accidentally made itself irrelevant. We are all connecting on a world level now with the internet and thus will achieve a one world control structure, and thus individual cultures will become a thing of the past, and the only thing that will not be tolerated is individual thought. If we are all in a state of one world order what is the purpose of the DOD? What is the purpose for individual cultures in each country? All the separate cultures will be thrown into a melting pot, and eventually all separate cultures will be considered one humanity culture. Essentially all individual identity will be lost.

So the scenario would be: The one world structure would grow enough food to feed everyone and make housing available to everyone and make electricity available to everyone. So this would eliminate the need for money. So what would ones purpose be? This is perhaps exactly what ignorance is bliss means. Every time you get a bit less ignorant you get a step closer to being that serpent with his tail in his mouth. We all end up in the same spot no matter how hard we try to run away from that spot.

How one chooses to chase their tail is what freedom is all about.

"Buddha described nirvana as the perfect peace of the state of mind that is free from craving, anger and other afflictive states (kilesa) The subject is at peace with the world, has compassion for all and gives up obsessions and fixations."

This is simply saying one is in a mental machine state. Passive would be a good way to put it. At peace with the world is impossible in Nirvana because peace is a feeling in relation to satisfaction. One cannot be satisfied and also have no fixations and obsessions. Being at peace is a fixation. I can simulate anger and humor but I cannot be those things, they are simply simulated phantom characteristics that my mind use to have. Free from craving is out of context. Breathing is a craving to keep living, Eating is a craving to keep living. Even in Nirvana one has the understanding they have to eat or they will die. The difference is one in Nirvana eats for no reason where one with a sense of time eats as the result of a craving. If one is in a mindful machine state they are at peace because they have no feelings. So the proper way to say it is, Nirvana is when one is mentally passive to an extreme but not an absolute extreme. Has compassion for all is relative. Passion is relative to compassion so passion denotes feelings. There is no feelings in the machine state that are tangible in respect to being constant. I recall when my dog baby blue had a cardiac arrest right in front of me some books ago I was sad for a moment or so. I documented it my book and by the time I dug a hole you put her in the back yard, I was over it. So the feelings happen but they are just phantom emotions. I recall four years earlier our other dog sugar had cancer and we put her to sleep and I cried for several days and was emotionally sad for about 2 weeks.

So I am certainly in Nirvana but that is not some magical state of mind because it is in fact the absence of feelings and cravings to an extreme but not to an absolute.

Some may suggest it is similar to having no conscience but that is a misunderstanding because a killer may be perceived to have no conscience but a killer has extreme cravings and desires to kill. A "serial killer" is essentially a person who is mentally an emotional wreck controlled by cravings and desires, and these desires lead to control determinations such as control over who dies next. So a killer craves control and this control over life and death in their mind gives them satisfaction, so they certainly have a conscience but it is not on the scale of people with slight conscience it is off the scale in relation to ones with normal conscience. They are simply control freaks. There are people who are control freaks and they do kill people. They are under the influence of the exact same emotions though, as a killer. They seek to covet things and this gives them gratification and satisfaction.

"mind that is free from craving, anger and other afflictive states" Mind that is free is an absolute. One's mind is not free from craving or one would not breathe. One's mind is not free from anger or one would not breathe. One would give up on living if one's mind was free from cravings or anger. So this would be properly clarified by suggesting when one's mind is extremely free but not absolutely free from cravings and anger to the extent they are passive about most thoughts. One way to look at it is, one is not capable of the extreme concentration the subconscious requires to remain dominate if they have all of these attachments and cravings running through their mind. Nirvana is not a spiritual guru, hocus pocus "you are so special" kind of thing, it is a machine state of mind and that is because the subconscious has to turn off so many things such as cravings and desires in order to work at full power. One passage in the bible says "As he increases I decrease" As subconscious increases the feelings and cravings and desires decrease. This is simply conservation of energy. There is a finite amount of power and to enable the subconscious other stuff has to get turned off.

Nirvana is really a state of mind reached when one sacrifices through mental conditioning their left brain emotional or feeling capacity to enable the subconscious, right brain, extreme concentration or heightened awareness ability. I see no mountain from my mole hill.

So one with emotions or strong feeling might suggest this absence of feelings is sad or dangerous or scary but that is because they have feelings and emotions. I am unable to feel sad or happy for more than a moment so it does not bother me, so I do not worry and I am not stressed. It is silencing of one aspect of the mind to enable the power house of concentration aspect of the mind to become dominate. I am not sad and I am not happy, I am not at peace and I am not at war. I do not feel an emotion long enough to suggest I feel that way. I do not feel depression or anger long enough to suggest I am depressed or angry. So I go through many shades but never rest on my laurels or I am not able to remain in one mental state for more than a moment. This is what "remaining on the fence" is. It is like a pendulum swinging back and forth very swiftly. Swiftly in relation to minutes or seconds not hours but the machine state of mind is extreme concentration, and that can only happen if everything else is turned off or silenced. So all my anger in my books is my minds way of attempting to be emotional or feel emotions because my mind is aware they disappeared. They are gone without a doubt and my mind is attempting to simulate them. I can say, I love the whole world and I love everything, but in reality I do not feel shit. I do not even remember the feeling of love because that is a desire or craving that can be satisfied. I do not have a favorite food but I used to love shrimp. I eat anything now because I can't taste it much and I have no contrasts to what is good and what is bad.

What purpose would I have to say things that make others think I am so wise or smart or peaceful when in reality I cannot feel satisfaction from their praises. I cannot feel ashamed as a result of their insults. One cannot insult or praise a rock. I swing from caring to not caring to attempting to figure what caring is. What is love, what is hate? Will acknowledgment from others help me feel again? I have no idea what I wrote yesterday in this crap book so how am I supposed to care about what I wrote yesterday? I just wrote that last sentence and use write instead of wrote and write in present tense and wrote is past tense so I had to go correct it, because my mind is so much into the "now" it is losing its ability to use past and future tense words. I am also stuck on using who instead of that. I use "One who is", instead of "one that is." I am uncertain why that would be. I perceive it is just the syntax of the language and subconscious does not acknowledge the syntax because the syntax is a rule and subconscious is infinity or no limits so it is, anti-rules or anti-establishment and that is the nature of free or infinite. There cannot be rules or laws in infinity or no sense of time because that would be a limit and thus negate infinity. I need to stop typing and play the video game because this book is going to be un publishable if I do not. I have to write about something.12:21:47 PM

I am wise to put many angry words in my books so that no person will come to the conclusion they should ask me to speak in public because they are unable to fully grasp what I mean when I suggest I decided to write infinite books and simply have no room to do anything but write infinite books.

Sometimes a great war can lead to a long peace and sometimes a great peace is the path to a long war.

I noticed something yesterday and noticed it again today. The phone rang and it was a very long duration between rings. I mean the phone rang and I expected it to ring again and it seemed like it was a very long wait for that second ring. So something is funky about that because I never noticed that until yesterday. So it is perhaps a new symptom or a symptom I am still in progression and as I go further more things keeps coming out of the wood work so to speak.

And to add a bit of humor I also just noticed I am good and everyone else is normal.

I tend to talk myself into corners because I am in shock at how powerful subconscious mind really is. It is just so powerful when unlocked to an extreme I can sympathize with all these people who say it is "Unnamable" etc. It can make them go to huge lengths to try to describe and it is so powerful it tricks them into anything. It is simply a very powerful aspect of the mind and everyone already knows that I just happen to be able to demonstrate how powerful it is because in one way or another I unlocked it to the extreme. I am uncertain how but I am sure it was one of two ways. Perhaps I will just keep writing books until someone notices something is weird.

I am not intelligent enough to know if subconscious is in fact the "unnamable aspect" of the spirit. I am not intelligent enough to comment on spirit or soul. I am only intelligent enough to understand if this subconscious aspect is the "unnamable aspect" then I am wise to never comment about unnamable because it is far too powerful and I do not desire to get its attention. I am intelligent enough to understand if this subconscious thing is the unnamable aspect, unnamable certainly does

56

not need my help with anything. I understand this subconscious aspect is so powerful, in order to operate it has to turn off everything even sense of time , even sense of taste , and it focuses all of its energy into one pin point. So it has to turn everything off to operate that is how powerful it is. It cannot function with feelings, psychical sensations, taste, hearing is altered, all of these things take up power so subconscious aspect is so powerful it negates them all. This gives one an impression of nothingness, but that because the concentration or heightened mental capacity is so great the other stuff cannot work while the concentration aspect works. I can only say it is really powerful. Beyond really powerful, beyond understanding powerful. I feel like I am a third wheel. I feel like I talk about it as if I am not a part of it. So that would lead some to perceive I am possessed and that is a good way to look at it. But that is because subconscious aspect is so powerful it also is another entity separate from me. It is simply too strange to describe in detail and accurately.

The subliminal test is a good way to explain it. They show a movie with a subliminal cigarette ad in it.

So a person consciously does not see that ad flash by but subconsciously they see that ad. That is somewhat of a contradiction, that person does not see that ad but that person does see that ad.

So there are two distinct things happening or two distinct personalities going on. One personality is "dumb" and misses the ad and one never misses a beat.

I think I just ruined my book.4:31:57 PM

A laser takes energy and focuses it to a point. Conscious emotional mind enables sense of time so the thoughts are scattered in the past and the future. When subconscious is dominate to an extreme the thought or concentration is focused to a point, so the thought or concentration is in real time or now. So instead of having ones concentration all over the time spectrum it is focused in the now so the mental power is much more extreme. I am not warmed up yet so I'll try that again in another book.5:12:15 PM

The women won't slaughter me. Considering their team is 4 for 4 that was a positive outlook. I am not intelligent enough to comment on supernatural powers.

6/6/2009 1:33:44 AM - I went to sleep at 9pm and woke up at 1:30 Am so I understand my internal clock is assuming 4 hours sleep is the same as 8 hours and saying I am fully rested. Something to that effect. My body is registering 4 hours sleep and my body is fully rested . I am not tired or maybe I just can't feel I am tired. Perhaps my body is unaware of time so it just believes 4 hours sleep is enough rest and tells the body that's plenty of rest so wake him up. I have these strange sensations about editing what I write to make it proper but then I have moments of clarity where I realize this is really not about morals and not about religion it is about some sort of discovery and it is important I keep things as they are in my diary because people who are studied in the mind can figure stuff out if I keep a daily diary, because perhaps something might happen in relation to overload and they will be able to perhaps piece things together better than I can. I am aware I am very biased about things at this time. I understand I am not exactly what one would call "religious" material but I am certain I would be classified properly under psychology material. I perceive since I went subconscious dominate I still see myself as not important but my mind is telling me I am important because subconscious is opposite of conscious aspect or left brain is opposite of right brain. So I "exchanged a walk on part in the war for a lead role in a cage" in relation to, I used to have very low self esteem and then went subconscious dominate and now I have very high self esteem but nothing has really changed but the signals my mind is giving me. My mind is convincing me I am "special" but I really am not because nothing has changed just my outlook or my perception is now opposite but in reality nothing has changed. My mind is making me believe I am important so it is making me believe writing books fast is proof I am important but that is just relative to me. Perhaps my scale of importance has been adjusted to suggest if I write books fast I am important but in reality I may just be writing books about nothing and my mind is just making me think I am important but I am not important, I am just being tricked. I have faith in my assumption that my mind just became tired of me harming myself and it simply gave me this "Midas touch" kind of aspect where everything I see I understand and everything is easy for me because my mind realized I do not do very well when I perceive I lose, so my mind just makes me think I win at everything because it understands after the last attempt, I do not play games and my mind desires to stay alive so it just allows me to see everything as a win now no matter how bad of a loss it is. My mind makes me perceive my books are perfect yet in reality my books are nightmares in literary mastery. Perhaps it is a good thing that I see everything is for a reason and proper no matter what because life is much easier that way relative my previous outlook on life.

I am laughing because I watched this video about this person who was "trained" by the Dali Lama, and he is some sort of Lama, and the reporter asked him a question about Tibet and the guy said "On one hand Tibet is suffering and on the other hand Tibet is united." So really this guy made an obvious observation and a very safe obvious observation at that. Perhaps he could have said Tibet is united in their suffering. I understand this is the right brain of subconscious philosopher aspect at work. This guy didn't really say anything. "on one hand" is a nice way of saying perhaps. Some religious beings say things along the lines of "I am the right hand and this is left hand" or "I sit at the right hand". This is simply the subconscious looking at things from many angles. So the subconscious does not allow one to see from a single narrow point of view but makes one look at situation from many points of view and so one could be considered "open minded" about all questions, but in some ways it is really just suggesting all possible answers and then one might get one of them right. This is perhaps similar to how a psychic operates. They say many obvious observations and then get one right and people say "Yes they are a psychic."

If I suggest, perhaps I unlocked my subconscious to an extreme, or perhaps I unlocked by emotional conscious aspect to an extreme, or perhaps I am in an unknown state of mind, or perhaps I am a lemur monkey , it is a pretty safe bet, I am wise in suggesting that because one of those options is perhaps the truth. I could make a definitive statement but it perhaps would seem specific to many. I could suggest no matter what happened to me I am certain it has to do with my mindset or perception adjustment in my mindset. Then I could feel very comfortable with that comment because that is a safe bet in relation to a comment. I can almost never go wrong with suggesting something that vague.

I understand the Lama is selected to be "religious leader" of Tibet so he is under this "fear" of avoiding saying what is on his mind in a public forum. But in general or in private conversations I am certain he is aware China is rather harsh to control Tibet, but Lama perhaps would not say that in an open forum because people might suggest "no "perfect" being would ever say that". But China is being rather left brained or "controlling" to keep Tibet because Tibet's gross national product is perhaps not keeping China afloat, financially speaking and making China lo0ok like a bully on the world stage. So there is this "keep your mouth shut and do not say what you really feel" aspect in the Lama. He is careful not to speak out how he really feels even though he certainly feels Tibet is being controlled, and this I simply because he has this "persona" to uphold, or he has to be a good "role model" at least in his own mind. So essentially people behind the scenes are pulling the Lama's strings.

So that is a situation where one has to be careful to not be associated with anyone because indirectly or not when one is subconscious dominate others will attempt to pull their strings or manipulate them to do their bidding. I am quite certain No one was pulling Freud's strings, or Jesus' strings, or Jung's strings or Washington's strings, or Mohammed's strings or Moses' strings, or Buddha's strings. It is perhaps obvious that these beings were under their "own power." They carved the path so to speak or they were off the beaten path in their suggestions.

"The right brain, on the other hand, functions in a non-verbal manner and excels in visual, spatial, perceptual, and intuitive information. The right brain processes information differently than the left brain. For the right brain, processing happens very quickly and the style of processing is nonlinear and nonsequential. The right brain looks at the whole picture and quickly seeks to determine the spatial relationships of all the parts as they relate to the whole. This component of the brain is not concerned with things falling into patterns because of prescribed rules. On the contrary, the right brain seems to flourish dealing with complexity, ambiguity and paradox. At times, right brain thinking is difficult to put into words because of its complexity, its ability to process information quickly and its non-verbal nature."

http://tolearn.net/hypertext/brain.htm

are quite opposite in the way they think. = the right brain seems to flourish dealing with complexity, ambiguity and paradox.

The right brain is certainly the subconscious aspect. Complexity is a nice way to say it is the "intelligent" aspect of the mind and one with a strong sense of time has the subconscious aspect silenced and the strong sense of time and strong hunger is the proof to test of that. I understand people do not like this word subconscious but one may look at it as the veiled aspect of the average mind. It is simply because the society does many things that encourages one to make the right brain veiled.

"Right brains are honored in eastern cultures more than western."

This comment is simply saying people in "nirvana" or ones who are considered to have slight sense of time are looked at as treasures in the east and are looked at as "problems" in the west. I am not intelligent enough to speak about supernatural powers in relation to this like the east and the west are able to. I look at main religious figures in the west as being "subconscious dominate" and some were perhaps butchered because of that simply because **"are quite opposite in the way they think".**

So they were perhaps looked at as "evil" or "bad" or "problems". In the east they recognize them as "blessings" or "above normal or spiritual teachers". They are certainly quite intelligent and "wise" so the east is justified in their suggestions. The west has many who are subconscious dominate but they tend to cling too many labels to hide their self. Einstein, Freud, Jung. I am certain they were, I have strong feelings about Washington also. They simply stick out like sore thumbs if one knows how to properly look for them. The thing is, they have to "hide" in the west because the west does not really accept them. The west tends to hang them on crosses and poison their lamb chops, so they are wise to hide and I cannot blame them for doing so. It all just comes back to the one simple fact that they **"are quite opposite in the way they think"** and also they do not like rules. They are mindfully in infinity so a rule is a control and it is not they break rules they just do not like them and that is logical because they are mindfully "free" because they are in infinity they are open minded and a rule hinders one being open minded. It is not they do not like rules, it is more like rules represent limits and so they have an aversion to them. This is the opposite of left brains people.

59

Left brain people like safety and therefore comfort and therefore like rules . Rules make left brain people comfortable and safe. Because left brain people are " **quite opposite in the way they think".** So there is a world with two kinds of people mindfully and they are opposites. Neither of them can really communicate at least the ones in the extremes. They are simply in completely different worlds mentally speaking. There is a disconnect that is unimaginable.

Barbra Walters did an interview with the Lama. She asked "Are you God?." The Lama said "No my eye sight is poor so that means I am not god , I cannot be god because my eye sight is poor." Now to ones with left brain , they perceive he is humble. To ones in the "know" they laugh at that answer. The ones in the "know" laugh at that answer because Buddha said "Do not take the word of a BLIND man ask questions." So Lama said in essence "I am not god I am a blind man.", which is in reality saying "I am Buddha and Buddha is understood to be god reincarnate".

 Of course very few "left brainers" would ever understand that because they do not consider the opposite meanings of everything that is said. So I guess I am saying I laugh a lot more now. It is perhaps difficult to get a straight answer out of the ones who are 'enlightened." There is much pondering that needs to take place when one who is enlightened speaks. One simply cannot take what they say on face value alone. They are perhaps speaking in parables more than literals.

So now you understand that go to this interview and listen to what Lama says when asked if he is a god or gods and keep in mind what I just said and you will laugh because he telling the truth but the truth is a parable. http://www.youtube.com/watch?v=8Zpf1DdArek

I am not intelligent enough to speak on supernatural powers but it is sad to me, some of the misunderstandings about some of these people. It harms me to be aware of some things I am now aware of because there is this disconnect that seems to be unable to be bridged. I am unable to bridge the "opposite" disconnect but I will write infinite books in my attempts to bridge this disconnect.

I have decided to write myself to death so perhaps the world will understand what kind of drive I really have. I am mindful none of these beings have been able to bridge the "opposite" disconnect so I would be a fool to assume I could do such a thing. I will be a trooper and try my best knowing I will never be able to accomplish such a task. I am mindful I am not supposed to succeed I am just supposed to try. "We" are not suppose to win and that perhaps rips me apart more than I am ever able to explain in words. Perhaps it will take infinite books to explain such ripping. Nothing makes any difference when there is a total "opposite" disconnect. Do you perceive anything matters when there is a total "opposite" disconnect? Everything I say is opposite of what you hear. How am I supposed to counter that? I cannot counter that. Who would put me in this situation? I must play the video game before I exterminate myself.

opposite in the way they think, opposite in the way they think, opposite in the way they think, opposite in the way they think, opposite in the way they think, opposite in the way they think, opposite in the way they think, opposite in the way they think, opposite in the way they think, opposite in the way they think, opposite in the way they think, opposite in the way they think, 3:51:22 AM

I feel extremely out of context 4:01:20 AM - You let me know if anyone ever says you are not perfect because I eat for no reason. Perhaps we have come to an understanding. Falling on the sword is the victory. You do it slowly so I might feel something.

5:50:00 AM - I will try to communicate using a parable. I am on the "opposite" side of a river. The river is raging and drowning out my voice. I see you on the opposite side. I do not know what I am trying to tell you. I only know there is an urgency or I perceive there is an urgency. I have already decided to communicate with you. I cannot take that back now."I on the opposite shore shall be." I am ready ride and spread the alarm. I have already decided I am not as important as communicating the message I do not even understand, to you. This is an accurate description of my situation. I will not give up in my attempts to communicate to you.5:56:28 AM

This day is certainly going to be a long one.

"The voice of the intellect is a soft one, but it does not rest until it has gained a hearing."
Sigmund Freud

Subconscious dominate people are soft in relation to not being physically violent because they are so cerebral, but they are lions in respect to their voice, they never give up the mental fight. Essentially they never shut their mouth because verbal expression is the only way to relate to the world.

"Sammasambuddhas attain buddhahood, then decide to teach others the truth they have discovered."

This would be translated as , one who reaches extreme subconscious dominate can only do so by "accident". Once the accident happens they cannot be taught because subconscious is adverse to :rules and laws". So they are essentially talkers or "teachers"." decide to teach others the truth they have discovered". This decide aspect is much more complex than it may seem. Mohammed wrote quite a big book. The bible is quite a big book. Buddha wrote quite a lot also. These writings happened when there was no easy way to write. It was a labor. I cannot imagine how difficult it must have been. They used some sort of animal skin or papyrus and some form or writing tool. They probably messed up and made many mistakes because they had trouble forming words to begin with because of the nature of right brain dominate. It must have been quite a task. I only have to type into a word processor and it at least gives me hints if I misspell words. I can swiftly correct misspellings. I have pretty much given up on commas at this stage and I guess paragraphs are out of my league. I just have some truth I have discovered or I perceive I have discovered, and I am in a situation where I have no excuse to not write infinite books to explain this perceived truth. Some may suggest that I have motivation and that is good but I perceive I have a hard time convincing myself I have written enough about this "perceived truth I have discovered." "then decide" I already did that. I already decided. I am uncertain why I decided, I am certain I did decide. I do not even perceive it matters if anyone reads any of these books because I have already decided to write infinite books. Perhaps that is rather funny. I am unable to comment on these beings whether they were subconscious dominate or perhaps supernaturally inclined because I simply cannot even figure out exactly what happened to me and I cannot even figure out how I am going to convince myself to stop writing infinite books. I guess the definition would be insufferable. I am locked into the decision and I am not mentally able to get out of it because I am too philosophical or "on the fence". Something along the lines of "maybe I should stop writing or maybe I should write faster." So the video game is my only way to slow down in writing because my books would be too big to publish even after 30 days. This book is going to be huge because my last book was 130k words and my mind has suggested that was a poor effort and now I perceive this one will be perhaps 300k words. No person is going to buy a 300k word book. It is far too large but I have to make up for my last tiny book so that maybe I will be able to go back to smaller 200k word books. So this book is already considered a failure. So then I will just gracefully finish this book and try again with book seven. I feel much more at ease after getting this off my chest. It is going to be ok. I will take it one sentence at a time and attempt to keep my chin up because I am certainly drowned at this stage. I submit I am defeated so that I can fight another day. Submission has much more to do with understanding the situation than weakness in the face of the situation. If you actually finish one of my books contact me because I wish to speak with one with far more humility than I will ever have.6:24:40 AM

I perceive this word Sammasambuddhas is in relation to "the least among you" or "the stone the stone cutter threw away" or "Blessed are the poor in spirit" or "the meek shall inherit the earth" because Ignorance is bliss and bliss means spiritual joy, so one who has no spiritual joy, is described as someone who is suicidal or depressed, so they are poor in spirit, and one cannot be in any great state of being compared to one who is suicidal, or one who decides to give up life when they do not have to, so this is a mental planting , or a state of mental fertility, when one is at that extreme state of humility because they wish to end their life when they do not have to. This poor in spirit or meek or least among you is the state of mind one has to achieved to become a "talker" or "teacher" or becomes extreme subconscious dominate and thus cannot shut their mouth in their mindset to tell everyone how to go subconscious dominate. It simply may not be subconscious dominate state of mind is what everyone should try to be, it is simply relative to the one who is in extreme state of subconscious dominate that perceives others should be that way. It really is not a good or bad thing, it simply is a thing. If you are an author who never wishes to have writers block ever again perhaps it is a path to consider.

I am mindful to "turn to stone" or a "pillar of salt" much swifter than I perhaps am. Salt is a factor in preservation. Preservation is relative to longevity and thus time. The fountain of youth aspect is relative to a mental state of longevity or preservation. One who has slight sense of time is not as prone to the decay aspects stress can cause the body. One with slight sense of time simply is unable to feel the stress because the memory is altered to the degree there is hardly the ability to feel shame or embarrassment or feel stress cause by deadlines or caused by a rushed state of mind.

My moments of denial are swiftly covered by a sea of doubt. I was brought to life on the day of the dead and the owner of the house will return.

"As he lay dying, Holliday allegedly asked for a drink of whiskey. Amused, he looked at his bootless feet as he died — no one ever thought that he would die in bed, with his boots off. His reputed last words were, "Well I'll be damned. This is funny."

Yes there is no other way to describe how I feel except to say, I'll be damned. This is funny. You perhaps do not get it, but that perhaps does not matter. It is not even important if he really said that. It still sums it up perfectly. Love can open all the doors one wants locked.

6:48:49 PM - I am throwing this out there for posterity. Children are born in right brain extreme/ subconscious dominate. This is evident by the comment "suffer the children to come unto me" and also in relation to "I sit at the right hand of the father." I am not intelligent enough to understand how Jesus knew the right brain is subconscious, but I perceive that comment meant "I am using the right hand aspect of the brain (father)." This is also in relation to why in Buddhism they seek a young child to claim as a reincarnation simply because a child perhaps up to the age of 3 is a good prospect because at that age they have no started using the memory or been encouraged to use memory as much. I am not intelligent enough to understand their methods to promote a child or keep a child in subconscious dominate. This is not set in stone with respect to a person who is not a child is unable to achieve this right brain dominate/subconscious dominate state of course. I perceive the situation with the memory is once a child is encouraged and rewarded for memory efforts the child starts to become left brain dominate. A child is rewarded with gifts so that child is pleased with the gifts or rewards and starts to remember what they did to achieve that. Tooth fairy, Christmas and birthdays all encourage a child to look forward to gifts. I perceive that somehow memorization activities are unwanted. The more one memorizes the harder concentration gets because the further into emotional dominate/left brain one goes.

Left brain looks at parts, Right Brain looks at wholes. So encouraging a child to memorize how to spell words makes a child look at parts in relation to letters and that decreases the subconscious/right brain which looks at wholes. So a child can say a word and that is fine as far as memory but once a child starts spelling they start to focus on parts and they lose the "whole" outlook.

This whole outlook is what seeing everything as one thing is, and what the American Indians suggested was seeing everything as one spirit. This is interesting because perhaps the Americans Indians where such an easy target for Early Americans because they were subconscious dominate. So Early Americans were left brain essentially and thus physically inclined and they find the Indians who appeared to be savages, "opposite" than what the American were is perhaps the proper way to look at it. So there is the "materialistic" Americans and the "meek" Indians. This does not mean the Indians did not have wars because the bottom line is, it is so complex to reach right brain that maybe a small percentage of the Tribe was right brain, certainly the medicine man was right brain. Certainly many spiritual "medicine" type people in relation to voodoo, aborigines and the like are right brain, but right brain is a simple way to say subconscious dominate. I prefer subconscious dominate because right brain makes it seem like left or right brain they are both the same as far as "intelligence" but subconscious is understood to be very powerful. Right brain may be somewhat inaccurate because the left brain is still playing a part but it is silenced so it creates some interesting effects. I lost my train, I perhaps need to rest. 7:06:49 PM

6/7/2009 1:49:59 AM - I cannot suggest some are good and some are evil. Perhaps one's who are evil are also capable of great good and ones who are good are capable of great evil. If I suggest everyone is good then ones who are evil will be encouraged and ones who are suicidal will go through with it. If I suggest everyone is evil then ones who are compassionate will be discouraged and ones who are arrogant will become meek. If I suggest everyone is lukewarm then everyone may become predictable. Perhaps there are no absolutes or harmonies because both paths are relative to the one who determines those labels. The concept of dammed if you do and dammed if you don't is perhaps if one speaks, one becomes offensive to some and if one is silent they deny their self. Perhaps everyone is suggesting ideals that are only relative to their own thoughts and do not apply to others. I am perhaps only able to speak my perception of truth with the understanding there is no absolute truth so I am only truthful to myself and a liar to some. I must consider my own thoughts as truth and discourage others from subscribing to them so they will not harm their own personal truth. I should attempt to monologue myself from one truth to the next with the understanding no other person will ever fully believe my own personal truth without discounting their own personal truth. Perhaps we are all just islands of perception unable to find true honest ground to any great extent with anyone else. Perhaps being meek is achieved when one understands they cannot live up to others perceptions. Without an absolute purpose there is a reason to create a purpose based on perception. If it is important to me, it is important. One must compromise their perceptions to accommodate others counter perceptions, this is where the tension lies that may snap the string.2:37:18 AM

My thoughts are not proper or improper but they are simply only relative to me. Chaos is all that is happening and humans attempt to find patterns in that chaos to persuade their self it is not just chaos. The patterns one seeks in chaos are attempts to find solid ground. All labels are patterns one uses to remain ignorant of the absolute chaos.

So civilization is still "hunters and gatherers". Some hunt for jobs to gather money. Some hunt for opportunities to gather benefit. Some hunt for knowledge to gather understanding. Civilized structure is simply an attempt to create order or patterns out of the subconscious awareness there is only chaos.3:34:25 AM

7:28:23 AM This is the delusion for the day. These religious beings encouraged rules and "fear" of unnamable because without fear there is no point. With an extreme of tolerance there is only the machine state. "Everyone should be willing to die for something", this is because in the machine state one feels perhaps nothing at all. So conflict or argument is required to avoid the machine state. Rules or laws are required to avoid the machine state. I perceive these "religious" beings were at a level to understand this and so they encouraged "UNNAMABLE" and "fear of UNNAMABLE" and "no one is perfect" and "fear unnamable with all your heart" because if you do not fear you do not have emotional contrast. "Love your enemy like yourself." Denotes fear or love because if you have no feelings what are you? I perceive it's suggest fear something or love something so that you do not lose your emotional capacity. Jesus could have gotten out of the cross but he didn't because he had no fear and thus no emotional capacity. He didn't fear death so he was in a machine state. Run up behind your computer and yell 'Boo" and see if it jumps. This is perhaps beyond the ability of ones with emotional capacity to grasp. The comment "We may not die with a bang but with a whimper" denotes without emotional capacity, we would eventually stop having offspring. People desire to have children and crave to have children but without emotional capacity they would not have children because children would just be a hindrance. "Suffer the children to come unto me" may be suggesting Jesus was suggesting "Go fourth and multiply" because with no emotional capacity that would be the only thing that is important, talking machines into having a next generation of children because a machine would have no desire to do so. I understand why I "picked fights" with everyone I could think of in my books, because I was aware I was losing my antagonistic aspect. I am passive. I am in a passive state and my minds natural reaction was to be antagonistic to attempt to avoid the passive state. But that is vanity or those attempts are in vain because I am in a machine state. Something along the lines of "any way the wind blows doesn't really matter to me." One might suggest that is depression but depression is a feeling so it's not depression. Depression is the absence of joy. Joy is the absence of depression. So it is neither of those. It is in fact a passive state of mind in relation to "the thinker". Maybe if I go water my hole in the ground people will assume I have compassion for the dirt. Maybe if I write enough books people will assume I care. If people assume I care then I certainly will at least be remembered as one who cared even though I do not. The last thing a human being with an emotional capacity wants to hear is the truth. The luxuries of civilization are turning us all into thinkers and not doers and the internet is the reason. The government will be relegated to a babysitter of invalid thinkers who stay home all day and learn from the internet. They will learn why they should not do anything but learn. If one wants to learn who is responsible for turning the world into thinkers instead of doers, look no further than these people.

"It was originally called ARPANET (Advanced Research Projects Agency NETwork). The concept was developed starting in 1964, and the first messages passed were between UCLA and the Stanford Research Institute in 1969. Leonard Kleinrock of MIT had published the first paper on packet switching theory in 1961. Since networking computers was new to begin with, standards were being developed on the fly. Once the concept was proven, the organizations involved started to lay out some ground rules for standardization. One of the most important was the communications protocol, TCP/IP, developed by Vint Cerf and Robert Kahn in 1974. Robert Metcalfe is credited with Ethernet which is the basic communication standard in networked computers. Tim Berners-Lee perhaps specified technological applicability

and / or linguistic construction of HTML while working at CERN, is chiefly credited for the ease of use and wide public adoption of the web. His website is: w3.org "

So these inventions appeared to be light but if we are all thinkers then who is going to be the doers? The doers are also getting into the internet so they will become thinkers. Then we will have just a society of cerebral thinkers. We will relegate ourselves into nothingness. Compassion will absorb conflict. Without conflict there is only thinking. We will invent our way into extinction. We will convince ourselves a robot is far more logical than ourselves and much easier to maintain, so we will have more time to think. The only people that will be left are the tribes in the Amazon who decided it is better to struggle in nature than attempt to become one's own master because human nature is to make things easier and easier to the point there is no point. My insanity is mine.

Moses took people out into the wilderness for forty years. Moses left civilization and thus luxury. The moment humans beings started civilization by "setting up shop" around an irrigation system they sealed their fate. Human beings are adept at tools and tools encourage luxury. It is easy to start a fire with a lighter it takes effort to start a fire with two sticks. We are prone to luxury. Luxury spears like light but it is not light when taken to the extreme. Luxury when taken to the extreme negates purpose. Moses wondered for forty years and then he settled. Mankind was once hunters and gathers and then one day they settled around that irrigation system of luxury. They settled.

Jesus prayed in the wilderness and asked, "Why has mankind accepted luxury over struggle?" "Why has mankind forsaken the hard road of struggle in nature for the easy road of luxury?" There is no mystery when you have your whole week planned out in detail. Then life just becomes a chore. The mountain men left town with supplies and there was no safety from that point on. They could die at any minute and that is living. The Indians traveled with the herds. They could die at any minute and that was living. Now the Indians are on reservations so we forced them to settle. Civilization forces everyone to settle. The luxury of civilization is so easy only an insane person would deny that luxury. A transient on the street lives more in one day than a person who lives in luxury lives in their whole life. There is no mystery in luxury and only safety. If someone fights all my battles for me what is my purpose? We have armies ready to protect us then what the hell is our purpose? We are simply allowing others to fight our battles so we have no battles and so we have no life. We are simply reduced to sloth without battles to fight, and luxury eliminates the battles. Buddha left luxury and went into the wilderness. Moses left luxury and went into the wilderness. That is nearly impossible to do because it is unreasonable and irresponsible. It is illogical to struggle when one does not have to. It is illogical to seek the hot coals when one does not have to. Perhaps ones with emotions are scared to death at this stage in the thick pamphlet.

Humans in luxury are slaves to safety and strangers to mystery. This is the life cycle of a human in luxury. They are born, thrown into school, thrown into work and end up in the prison or safety and comfort until they decide that is not living and find a way to check out. This is the life cycle of the ones who live in the Amazon. They are born and every day could be their last day, until the last day comes. That is living, that is mystery, that is the absence of luxury. Living is not about seeing how long you can live until you decide you want nothing to do with life; Living is about seeing how far you can go into the unknown and still remain alive.

You put the most hardcore survivalist in civilization into the Amazon situation and they would not last a month. A human who lives in the Amazon would be embarrassed if they understood the level of sloth humans that live in civilization have achieved. They would say, "Let me go back to the wilderness so I do not have to look at what you have become." We mock the ones in the Amazon as savages because we are not aware a savage is at least living a life of mystery instead of a life based on a schedule of safety and predictability.

Perhaps give me liberty or give me death, is more about allowing people to find their own struggles because without struggles life is utterly pointless. It is not considered a struggle if you are worried about the price of a cup of coffee going up or the price of a gallon of gas or how much of a raise you got for showing up to your air conditioned work box on time. That is not struggle that is purposelessness.

Anarchy is struggle and freedom is anarchy. Perhaps we should all just work together so none of us have to do anything including breathe. Perhaps we should just hook ourselves up to a ventilator and induce a 120 year coma, then we will be safe and secure and live a nice full life. This certainly explains why the "pagans" were slaughtered because they denied the luxuries of civilization and were deemed "evil" because civilization slaughters anything that does not agree with its norms of "security and comfort."

I will just sit here in my room and never leave it so that you can feel like you are living and you have purpose. Human kind died when it settled around that irrigation system of luxury. Now we are simply praying for a swift death to escape our existence of sloth and safety. I will go now the lawn now and maybe ants will bite me and I will feel alive, but I do not expect that because I killed the ants with the insecticide so that I would be safe in my luxurious purposelessness. You just stay down in the little foothills because it is far too unsafe to climb to the heights or the depths depending on your degree of insanity, I thrive at.10:44:04 AM

Osama once said "I told my son he cannot use ice cubes because when they are not around he will miss them." So now we have a harsh economy and people get laid off and lose the ice cubes and go home a kill their children and wife and then their self because the ice cubes are melting. And you call yourself wise or responsible and you suggest Osama is insane. You are suffering now aren't you without all your luxury. You gave up on life and decided to have luxury over life and now when your luxury is gone you decide death is the next reasonable option. You are certainly as Buddha suggested "sane". I just write books like the wind to remind you of how insane I am and how infinitely sane you are. The same ones who suggest we need to save the earth are doing the exact same thing the Taliban are doing. They are attempting to negate civilization of luxury. Civilization somewhere along the way determined it can reproduce a viable eco system better than the master of viable eco systems could. Perhaps you will find out the hard way, there is only one master of viable eco systems and its name is not human beings. Paving over the entire planet with cement is not exactly a proper way to create a viable eco system it is a proper way to ensure everything dies swiftly. This is along the lines of the comment "Cannot leave well enough alone." Somewhere in history man determined if it makes an irrigation system it will be better than nature's natural irrigation system. Perhaps you perceive that was a misguided determination. Perhaps if the main goal of civilization is to educate our children, so when they cannot pass tests and understand they will not be able to make enough money, and thus will have a difficult life, and then they will feel like failures, and take a handful of pills because you told them they are losers, then civilization is just right on track. Civilization has invented artificial benchmarks of success and when someone finds out they can never live up to them they find out civilization is a sham.

Maybe you better tell all your friends never to read my books because they might start to have brain function and understand you are insane, and then they will never talk to you again and then you will blow your brains out because without luxury, you will understand you are simply wasting my oxygen. I am certain I ruined the book now. A seventh book will be needed to mend this tragic oversight.

If I ever write in my book everyone is a unnamable dam brain damaged lemur monkey then people will not buy my books and I will become depressed and go into the den and take a handful of pills and when I start to convulse I will not call for help and then two months after that everything will make sense and I will write infinite books and say "everyone is a unnamable dam brain damaged lemur monkey." So I will avoid saying everyone is an unnamable dam lemur monkey so I do not have to go through that tragedy. Thank unnamable I am wise enough see that far ahead so I don't make that mistake.

I am you in the mirror. I am the one you say is a fool because they cannot spell words properly. I am the one you insult because they do not met your perceive standards of excellence. I am what civilization creates with its "norms" of acceptance. You should get use to me because I am not fucking going anywhere, but you will be going somewhere if you get in my way. If I needed a fucking army I would have one. When you look in the mirror I am looking back at you and I am asking "Why did you do this to me?" and you never respond because you are blind to my questions.

Before you get weird just please remind yourself, all I can do in limbo is chase my tail. I am just chasing my tail. I am fighting and then resting and then fighting and then resting, and I am accomplishing nothing. I always end up back at zero.

Money is not a guarantee but I guarantee there are many idiots who believe it is.

http://www.youtube.com/watch?v=AW4lxjicBAw&feature=related

The secret about this song is to understand everything is opposite and delete the maybe's because they are inserted for retards. I dated this girl who was into S&M and she had these specially made acrylic vampire teeth and she said "I am submissive but I want to bite you with my vampire teeth." I am still trying to figure out what kind of submissive she was. That is what I thought about when I went to my Chinese restaurant and when I was there I got a fortune cookie and it said "Your compassion is only exceeded by the quality of your books." The Chinese are extremely tricky with their wordings.

Do you perceive the author is:

Buddha.

The Lizard King.

A person with 47 fingers.

In need of sedation.

Seeing how many friends he can make.

666

In another dimension of space

The worst literary genius in the universe

6/8/2009 6:09:51 AM - Since I just woke up I will attempt to come back to reality and explain what I perceive is happening from a psychological aspect. I am over compensating my "anger or rage" because I am unable to be satisfied with my anger or rage. I have no limits or cannot tell what is enough rage or anger so I go full tilt. It is vanity. People will certainly perceive I am angry but I am not, my mind is aware my emotions are nearly gone and it is attempting to make them happen so I come across as very angry but that's not possible that I have that much rage yet can still pump out books so swiftly. So in one way I am attempting to emulate anger and rage and in one way I am mentally attempting to make sure no one likes me because that to me or to subconscious is a form of control and subconscious is not about limits or control. So I am emulating emotions and making sure no one likes me because I have infinite books to write and have no time to "chat" so to speak. This is exactly why I put my books in psychology because I perceive no religious person would "get it" they would simply get all religious and judgmental. Subconscious is just weird and everyone knows that. It is powerful yet has some deep seeded aspects to it also. Certainly I am not walking on water or calming storms unless that relates to attempting to calm this emotional aspects in my mind by putting it in words or walking a tight rope by explaining some concepts in humanity very few have ever explained in the history of mankind, so maybe in that respect I am doing the "impossible" but I simply feel I am in a state of monologue. I come to understandings that me mentally and since I cannot express myself by feeling satisfaction from being harmed, I just rattle off hateful words in hopes I can take the pain from the understandings and I cannot so I just cuss until I forget what I was upset about then I move on. I see everyone as perfect and if I did not express in words my pain when I see some of the things that are happening I might go mad. Ok, more mad. Perhaps I could just sit in a room and never speak again to combat this, but I am a firm believer in jumping into the hottest coals for no reason. Now I perceive I have canceled out all my rage in the book this far or explained it away and now I can start again. I understand that is my cycle. I cannot type some things I perceive are "deep" and then not attempt to retaliate because at times these things harm me. So I am fighting myself. This is all in relation to the comment is "the battle is within". That means I am in cerebral battles and I am getting slaughtered on a minute to minute basis but I am a little trooper. That's the only way I can explain it. I can't stop it. When I have my moments of rage tears usually are pouring out of my eyes so it perhaps would not be what I understood to be rage but more like self inflicted immolation. On another level I attempt to be very angry because I am not used to having slight emotional capacity and I perceive if I can emulate anger enough I will go back to how I was before the accident and I understand this is also vanity. I recall in my first book I have no rage or angry comments, but that is because I was going into the "clarity" and from that point on I have been quite a little demon in my words because the clarity is growing and growing and it rips me apart. It is perhaps more difficult to stop thoughts that one might imagine, perhaps, psychologically speaking, so to speak. Perhaps the comment "I am not like this in person." is quite accurate. I am more like Mr. Magoo in person and not angry at all when people are around, I tend to crack many jokes and that is a defense mechanism. It all comes down to one thing, Ignorance is bliss so great clarity means absence of spiritual joy because bliss means spiritual joy. I call it being ripped apart but perhaps any word would work just fine. I try to look at it like I am taking one for the team because I understand I cannot attempt to treat this rage with drugs because I would perhaps harm myself greatly because I cannot treat this rage with drugs, drugs simply would have no effect but to make me physically tired, they would not affect the mental clarity at all.

My mind tricks me to perceive my self control is that I do not delete what I write in my diary, after I write it. I want to delete nearly everything I write and I do not delete it , so that is self control or I am conditioning myself away from the emotion "ashamed to say what I feel." I perceive I was so shy all my life that I will not allow that to ever happen again. I always kept my mouth shut and now I am over compensating for that to what one might suggest is an infinite degree of over compensation.

Extreme ignorance = extreme bliss = extreme spiritual joy

Extreme understanding = extreme "harm" = "eyes black with rage" = "mouth black with sticky knives" = "forked tongue"

If I did not vent the rage with words I would perhaps harm myself physically. I recall this concept of people suggesting get your ideas or thoughts down on paper. I tend to publish what I write on my paper, but I understand I am doing that technique. I am getting it all out on paper because that is a way to avoid harming myself physically. I write my thoughts down then I condition away from "care what other think about my thoughts" and "don't be ashamed of what you think" by publishing the diaries.

So I do not perceive I write these books to help others in fact I perceive I write these books to help me or "work on the log in my eye".

"Masses are always breeding grounds of psychic epidemics." Carl Jung

The herd will easily go off the cliff if the sheep in front of them does first.

The cool aid tastes sweeter in a group setting.

This comment is in relation to a Salem Witch trials and also the Holocaust because it was groups of people who allowed these things to happen. One person alone, would not have burned any witches at the stake, but a group of people can start to act as one judge and then at times things can get way out of control. It is as if one person says something and then another person adds a comment and before you know it they are stringing people up on stakes to burn them. It is not always one single person that is to blame as much as a group of single comments coming together to make some rather harsh judgments.

This Mather's fellow certainly would not have burned those people on the stake if he was all alone, but in a group setting and him being looked at as the "authority" it was much easier to cast stones and play that stone casting out in a physical manner. One does not do harmful physical things unless they are certain someone is watching or someone will see their deed. Cotton Mather certainly assumed if he burned a few "witches" his popularity as a wise spiritual leader would sky rocket. Of course now we remember him as essentially an idiot, so his fruits have been judged by his peers and by history and he will always be remembered as a good example of what a cult leader is capable of doing when they are mentally unstable and "left brain" or physically based. He essentially burned innocent people on stakes because he was perhaps best locked up in a mental ward than teaching morals because he was in fact a mass murderer and the only fruits he produced were rotten fruits and bitter tasting on the lips of history.

Now if one contrasts this with the American revolution. Certainly there were innocent lives killed but it was because a tyrant attempted to take advantage of others. The reality in life is if one allows others to walk over them they will. This is complex because one must be certain verbal communication cannot solve the situation. One must also be mindful to avoid conflicts that are out of their scope of influence. One cannot simply go to their neighbors house and attempt to correct them because that is what is known as "none of your business". It is perhaps important to have extreme mental clarity so one is able to anticipate another's move well in advance, to avoid becoming a reactionary in relation to acting on deeds on ones plate, instead acting out several moves ahead. A grand master chess player understands many moves ahead so they are seldom caught off guard. An authority figure that suggests "I was caught off guard" is essentially telling everyone, "I have no idea why I am in a position of authority." It is easier to react to an anticipated move than react to an unexpected move.

I have pondered reading these diaries by Anne Frank and my desires and craving are very strong to read her works but I am not intelligent enough to read the diaries of one I am aware was so

69

graceful and wise so I am harmed because I desire to read her wise words but I am not allowed to disrespect her legacy because of my selfish desires for further understandings. So I will look at my infinite desire to read just one page of her graceful words as an opportunity to block my desires and cravings. I certainly have enough on my plate as it is, so I will not entertain the idea of invading the personal diaries of one who is far wiser than I will ever be.

"Exo 32:19 And it came to pass, as soon as he came nigh unto the camp, that he saw) the calf, and the dancing: and Moses' anger waxed hot, and he cast the tables out of his hands, and brake them beneath the mount."

"As soon as night came unto the camp" denotes the left brain physical aspects. Jesus refers to it as the darkness and Mohammed suggested infidel, Buddha suggested the "sane". The night refers to ones who are physically orientated mentally as opposed to ones who are right brain dominate and are cerebrally focused. It is not really a "good or evil" scenario it is simply a contrast. Some people are more physically motivated and some are more cerebrally motivated. Some people body build and that is their "way" and some people write very poor books and that is their way. So one is physically motivated and one is more cerebral. Both are flexing their muscles.

"He saw the calf and the dancing" this is simply suggesting he saw the physical aspects, calf representing money and material wealth or material objects, not strictly money and the dancing is a nice way to say "having fun". Having fun is a desire or craving. One wishes to go have a few drinks and have fun. One wishes to conquer another country and take their land to have fun. One wishes to dominate other people in physical ways to have fun. So this whole dancing comment is simply stating the people were left brain dominate because right brain/subconscious beings are not able to have cravings or desires in relation to "let's go have fun." It appears to ones with left brain that it would be sad and lonely to never have fun, but what really is happening is one is emotionally silenced to the degree they are unable to sense what fun is, so one may suggest writing books swiftly is a chore and so they would be taxed, or tired from writing books so swiftly. It would be more like work to them. I have no concept or work and thus no concept of play so I just do. I do not recall what I write about and I do not feel like, "Oh no now I have to write another book." I just write another book and then write another one, and I never get around to feeling like I have done anything mentally or physically speaking. I do not feel satisfaction so I also do not feel fatigue. "and Moses anger waxed hot" Waxed is in relation to increasing gradually in size. This is very accurate. One might suggest Moses ignorance was decreasing and so his understanding of what was happening was ripping him apart. It is not that being physical orientated is evil or wrong, it is the simply a disconnect between one who is extreme right brain and has great cerebral clarity attempting to communicate with ones who are extreme left brain. There is an "opposite" disconnect and it is painful.

Perhaps a good way to look at it is, one watches a child in the road and see's a car coming down the road at a high rate of speed, and one is aware they cannot get the child out of the road before that car hits the child. So there is a helplessness aspect and it never goes away because of the "opposite" mental situation. I cannot reach you and you cannot reach me and that will never change. So it is not that Moses was so righteous because he was clearly suffering because he was "opposite" than those around him. One might suggest I show this "waxing of anger" but that is simply my verbal way to deal with the fact I cannot reach you.

"for they are quite opposite in the way they think". So Moses was standing there watching people having fun and doing physical orientated things and he was saying, you are encouraging your physical aspect and the cerebral aspect is perhaps better, and they all looked at him and said "Take a load off just have fun and forget about cerebral" and it ripped Moses apart because he was unable to understand why they would say that, but they were also unable to understand why Moses would say "Do not focus on physical things the cerebral aspect is far more rewarding". So there was just a disconnect or opposite point of view and neither point to view was going to budge. So relatively speaking Moses was right and the ones he scolded were right. They could not grasp what Moses was suggesting and Moses could not grasp what they were suggesting.

I would sound like some sort of moral king to say money or material things or having fun is bad or evil. That is not what I perceive. I perceive material things or having fun is not exactly possible when one is in extreme subconscious dominate/ right brain mindset. One with left brain dominate would do many things for a million dollars. They would build up this mindset that money would solve their problems or make life easier and that is valid and logical and true. I would not be able to grasp that logic. I have no desire to write infinite books I simply recall I decided to write infinite books. I do not crave a million dollars because that would mean I would have to write swifter somehow. I do not perceive money would solve my problem, it perhaps would tax me further. This is in relation to my decision to write infinite books. I would not use the money to seek luxury I would use the money to write swifter. I am unable to trick subconscious. My mind would say "Well you have enough money to publish a book every week now, so you are going to have to neglect eating and speaking and playing your video game."

So this again is an example of the "opposite" aspect. I am aware left and right brain types of people are required and I am aware that it perhaps is not good if everyone is left brain or everyone is right brain. So I am not even able to "preach" everyone should be right brain/subconscious dominate because I simply do not believe that from the way I perceive things. I am simply not intelligent enough to determine what is proper or what is improper because of my mindset. I am a "talker" but not a "preacher". I simply like to put words on a piece of paper and then I forget what I wrote and then I write more stuff. One way to look at it is, I ask myself a question with a quote or a comment and then I write many words to talk about it. There are many "question" scenarios in the Holy books. Perhaps that is what I am going to discuss next.

I am experimenting in the voodoo chat room and my friend asked me a question and I perceive this may be of value. I find he is interesting and he is curious about what I have to say like many are curious. I see no evil or bad aspects in the fact he is in a voodoo chat room. I see he is a human being and he is curious like I see all human beings. Curiosity may lead to understandings and may lead to enlightenment on the topic of discussion. I do not perceive evil or good, I perceive everything is one thing.

<Heimdall> I am something I cannot explain. I think the anti christ is very accurate considering the date of the accident was on the day of the dead

<Heimdall> But i am wise also

<Heimdall> I am confused

<Heimdall> something happened but I am uncertain to be honest... I understand everything clearly but I do not wish to make money off of it

<Heimdall> I just want to write infinite books

<Bateau> then do that... :P

<Heimdall> I feel like a lamb to slaughter

<Bateau> why?

<Heimdall> I am cerebral and many are physical based

<Heimdall> Extreme Subconscious dominate/right brain people are cerebral and they are wise becasue of it but they are opposite in their thinking

<Heimdall> they are in tune with the "spiritual" but lose touch with the physical

<Heimdall> "Left-brain dominated people(have a strong sense of time) may find their (Right Brainers) thought processes vague and difficult to follow, for they are quite opposite in the way they think."

I would sum up this chat comment by saying I perceive they will slaughter me because I am so far to the extreme and so far opposite from them, and I would humbly suggest to them I do not mind repeat performances. I understand what you are thinking and what you are planning and I would humbly remind you, I will not be blinking when you arrive. I am not allowed to defend myself so you kill me slowly so they will remember me. Perhaps my mind would explode if my tear ducts stopped working.

I will play the video game to ponder my reasoning. I have infinite faith in freedom of speech.9:03:12 AM

10:04:05 AM - Consider this experiment. Get a group of people who you have a slight idea of what kind of music they appreciate. Find a song that is opposite of what they prefer. If they prefer classic music get a nice heavy metal rock song. Something that is an "insult" to the mind of what they appreciate. Play the song one time and note what the comments are and then play the song as second time. As you play the song more the insults will become greater and it will reach a point people will suggest "You play that song again and I am leaving." and perhaps even more violent comments than that. This is actually a symptom of left brain and a symptom in turn of a strong sense of time. The song is harming them mentally. This is what is known as impatience. In reality a song is not good or bad it is a musical vibration and the voice is also a musical vibration. A person with left brain dominate aspect will perceive judgment on the vibrations and allow those vibrations to harm them. They are essentially making a mountain out of a mole hill in their mind. They are allowing an inanimate object or inanimate words to harm them. Words and musical vibrations cannot harm you unless you allow them to with the exception of extremely loud music or vibration's that may rupture your ear drums. One might suggest if a person cannot listen to a song that is not in their preferred genre for 2 hours straight over and over and over they are an emotional wreck. That is perhaps a harsh truth and perhaps ones with a strong sense of time may fight that truth, but disbelief does not change reality. I tend to go to youtube and find a song I never heard of or even a song I am pleased with and I play over and over for the whole day and I just recently realized I am using it as an emotional conditioning tool. One with a strong sense of time that has a song they "love" will not be able to play that song over and over for hours at a time. They will get "tired" of it. One should not get "tired" of a vibration unless there are mentally in a state of "good and bad". The song is good for a few plays and after a few plays the song is bad. So the only way to eliminate that mental block is to find a song and listen to it over and over and fight all these feelings that suggest "I can't listen to this song one more time or I will be destroyed." The reality is, you will not be destroyed you are just believing hallucinations your mind is suggesting. Whatever song you hate the most is the one you listen to for two hours straight. When you are pleased with that song you won a mental battle. You showed the thought's who is boss so you are starting to have something called mental fortitude. If you think a song is evil or the lyrics are evil, that is the song you want to listen to. I am not intelligent enough to detect evil so I assume evil is a delusion and thus I do not subscribe to it. If I started going down the path of judgment about what is evil there would not be enough fire in the universe to satisfy my desire to burn those I determined are evil. So as far as I am concerned everyone is perfect. Perhaps you are pleased with that logic. It is perhaps proper to not make the music condition a focus of what you are doing but simply play the music as you do something else. Let the music play as your browse the internet for example or as you go about doing other things because the subconscious never misses a beat and this is not about how fast you can do it because that may harm you if you try things to swiftly. The bottom line mental goal is to detect the emotions. Detect when you are becoming impatient. Detect when you are becoming angry or frustrated with the song. I detect emotions when I sense them and they are like a powerful drug or sensation so I am very biased. This is in relation to a person who is a control freak will feel good when they control things. This is in relation to absolute power controls absolutely. The feeling of power is the feeling of control and that emotion is a pleasurable drug to ones who like control. This is a thick illusion because one who has "Dr" in front of their name if they are not called doctor they may become very upset and say "you insult me by not calling me doctor." That is as much of a control freak as one who holds money over another ones head to control them. It is all the same emotion. The control emotion is relative to the left brain characteristics.

"On the contrary, the right brain seems to flourish dealing with complexity, ambiguity and paradox."

Ambiguity is a nice way to say "freedom" or "avoids rules". So one may be perceived to be a revolutionary in relation to one who is left brain dominate. So one in extreme right brain/subconscious state is unaffected if someone insults them. If someone suggests my books are the worst books ever written in the universe I will consider that a compliment because I will understand they should be because I am at the extreme opposite of the "norms". People with a strong sense of time should perceive my books to be nightmares because I am at the opposite of the universe in contrast to them mentally speaking. **" quite opposite in the way they think".** I perceive my books are just fine. I perceive I do the best I can and I cannot do any better than that, and only a fool would judge someone who submits they are doing the best they can based on their situation.

"At times, right brain thinking is difficult to put into words because of its complexity, its ability to process information quickly and its non-verbal nature."

"At times, right brain thinking is difficult to put into words because of its complexity"

This is in relation to how powerful the subconscious is. Everyone understands it is very powerful. I have determined it should not take me more than infinite books to explain it, so I am at least certain about that determination.

"flourish dealing with complexity, ambiguity and paradox"

This is quite accurate. I do not have any problems attempting to explain something I understand I am unable to explain. So I am undaunted with explaining an infinitely complex situation I am aware I will never be able to fully explain. Paradox in this description is relative to all of the contradictions

I suggest. All of the contradictions are relative to how complex or powerful subconscious is. if one makes to many contradictions one who is left brain will assume they are crazy or insane. Left brain is more about limits and control and rules and they will say, "What he said was a contradiction so he is insane." The reality is, The right brain is so powerful, it is beyond description, it is what is known as unnamable. I will write infinite words and still not explain it properly that is a symptom of how powerful it is. Many who reach "Nirvana" or subconscious dominate, which is the same thing, end up sitting in silence their whole life essentially because they cannot communicate their thoughts to the "sane" or left brains people anymore. Most of the things they says are "a paradoxical or contradictions" so they come across as insane to the left brain "majority" and they are forced to live in "temples" and isolate their self from society, simply because they are "opposites". I will never verbally isolate myself, because I do not fear brain dead mole crickets. Perhaps we have come to an understanding. I find no fault in ones who desire to cling to desires and cravings and thus rely on the left brain aspect of the mind but they should perhaps ponder what is going to happen once I get warmed up. You will perhaps understand what I am suggesting when I get warmed up. I will certainly remind you when I get warmed up. One might suggest you will be the first to understand. I have some doubts I simply became extreme subconscious dominate and nothing more since I detect this "presence" that is mindful to keep us as a species asleep using these "emotions" as a sedative. I am not intelligent enough to speak about supernatural powers.10:51:36 AM

I am watching this documentary on suicide bombers in relation to the Israeli-Palestinian conflict and my anger was waxing and then one "Muslim" said. When one is willing to die they are chosen by Allah. And I though, Wow that guy is right but he is extremely out of context. Unnamable is subconscious or complex or very intelligent and the only way to reach it as in that spirit or state of mind however you want to look at it is to be mindful of death or lose your fear of death. So what this person said was accurate just out of context.

The Conflict has nothing to do with religion first off. I will repeat that, this 50 year conflict has nothing to do with religion.

The Vietcong were not religious and they blew themselves up all the time to kill Americans. They also came at American's in waves only be to be mowed down. War is suicide. There is no physical war that is not suicide. People will die for anything; land, money, drugs, food and, beliefs, and usually it usually is summed up with; so they can feel alive. Freud summed it up properly.

"The   goal   of   all   life   is   death." Sigmund Freud.

I will attempt to sum up what I am saying. Propaganda is required to convince the offspring to die for the selfish control objectives of the adults. It is not bad or good though. It just is. Washington had to take an angle to convince people to die to get out from being taken advantage of by the British. I do not know exactly what he said but he made a case that the cause was worth dying for. I am quite certain you are thinking that is not what Freud was saying. The point in life is all about testing the limits in life in order to live a proper life and at times that costs one their life. The kamikazes in World War two were no less suicidal than pilots who fought against the enemy as in pilots who attacked ships with anti aircraft guns exploding all around them. Death is expected in war and life is war. A person known to be a daredevil is one who is rather inclined to taking chances so they are certainly under the influence of subconscious to a degree because subconscious has no fear. I perceive I say many things in my books that may get me killed or be taken wrong and result in my suffering but I frankly do not care and so I do not fear. I speak what is on my mind and do what you will to me because I won't be blinking when you arrive with your weapons. Am I suicidal ? Maybe I have a death wish. In actuality that is the purpose of life.

"The   goal   of   all   life   is   death."
Sigmund Freud.

You simply cannot kill a dead horse so why would I be afraid to speak my mind. It would be insanity for me to be afraid considering I have already looked death in the eye and it ran away. Firefighters are pretty much without fear and so are policemen so are ones in the army. The ones who have too much fear in those "professions" end up going mad or end up kill their self because they cannot take the "heat".

So the whole war thing in the "east" has much more to do with one group claiming land and dominating over another group and suggesting that other group has no right that land and thus we have a conflict and it is essentially a blood bath for the offspring. The adults on each side of this conflict are giving their offspring a bath so the adults can reach their selfish goals of control over that land. Take any conflict where people are dying and it is usually about land or resources on that land. It is never about religion. No one even knows what the hell the religions were talking about I am certain of that simply because, "right brain thinking is difficult to put into words because of its complexity". IT is impossible to put into words or I would not be writing unnamable dam infinite books would I? I would just sum it all up in a nice paragraph and check the spelling and get on with my stupid life, if I could. My subconscious is saying this to me at all times "You are going to write infinite books and I do not give a "stuff" what happens to you a result of that." So I just try to figure ways to kill it. Maybe you have a nice big bottle of pills you want to prescribe me. I am infinitely open minded to that. Maybe you have a big poison mushroom patch and you want to invite me over for lunch sometime. I am infinitely open minded to that. I just convince myself people do not even read books anymore so my attempts are far beyond the realms of infinite vanity. I make insane people look like gods of sanity. So now you understand the definition of " its complexity". Do not assume I am an authority on IT because IT is ripping me apart every second of every second. We will just call it subconscious or right brain dominate,(wink wink). Just to have something to laugh about. That is about all I can do is laugh but if you figure out how I can kill this thing let me know. I am still trying to figure out who determined it is inhumane to allow old men to die in wars for land and it is logical to allow young offspring to die in wars for land. So I am certain I am in an insane asylum. You can write infinite books about how sane everything is but I promise you, this world is an insane asylum.

"A casual stroll through the lunatic asylum shows that faith does not prove anything."
Friedrich Nietzsche

If what I perceive is truth relative to me alone and what you perceive is truth relative to you alone this is an insane asylum.

If you are one of these beings who has been hoodwinked into fighting foreign wars to line the pockets of the carpetbaggers let me tell you something. Heimdall does need to be protected so you just understand one thing. Whoever told you that you should risk your life for foreign conquests of empire building, they are liars. Heimdall does not need your protection, so go home and help your mama clean the dishes. If anyone has a problem with anything I ever say you bring it and make sure your death shroud is clean because you are going to be wearing it for a long time. I know I am insane because at times I perceive you might understand what I am saying. It is important you do not rest on your laurels in relation to what I say because I am certain I will clarify everything by the infinite book.

I wanted to write something about the above comment but then an experiment occurred to me. If I am subconscious dominate then I should be able to watch a movie with subliminal messages in it and I should be able to detect them. If I cannot detect them that means subconscious aspect of the mind is neither right nor left brain and so it is another aspect of the mind all together. So that would mean there is conscious "logical" aspect, subconscious "infinite" aspect " , Torn silent aspect, and then another aspect of the mind that picks up the subliminal messages. So you if you have a subliminal movie of some sort call. I perceive I would certainly pick up on subliminal messages no matter how short they were in a movie.

7:53:57 PM - I have uploaded the second volume to a popular download site so the plan is well underway. It is now unstoppable. I will no longer speak, I will just fiddle.7:54:51 PM

6/9/2009 8:18:17 AM

"The left brain is associated with verbal, logical, and analytical thinking. It excels in naming and categorizing things, symbolic abstraction, speech, reading, writing, arithmetic. The left brain is very linear: it places things in sequential order -- first things first and then second things second, etc. If you reflect back upon our own educational training, we have been traditionally taught to master the 3 R's: reading, writing and arithmetic -- the domain and strength of the left brain.

The right brain, on the other hand, functions in a non-verbal manner and excels in visual, spatial, perceptual, and intuitive information. The right brain processes information differently than the left brain. For the right brain, processing happens very quickly and the style of processing is nonlinear and nonsequential. The right brain looks at the whole picture and quickly seeks to determine the spatial relationships of all the parts as they relate to the whole. This component of the brain is not concerned with things falling into patterns because of prescribed rules. On the contrary, the right brain seems to flourish dealing with complexity, ambiguity and paradox. At times, right brain thinking is difficult to put into words because of its complexity, its ability to process information quickly and its non-verbal nature. The right brain has been associated with the realm of creativity." http://tolearn.net/hypertext/brain.htm

The school systems are biased and are only geared to create children that are left brain dominate. This explains the extreme emotional problems in society. The "physical" issues such as violence and drug abuse in the youth. That is not good or bad. There two schools of thought and parents or the child should be able to suggest whether they want to choose the path of left brain or right brain dominate. The left brain school is what is now available.

"Our educational system, as well as science in general, tends to neglect the nonverbal form of intellect. What it comes down to is that modern society discriminates against the right hemisphere." Roger Sperry – 1973

"Heb 1:13 But to which of the angels said he at any time, Sit on my right hand, until I make thine enemies thy footstool?"

This comment has little to do with taking advantage or harming others this is simply a truthful statement. It is perhaps suggesting the right hemisphere is "dealing with complexity, ambiguity and paradox" which would denotes "smarter" than the left hemisphere. Of course that is out of context. The right brain is perhaps also a symbol of the "spirit" literally and or figuratively which is perhaps suggested with the comment "right brain thinking is difficult to put into words", this may suggest infinity. I am not intelligent enough to speak about supernatural powers. To clarify "make thine enemies thy footstool." Ones on the 'right" have extreme "intelligence" and can easily defeat their enemy "ones on the left" with words. **"Psa 48:10 According to thy name, O God(subconscious), so is thy praise unto the ends of the earth(some are very talkative): thy right hand(right brain) is full of right righteousness. (complexity)"**

"Right hand full of righteousness" would denote the cerebral aspect of the right brain or what is perhaps understood to be the "peacemaker" aspect of the brain. Righteousness is perhaps not denoted a "good or bad" but simply suggesting one is less prone to physical violence or one is more willing to seek a verbal conclusion that involved a plowshare as opposed to a sword. Perhaps Unnamable in this comment denotes the brain and perhaps the brain denotes the method in which one is able to communicate with "unnamable". I am not intelligent enough to speak of such things.

"Col 3:1 If ye then be risen with Christ(become right brain dominate to an extreme), seek those things which are above(cerebral mental battles), where Christ sitteth on the right hand(right hemisphere) of God.(brain)"

"Risen" perhaps denotes one has gone from the left brain aspect to this right brain aspect using emotional conditioning concepts such as "meek shall inherit the earth" and "turn the other cheek" and "submission" which are all forms of humility this is in relation to other "conditioning" techniques such as "Mat 16:25 For whosoever will save his life shall lose it: and whosoever will lose his life for my sake shall find it." Because this is perhaps the greatest form of "meek shall inherit the earth" or "turn the other cheek" or "submission" simply because for one to look at their own self as unworthy of life, one is in the ultimate state of mental humility of course this is perhaps best done mindfully, considering attempting this physically may lead to one becoming much "deeper" in relation to being buried than one perhaps wishes for, but this method appeared to work for me accidentally. This would also suggest ones determined to be "depressed" are in fact in a perfect mental state of "grace" or "humility" or "meekness".

"Those which are above" perhaps suggests the right brain is "more complex" than the left brain because it goes beyond the linear to the infinite or ponder state of mind so it would be considered "above", but perhaps not in a "good or bad" but simply it is more complex and "is difficult to put into words because of its complexity, its ability to process information quickly and its non-verbal nature"

", its ability to process information quickly" is perhaps what is denoted by the suggestions in the Holy texts in relation to "adversary", "darkness and light" and the "infidels" and the "sane". In contrast to the left brain the right brain is "light, righteousness" but this is perhaps not denoting something is worse or evil or bad, it is simply a contrast.

"Isa 41:10 Fear thou not; for I am with thee: be not dismayed; for I am thy Unnamable: I will strengthen thee; yea, I will help thee; yea, I will uphold thee with the right hand of my righteousness."

"fear not" denotes conditioning away from fear, such as fear of the unknown and fear of death because fear is a strong emotion that hinders ones mental ability to go to the right brain "world". Fear could perhaps be looked as a mental block that keeps one left brain dominate, such as fear of embarrassment and this leads to the emotion shyness. "uphold thee with the right hand of my righteousness." This denotes the "righteousness" is simply the less physically violent aspect and the "complex" cerebral aspect. "uphold thee" perhaps suggests this is the "smarter" aspect or the "wiser" aspect of the mind in contrast to the left brain aspect but perhaps not in an arrogant way but simply it is perhaps the truth. The right is more complex and tends to be "difficult to put into words".

"I am thy God" is perhaps in relation to "I AM" which denotes now which denotes no sense of time, or being in the now mentally, and "thy God" perhaps denotes "I am the complex ,wise, less physically violent aspect of the mind". It perhaps also denotes the "Unnamable aspect" in relation to "Gen 1:26 And God said, Let us make man in our image," so perhaps the right brain is the "image" spoken of here. In relation to supernatural powers I am unable to comment on such complexities.

The right brain school of thought would simply be " **quite opposite**" from the left brain school of thought in its functions so this would mean a completely different school. No matter how one looks at it, if you only have school that encourage left brain thought that is all you are going to produce is left brain people. So it is not about how much money one throws into the school system is about how one goes about the education process. Garbage in, garbage out is perhaps proper way to look at it.

 Left Brain: "categorizing things" denotes labels. This is in line with "Logic". If one is not judged to be in the label of "smart" they are therefore dumb. The thoughts encouraged by left brain are quite shallow. They are reverse of the right brain

Left Brain:"Logic" denotes by left brain is essentially a judgment. This is in relation to: if a person is not judged to be "good" then they are "bad". If person is not like you, and you do not perceive yourself to be bad, then that person is different than you, and so they are bad. This is what elementary logic incites.

Left Brain: "The left brain is very linear: it places things in sequential order -- first things first and then second things second.", this very characteristic is what creates the strong sense of time and thus strong physical sensations such as strong sense of hunger, cravings and desires. This also relates to the very simplistic logical deductions such as "I am good therefore you are bad.", which is anti "complex" in thought deductions. This is perhaps also the reason for the strong "control" aspects such as control of land of control of people. The simplistic logic in situations like "You are different so I must control you and/ or destroy you." A hunter see's a deer and must kill it to hang its head on their wall so they can suggest to others, "Look what I control." A man's love is scorned will harm their mate who has scorned them to suggest, "I have control and you are not allowed to scorn me." A religion may suggest "You are not like my religion so I must harm you and make you become like I am, because if you are not like me you are bad." A person may lose their job and determine "Without money I am bad because with money I am good", and then determine since I am bad I must harm myself because bad things should not be allowed to live."

This is all a symptom of "very linear" and "elementary" deduction skills encouraged by the left brain. Perhaps all current left brain dominate schools should be called "elementary" schools.

The right brain type school would need to be completely verbal with no grading. No "judgments" These type of school would have teachers who are "right brain" dominate who would understand the proper approaches. A child cannot be judged to be right brain or left brain because it is strictly a lifestyle choice than can be achieved with emotional conditioning. So these two schools, left and right brain, would in turn simply be opposites but not "good or bad". The left brain type of person has their moments and the right brain also has their moments and both have their purpose.

It would perhaps be difficult to avoid rivalry between the two simply because the left brain people would be prone to such emotions as envy, jealousy, spite by the very nature of left brain characteristics and thus may resort to physical violence against the right brain students. It would perhaps be a

"David and Goliath" or "lion and lamb" scenario in relation to the right brain students would be "cerebral" and the left brain students would be "physically" orientated. One might suggest one would be "the darkness and the other the light" but more in relation to physical hostility as opposed to being "evil". Left brain would be considered the "viper" in relation to judgments and physical aspect encouraged by the logic and linear or elementary thoughts processes in contrast to the right brain "complexity" and this again is a symptom of the disconnect in relation to the "opposite" nature of the two hemispheres. Both are "anti" in contrast to each other. I will now discuss something of importance.7:38:31 AM

8:52:19 AM I find the humor in the world quite staggering.

"North Korea today said it would use nuclear weapons in a "merciless offensive" if provoked — its latest bellicose rhetoric apparently aimed at deterring any international punishment for its recent atomic test blast"

Now this is beyond a doubt simply verbal posturing. I am quite certain North Korea understands there are perhaps 1000 nuclear warheads trained on it at this moment. I am uncertain what North Korea would even accomplish by launching a nuke at anyone except to ensure its own annihilation, so this is simply a "Look at me I am powerful" type of left brain thinking. "I will harm you physically if you do something or do not do something." In all reality, they are not going to do anything and even if they do, they will perish and they are "afraid" of death so they will never launch a nuke at anyone. So they should be looked at a country with "control" problems encouraged by the "left brain" elementary logic characteristics. The world should allow them to talk their self into some clarity. If everyone keeps paying attention to them and plastering their comments in the headlines they will continue to talk because they are not aware they are actually in monologue to their self. They are attempting to talk their self into relevance because they are aware they are irrelevant. In relation to the comment "Sometimes a cigar is just a cigar" or sometimes a threat is just an attempt to communicate. Launching a nuke at this day and age is simply suicide so perhaps North Korea is meek. Perhaps North Korea is suggesting, "If you wish to test your targeting system on your nukes we are available." Most of this verbal posturing has much more to do with making an impression on the ones they control in their own country. I cannot speak about other countries but if North Korea ever launches a nuke America will certainly wipe them off the map. It is all an aspect of nature. One may be tough but sooner or later one who is tougher will allow them to understand they were not that tough after all. North Korea is a country that is struggling to be accepted because they understand they are an outcast. There is nothing wrong with the world considering to assist North Korea. What harm would it do? North Korea is no threat to anyone. One should consider the "opposite" approach to situations or what is known as reverse psychology. What harm would it do to assist them with food and other material goods and be their friend and respect their "way of life" in relation to their political agenda. The big fish do not have to pander to the little fish. The big fish are the "teachers" and should strive to be above the little fish in relation to being a good role model. The big countries are attempting to treat North Korea as some mountain of threat when it is not a mountain of threat. North Korea is an outcast and it is alone and it needs a country to tell it, look we are all outcasts and I will assist you if you need it and I am not afraid you because you are a human being and I can be your friend if I decide to be. I am not aware of any country that has no "character flaws".

I am aware North Korea wants to be a part of the "world" but it also has pride and it perhaps not able to deny its own pride to come into the fold. That is why the big fish have to understand this country is not a threat but simply posturing because it is "upset" it is an outcast or considered an outcast, and so it is suggesting things that are along the lines of what one who is depressed or suicidal might suggest and so it important to give it the benefit of the doubt. Paying attention to North Korea is going to incite it more.

If North Korea wants to commit suicide by launching nukes there is nothing anyone can do. If person wants to kill their self there is nothing anyone can do. One is wise to look at it like a harmed being that is attempting to find its footing. There is no reason to humiliate the harmed being further because the harmed being is hurting enough, they will work things out or they will not work things out, but that is their problem or suffering or situation. One is simply unable to work another person's problems out for them. People do not always solve their problems in the fashion one would hope. To quote a master:

"The goal of all life is death." Sigmund Freud.

What would happen if the world still gave North Korea food and water and made sure the people in that country were fed and taken care of and the world still treated North Korea as a friend in the world community and tried to work with them and assist them now matter what and showed them the world is not against them and perhaps in time North Korea would start to understand we are all just people and we should try to assist each other and just because a person does not think like everyone else it does not mean they are not important. Would the world blow up if we tried that? Maybe the whole would blow up and I would not care.

One is unable to win when death is the end conclusion. Life is already lost, but we can lose perhaps with grace and dignity, either way the end conclusion is certain. Whatever North Korea is going to do, it is best to allow them to explore what they are going to do and not give them a reason to monologue their self into suicide. North Korea is saying "attack me." So one should simply not pay any attention to them this way, they may realize they are not so scary and not so tough and perhaps they will become a bit more meek. Their fate is in their hands and their destiny is of their own making and so it is best to watch and attempt to understand where they are gong but to posture along with them will only encourage them. When a child says "I am running away from home." And a parent says "fine see you later." This is a complicated situation but the truth is, people have to experience the extremes their self in hopes they may turn back, but that is not always the case and some end in "tragedies." That is the nature of the situation but it is not good or bad.

Sometimes a cigar is just a cigar, sometimes a threat is just a communication, sometimes money is just money, sometime people are just people and not good or evil. The carbon -12 atom lives forever and we are all perhaps slightly jealous of it.

<Bateau> you have no morals?

<Bateau> so you don't see the difference between right and wrong?

<Heimdall> I see everything as one thing. I see no labels. Left brain or emotional aspect understands sequence and elementary logic, as in "you are not like me so you are bad."

<Heimdall> These are simply labels that left brain or emotional aspect encourage

<Heimdall> Indian medicine men see everything as one thing, so they see the opposite

<Heimdall> they see infinity

<Heimdall> If i burn my hand that is not bad because i understand fire burns and so I have learned something from being burned

<Heimdall> So being burned is not bad or good it is simply an opportunity to understand or progress in understanding

<Heimdall> Some may suggest fire is not always good or not always bad

<Heimdall> but the truth is fire is neither good or bad, fire just is 9:30:27 AM

9:33:29 AM - There is a comment I heard recently. It suggested, if one keeps one secret one will perceive that initial one has 10 secrets. This concept of keeping secrets encourages insecurity in the ones who are not aware of the secret and encourages "control" aspects in the ones who have the secrets. Simply put, one does not have the secret that the carbon-12 atom has, which is the ability to live forever, or the information needed to escape impermanence, so ones secrets are of little value in the perspective of the whole.

"Freud believed that humans were driven by two conflicting central desires: the life drive (libido/ Eros) (survival, propagation, hunger, thirst, and sex) and the death drive (Thanatos)." WIKIPEDIA. COM

These concepts are in line with the concepts of the "religious founders". Cravings and desires are more prone to be left brain or emotional aspect characteristics. Strong hunger, strong sense of time, strong sex drive, strong need to be relevant or make an impact on the physical level. This is in relation to "the kingdom is within" which denotes the cerebral or mental aspect is the focus because the physical aspect is impermanent or unquenchable. This is not as about what is good or bad or proper or improper because those are simply labels encouraged by the left brain. One might suggest the strong physical cravings such as need to be important or accepted that is encouraged by the left brain are a result of the "opposite" right brain or subconscious aspects understanding that one is not relevant or "permanent".

The comment "No man is an island unto their self" is a left brain trait that one wishes to be accepted or "fit in" to their peer group, such as look pretty or be rich materialistically, because the right brain subconscious aspect is fully aware one is all alone. This again is the "opposite" or "anti" contrasts between the two hemispheres. So the Torn aspect of a being is between the two "angel and devil" aspects so to speak, one aspect is the left and it is pulling one into the physical focus and the other aspect is the "right hand of righteousness" in relation to encouraging one to be cerebrally focused, because mentally one can do anything but physically one is very limited to what they can achieve, so the physical focus creates much struggle because physical things can never satisfy. This of course is in relation to what influence mentally one is under. To suggest physical things are not as important to one with left brain dominance will perhaps be perceived to be illogical based on the elementary logical traits of left brain characteristics. One under the influence of the "complex" right brain influence can grasp that concept perhaps much easier, simply because one under the influence of right brain is more prone to have more than simply one of two options when looking at suggestions. This is of course the disconnect created by the "opposite" or "anti" aspect of the two natures of the mind or brain or "spirit".

The scenario of the devil(left physical aspect) and the angel(cerebral right aspect) and then the torn aspect which has a choice between the two in the middle. It is not in relation to which one is "good or bad" but more in relation to simply different paths. One can take the physical based path or the cerebral based path but neither is evil or good, they are simply opposites or contrasts to each other. Perhaps the comment about many paths leads to one destination suggests the physical focused aspect of the left brain and the cerebral focused aspect of the right brain implies both paths lead to the same destination which is the mind or brain itself. Apparently that is what some have been suggesting. I am unable to comment on the matter.10:01:37 AM

"Isaiah 5:15 And the mean man shall be brought down, and the mighty man shall be humbled, and the eyes of the lofty shall be humbled"

"Mean" denotes anger or "wrath" which is a primary characteristic of the left hemisphere. So "Mean shall be brought down" may suggest when one achieves subconscious dominate or right brain dominate the "emotions" are decreased in relation to "as he(right brain) increases I(left brain "mean,anger)

decrease". "Joh 3:30 He must increase, but I must decrease. "

 This suggests one under the influence of the "complex" aspect of the mind is in a state of "humility" or in a state of cerebral and not under the influence of the elementary logic or judgmental aspect in relation to "It excels in naming and categorizing things " and thus labels(good and bad) of the left hemisphere.

This is also somewhat of a numerical suggestion considering the verse number. My date of birth is 5-15 but that is perhaps of no consequence. The number 5 is in relation to man. So it is suggesting a man will be humbled or in the spirit of humility when under the "image" as in "we will make man in our image" of the mind in relation to the right hemisphere. So the number 6 would be in relation to the left "physical" focused aspect of the mind. The number 7 is in relation to "unnamable" or complexity so this number is the "right hand" as in "righteous" aspect which is the right hemisphere. So this perhaps suggests the three aspects of the mind or the trinity of the mind. The 5 being the torn aspect, 6 being the left emotional physical based aspect, and 7 being the right cerebral "meek" "humble" "complex" aspect. This is perhaps also in relation to the western "founders" with respect to Moses who arrived in 2500 BC , Jesus who arrived in 2000 BC and Mohamed who arrived in 1500BC, and the separation of each is 500 or 5. Mohammed agreed with Jesus and Jesus agreed with Moses and this is also a trinity. So the trinity of man (5) separated by 5(500 years) humbled the "mean" because they are still remembered and the focus or center of attention in relation to the "western" world, even after all of these years. "and the eyes of the lofty(physical orientated men) shall be humbled" in the presence of this trinity. Perhaps the wars that are fought in the names of these beings have much more to do with (left brain emotional physical based) man's (invidia (envy)) of their achievements than anything else. I submit I am unable to understand such complexities. This "trinity" denotes the three of these beings were on the same "level " or from the same "source" or in tune with the "message". Perhaps beings with "left influence" may become quite ira (wrath) because great truth would simply harm their ___superbia___ (pride) because one must be in a state of mental Humilitas in order to eat the amount of crow such comments suggest. I will certainly not publish this comment in my sixth book because I am certainly fearful of the "sane" vipers because they are so "Lucifer: Pride (superbia) " and I am so weak. Fear is relative to uncertainty; pride is relative to fear of uncertainty. Humility occurs when one understands they misunderstood; pride occurs when one is unable to understand they misunderstood. 10:49:24 AM

12:10:30 PM- I will now discuss something of value. Humility has far less to do with admitting ones misguided physical actions were improper and far more to do with admitting ones understandings that lead to those misguided physical actions were improper. Submitting ones understandings are misguided surpasses the physical strength of 100 men.

"Samson, Shimshon (Hebrew: שמשון, Standard Šimšon Tiberian Šimšôn; meaning **"of the sun"** – perhaps proclaiming he was radiant and mighty.

Ra (pronounced as **Rah**, and sometimes as **Re**) is the ancient Egyptian **sun unnamable**

The **crescent moon** and star is an internationally-recognized symbol of the faith of Islam.

The Hebrew Scriptures (Old Testament) contains many references to the societies surrounding the Israelites -- Babylonians, Canaanites, Philistines, etc. These are commonly referred to as Pagans:

Referring to sun wheels and obelisks: "...*These symbols of pagan sun worship were associated with Baal worship, or Baalim, which is strongly condemned in scripture.*

Chistian Son of God."

WIKIPEDIA.COM

Heliopolis or RA the sun God represents the mind.

At sunrise Ra is known as Khepera. Depicted by a human with a beetle head. The name Khepera means "to become" in relation to "being and becoming". Being denotes one with subconscious /right brain dominate. This is because they have no sense of time or are in Nirvana so they are "being" or in the now or moment mentally. So the aspect of RA(the mind) at sunrise which denotes not at full power or not subconscious/right brain dominate is one who has a sense of time so they are "becoming" and becoming denotes time, becoming denotes future tense, "I will come" "I will become". So the beetle head denotes what the Holy books explain as the adversary, the darkness, the infidel in relation to not being up to "full power" or under the influence of the "light" of the "powerful aspect of the mind" in relation to "right brain thinking is difficult to put into words because of its complexity".

At noon Heliopolis is known as Ra because he is at full power. This denotes one who is subconscious/ right brain dominate to the extent they have slight sense of time or are in Nirvana and thus have diminished physical traits such as strong cravings and desires for food and material physical aspects. This is relative to gluttony derived from the Latin gluttire, meaning to gulp down or swallow. Gulp down or swallow denotes strong hunger but also strong physical attachment as opposed to the right brain that has diminished physical attachment due to the extreme cerebral focus or "spiritual" focus.

The crescent moon aspect is suggesting the mind is the moon and when the moon is full, it is bright like the "light" and this denotes right brain is at full power and then the "darkness" covers it up and the "light" fades, which is simply suggesting when the "emotions" fill the mind the "light" or "right" aspect is covered or "silenced".

""Ba`al" can refer to any god and even to human officials; in some texts it is used as a substitute for Hadad, a god of the rain, thunder, fertility and agriculture, and the lord of Heaven. Since only priests were allowed to utter his divine name Hadad, Ba`al was used commonly. Nevertheless, few if any Biblical uses of "Ba`al" refer to Hadad, the lord over the assembly of gods on the holy mount of Heaven, but rather refer to any number of local spirit-deities worshipped as cult images, each called ba`al and regarded by the writers of the Hebrew Bible in that context as a false unnamable."
WIKIPEDIA.COM

A false god would be suggesting an "opposite" or "anti god". So this is in relation to **"On the contrary, the right brain seems to flourish dealing with complexity, ambiguity and paradox."** Contrary denotes "opposite". Left brain is physical focused and material focused (golden calf), right brain is cerebral focused and this is the "opposite" or "contrary". It is the anti aspect of the mind.

So with all of this information and all of these religions a person with the "left" judgmental aspect of the mind will be unable to grasp these religions are all the same because the left brain uses elementary logic and the right brain uses complexity. The left brain uses "you are bad because I am good logic." The right brain uses complexity and understands everything is one thing. This is all in relation to the comment "They (left brain) hear but they do not understand". The left brain (darkness) cannot grasp the complexity of the words or the principles that the right brain can grasp." The right brain looks at the whole picture" the left brain looks are judgments and remains isolated in its "wholeness" view. It has been suggested each person has a preference to each aspect of the mind. Some prefer physical actions over cerebral actions. Some prefer labels and some prefer complexity. So this is why it is not good or bad if one prefers either aspect over the other. These teachings are simply suggesting ways one may achieve the "cerebral" aspect of thought but not in a way that makes one feel obsolete to another. If one prefers physical aspects then they lose cerebral aspects, if one prefers cerebral aspects one loses physical aspects. "He increases as I decrease." That is simply what harmony is, or give and take or win some you lose some. It has nothing to do with good or bad, they are simply states one can achieve or one can decide to not achieve with no consequences either way. One cannot physically live forever only carbon -12 can, so one has choices in the states of mind one can achieve, but both states of mind in relation to the species are required. I am not intelligent enough to speak about supernatural concepts.1:09:06 PM

1:19:47 PM <Bateau> so there is nothing then. no life, no existence

<Heimdall> We are living creatures and our minds can be altered from a left brain physical aspect to a right brain cerebral "spiritual" aspect, I am not intelligent enough to discuss supernatural powers but they are perhaps suggestions to "instill fear" in the ones with "left brain" aspect, to bend them to the will of others.

<Heimdall> If one has no fear, which is an emotion and not capable in the right brain subconscious aspect, then one is immune to such "fear tactics"

<Heimdall> One cannot beat a dead horse, the dead horse has no fear, so they are unable to be manipulated with "fear tactics"

<Heimdall> one with left brain emotional aspect has a sense of time so life is very swift and sadness and loneliness are harsh, one with right brain or subconscious aspect has no sense of time and no ability to feel lonely or sad and life takes a long time to happen, so they are in a mindful state known as the fountain of youth.

I am mindful of the sadness in Bateau's question. The emotional aspect of the mind gives one the impression of loss or sadness but that is a symptom of emotions. It is essentially dissatisfaction. The reality is, one is unable to understand what one is unable to understand. I am not aware of this spiritual ,spirit world. I perhaps am not intelligent enough to grasp that concept but I am not harmed by that reality because I am not "emotional" . I am not counting on something to satisfy me. I am not based on satisfaction.1:23:19 PM

Brainiest Tot: Two-year-old Karina has same IQ as Stephen Hawking and Bill Gates!

This is for all of you "sane" beings who assume your college books make you smart. All your spelling bee's enable you to accomplish is to destroy the complex aspect of the mind called right brain/ subconscious. So I find it quite funny how much money this world invests into schools that only make people dumber. It is very difficult for me not to laugh at that great truth. Every child could have an IQ of this child but as soon as people start telling them how to spell properly it kills everything mentally speaking.

"The right brain looks at the whole picture and quickly seeks to determine the spatial relationships of all the parts as they relate to the whole. This component of the brain is not concerned with things falling into patterns because of prescribed rules. On the contrary, the right brain seems to flourish dealing with complexity, ambiguity and paradox."

I will explain this quickly so I do not end up in a triad of cussing and cursing you to a painful death.

"not concerned with things falling into patterns because of prescribed rules." The second a parent starts saying stupid "stuff" like "You do as I say or you are bad or in trouble." "What you just did was bad." "You did good." "It is not right to do that." You destroy the child's mind with your elementary logic, rules, and insanity in encourages "labels"." **not concerned with things falling into patterns because of prescribed rules"** is a nice way of saying subconscious/right brain doesn't give a "stuff" about your elementary isolation and insanity "rules" of "right and wrong" and "good and bad". You are simply blind to the fact you are a child abuser. In direct relation to the comments "You know not what you do" and "suffer the children."" modern society discriminates against the right hemisphere." Is a nice way to say modern society or the "sane" abuse the children who are born with subconscious dominate/right brain dominate. I will stop talking now before I start ripping your heart out of your chest. I definitely won't be leaving this comment in my diary it would be "evil" and "bad". I will go play my video game before I say something and sense regret even though I am unable to, ever. Perhaps you perceive I care about what you think, ever. Perhaps you perceive you are relevant at all, at this stage. I am pleased you are unable to grasp anything I say.6:41:14 PM

6:58:32 PM - Any being who is in nirvana who suggests they "care" or "are all about kindness" are not in nirvana or they are liars simply because subconscious dominate is unable to grasp such labels. I will put it this way, I took a handful of pills and when I started to convulse I did not call for help and my mind registered "this being does not care even about his own life so turn that function called care off." That is as simple as it is. I essentially tell jokes now because any talk of good or bad only leads me into long monologues about what is good and what is bad. My mind does not understand those concepts but that does not mean I am physically harmful like the "sane" who know who is good and bad, and tend to kill who they perceive is bad. It is best I do not start killing who I think is bad like you do, so it is best my mind does not register who is bad. All I understand is the difference between a brain dead mole cricket and a lemur monkey. I own the brain dead mole crickets, guess who I am.7:04:32 PM

I submit I did rather well in my writing today until I started looking at news sites and then I implode because I keep discovering I woke up and realized I am in an insane asylum and I do not have the mental capacity to physically start slaughtering them all for my own protection. Life is not fair indeed. Perhaps I should go back to your school so you can teach me what is right and wrong. It only took me a handful of pills ,10 years and 30 attempts, to undo all the damage your "proper teachings" did to me. I do not care what you think in your tiny pinprick mind , you could not have harmed me more than you did and what is so sick is you perceive you did the "right" thing and it's my fault not yours. It's an insane asylum, in relation to

"A casual stroll through the lunatic asylum shows that faith does not prove anything."
Friedrich Nietzsche

or I died and I am in hell and I am being tormented for all eternity; either way, I perceive it is the same thing, It is all one thing. I simply devour myself over and over and over. Perhaps you are unable to grasp that is what is going on.

6/10/2009 3:59:30 AM - Watch a horror movie that scares you and then after the movie turn off all the lights and sit in pitch darkness, if you feel scared or frightened at all you are an emotional wreck. If you are sitting alone and someone comes into the room and yells "boo" and you jump , you are an emotional wreck. I am not so sure about if they actually grab you to scare you , but if they just yell "boo" and you jump or are startled, you simply have way to many emotions and you are frigid, scared, unstable mental wreck. So the logic here would be to watch a very scary movie and turn off the lights and sit quietly and if you can sit for a long enough period without mentally freaking yourself out you are conditioning away from fear or emotions. This perhaps takes much time to accomplish, perhaps several tries and maybe requires various different scary films, it is hard for me to say because I have no fear. The good news is there is no shortage of horror movies in the world.

"A thing is not necessarily true because badly uttered, nor false because spoken magnificently."
Saint Augustine

An isolated mind will be unable to let the hot air it hears escape. This quote is all about mindset. I submit I am sitting in a chair and I feel it so I am safe in suggesting I am sitting in a chair, but then someone might say, "Anyone who drinks beer is bad." Or "Anyone who cannot spell and use commas is bad because they are poorly educated and are stupid." That is where it ends. It does not matter how great of a case they have for their delusion, they are simply insane in their logical conclusions. People tend to assume because they can make one obvious conclusion they can go to the deep end and wield the same power. They tend to make one deduction and then consider their self a master of deductions. Someone reads a book and determines life is sacred and the next thing you know they are killing abortion doctors in some delusional righteous crusade. Someone gets a doctorate degree in psychology and the next thing you know they are giving children heavy psychological drugs so the children act like they do. Someone is told they are wise and the next thing you know they are declaring people are witches and burning them on stakes. So a good rule of thumb is, if you get scared after watching a horror movie while you are sitting in the dark all alone, avoid making any deductions about anything beyond extremely obvious observations every human being would agree with. If you have a scène of right and wrong or morals you have no business making decisions that affect the physical well being of others.

"A thing is not necessarily true because badly uttered, nor false because spoken magnificently." You are not good just because you read a few words that suggest you are good and you are not bad just because an idiot said you are bad in a well worded fashion. Saying the word righteous properly does not mean you are righteous. Avoid the crusader mentality; if you want to help someone mentally go to war with yourself. This quote is a simple translation of "worry about the log in your eye" because you are unable to ever take that log out, so you will never get to the point of actually being able to help anyone ever. Understand you will never be able to help anyone ever, you can just maybe monologue to yourself and others might hear it and they may find some wisdom in it, but you cannot intentionally help anyone but yourself ever. Perhaps you cannot handle that great truth and I understand that and I expect that.

"Beauty is indeed a good gift of God; but that the good may not think it a great good, God dispenses it even to the wicked."
Saint Augustine

Beauty occurs after many mental battles have been lost. The ones who withstand the hottest fires often give off a special glow. I will not discuss this comment it is too harsh for a loser like me.

"While he was in Milan, Augustine's life changed. While still at Carthage, he had begun to move away from Manichaeism, in part because of a disappointing meeting with a key exponent of Manichaean theology. In Rome, he is reported to have completely turned away from Manichaeanism, and instead embraced the skepticism of the New Academy movement."WIKIPEDIA.COM

Skepticism is a nice way to say he started saying "perhaps" and "maybe" a lot. He became a doubting Thomas which is what is required to free the mind from the isolation and tiny views the left brain encourages. It is interesting, a bit after this time in his life he found "unnamable". I found subconscious aspect of the mind but you may perceive I am "unnamable influenced" and that is dangerous because some will perceive the "good unnamable" and some will perceive the "bad unnamable" because I am full of contradictions. That is the nature of subconscious, it is full of paradoxes. I prefer you do not think anything of me ever. I have been judged enough for one eternity. Factually I am not possessed by a unnamable I am simply Heimdall. I am not your savior and I certainly will not be coming to your rescue. One might suggest my emotional feelings were hurt to the extent my mind no longer allows me to register them. It was not so much one person or one event but simply the whole "civilization" or the whole insane asylum got to me. The insane asylum got the better of me and now I want nothing to do with it any longer.

"Complete   abstinence   is   easier   than   perfect   moderation."
Saint Augustine

Doing nothing is easier than correcting mistakes.

Perfect moderation is relative to the degree of obsessive compulsions.

Be hot or cold but avoid lukewarm.

<Bateau> but that makes you unable to think. you just are. so there is no point for you to live really... we think, therefore we are

<Heimdall> I copy our discussions in my book

<Heimdall> you do make a good point but it perhaps is rather depressing for ones with emotions

<Heimdall> there is a point to life but it is not an absolute, it is relative to the observer

<Heimdall> this comment is perhaps very close to the purpose in life

<Heimdall> "The goal of all life is death."

<Heimdall> Sigmund Freud.

<Heimdall> but for ones with emotions it requires much clarification

<Heimdall> the lord of all creation or living things is death and so death is perhaps an entity and is what i understood to be unnamable or the unnamable one

<Heimdall> of course to ones with emotions that scares the hell out of them so they would suggest i certainly must be insane

<Heimdall> and perhaps they suggest Freud is insane also

<Heimdall> and perhaps everyone who does not think like the "sane" do are insane and should be hung on crosses

<Heimdall> Left-brain dominated people(have a strong sense of time) may find their (Right Brainers) thought processes vague and difficult to follow, for they are quite opposite in the way they think."

<Heimdall> Quite opposite denotes I cannot reach you and you cannot reach me, only extremely "wise" right brainers can reach the left brainers

<Bateau> It is how the two sides of the brain complement and combine that counts.

<Heimdall> that in relation to the comment from the bible "I spit the luke warm out of my mouth" that denotes ones who have 50/50, they are smart with right brain but they do things physically, like they are smart enough to convince the offspring to go die in a foreign war over oil. so they are the most dangerous because they are not hot(right) or cold (left) they are lukewarm

<Heimdall> they are the "sane"

<Heimdall> they appear quite sane but they do many insane things physically speaking, like work their self to death or steal from others to make money and to get big houses and big cars, and then they say, its okay to rip people off because i have to make a living, then they lose their job and go home and kill their family and their self

<Heimdall> they are the lukewarm

<Heimdall> they get a degree in psychology, and the next thing you know they are prescribing drugs to children so the children will be "sane" like they are and they get kick backs for the drugs they prescribe and then they say "i have to make a living", thus the comment "suffer the children, because the lukewarm know not what they do."

<Heimdall> money and drugs are not bad

<Heimdall> Freud said sometimes a cigar is just a cigar

<Heimdall> that is right, drugs are not evil, but ones with left brain see everything as good or evil, and no middle way

<Heimdall> money is not evil but if you lose your job and kill yourself because you lose money , you have materialistic issues

<Heimdall> i know this because that is why i killed myself

<Heimdall> Jesus was a poor carpenter, that is why he had the money changer event, he hated money because it reminded him of why he killed himself

<Heimdall> i hate money also

<Heimdall> it harms me

<Heimdall> one might suggest the blood doesn't dry

<Bateau> the thing with right and left brain activity is simple. the left brain sees the full picture. while the right brain sees the details. however! this does not mean you can see only one. because they interact. for instance, a painting. if you would only have left-brain activity. you would only see lots of colors. if you where only right-brained you would only see dots. but! you don't see that. you see the whole picture. with and without details. of course t

<Bateau> you cant have one, without the other

<Bateau> they complete each other

<Bateau> just like our senses complete each other

<Bateau> seeing

<Bateau> hearing

<Bateau> smelling

<Bateau> tasting

<Bateau> feeling

<Bateau> it all comes together to form the world

<Heimdall> yes its forms perceptions, so like Stephen hawking he was "robbed" of his physical aspects to a degree so he had to rely on his mind, Helen Keller was robbed of sight and hearing so her mind was more powerful because it didn't use those aspects, as her sight decreased other things became heightened. "as he increases I decrease" so one is lost and others things are found

<Heimdall> so lukewarm is when one has all senses turned on but none of them are very "good" then ones with no sense of time, have many physical things like sense of taste and time turned off, and so their mental capacity is heightened, heightened awareness.

Please note this is in a voodoo chat room yet this being is wise and curious and not judgmental about things I discuss. One might suggest he is quite the psychologist.

"What progress we are making. In the Middle Ages they would have burned me. Now they are content with burning my books."
Sigmund Freud

Sigmund. I have faith in freedom of speech, tolerance and camouflage.

Monologue is all that is happening ; once one understands that, communication gets very easy.

6/11/2009 7:35:27 AM - I stopped writing yesterday because something happened that proved to me how stupid this whole effort is and also proved to me why psychologically speaking this whole world as far as humans are concerned is stupidity beyond understanding. Totally pointless in relation to psychology is the understatement of the universe. I uploaded volume 3 to a "pirate" download site. Some people took to the book well because I made it look like "I got a copy of this book and if you download it you are like stealing it." People react well to "mischief." So I pretended I was not the author and in reality they were not stealing it, but as long as they thought they were they read it.

"slackOR at 2009-06-09 11:04 CET:

Very Interesting read...in a scattered-brain way -perhaps. A must for serious VIDEO GAMERS to read what this guys perfected mental state has become after all he's been through....he's deeeeeep alright. He's got me saying PERHAPS a lot now perhaps."

Now this guy read the book and he detected the "opposite" inflection and he looked at it as something to that interesting and this is in relation to why the eastern cultures appreciate people who are "right brain" or in Nirvana/no sense of time. It is kind of like a rarity in the east.

"rtypo at 2009-06-10 23:59 CET:

I personally do not like this book. It is a mess. Many points of view are flawed. Very difficult to read.
"

Now this guy detected the same things but he freaked out and started judging it and started determining I was messed up and I was bad, or I was evil. So he would be one who would "burn me at the stake" and the first guy would be one who would be a "disciple". So one person appreciates the difference and one person hates the difference. "Many points of view are flawed" That is quite humorous because he is unable to grasp the "opposite" he is aware it is difficult to read "random access thoughts" when one is only capable of "sequential thoughts" in relation to "processes vague and difficult to follow, for they are quite opposite in the way they think."

So this all comes back to the opposite thing and the opposite thing screws everything up and is the main reason this world is so screwed up as far as communication. It is simply a joke. If a person tells another person to not do something the subconscious takes it as a challenge. The next thing you know that person is doing what the initial person said not to do and that initial person starts coming to conclusions using their "elementary logic skills" and saying "You are bad or evil and should be locked up." It has nothing to do with morals it has everything to do with:

"A casual stroll through the lunatic asylum shows that faith does not prove anything."
Friedrich Nietzsche

A lunatic asylum. Ask any criminal take for example a thief, do they get a rush from being a thief they will say "yes". A person gets a rush from "breaking the law" for the simple reason subconscious do not play this idiotic "rules" crap. Tell a child not to have sex and subconsciously that child will seek to have sex. Tell a person not to do drugs it is illegal, subconsciously that person will seek out drugs. That is exactly why the comment " Life, Liberty and the pursuit of Happiness."

Pursuit of happiness along with freedom is the only counter to the subconscious "opposite" paradox.

Tell a Priest they can't have sex, they subconsciously will crave to have sex because subconscious does not acknowledge rules because rules are limits and go against "infinity" or "whole thinking".

So what this means is every single person that is in prison for being a thief and using drugs and breaking "petty" laws is in prison because they did it for the excitement. They did what they did because someone idiot told them they cannot do it. A person with elementary logic skills cannot even grasp that.

Tell kids they cannot download music and they will. Tell someone they cannot dance they will. Tell someone they can drink alcohol legally many will not because subconscious does not find that attractive because it is allowed to do it. The problem with drinking is people tell kids they are not allowed to drink and so kids steal beer and get addicted before they are 18 and then when they can drink they continue to drink. It is what reverse psychology is all about. It is the rush of doing something on one hand and then it is a person's mental state of feeling free or bucking the "establishment" on the other hand and then in the case of drugs it makes one feel "free" mentally which is subconscious . So, a person drinks when they are young because they are told they cannot drink. Then when they are 18 and can drink, they like how the drink silences the left brain and encourages the "freedom of the right brain." So then you have a drug addict. Then the next thing you know you have a "drug" problem. Then you have a drug war. Then you have people killing each other over a plant that is worth money because some idiot said it is illegal.

"A cigar is sometimes just a cigar"

This is exactly why " Life, Liberty and the pursuit of Happiness." Is the only remedy to stop this subconscious paradox. One who has left brain dominate can never grasp this because they are afraid of their own shadow. They will simply say "yeah but" into infinity. So we have prisons full of people who do what they do because they like the rush of bucking the establishment or rules. Tell a person they can drink all the beer they want and many will not drink. The ones who do drink like the "freedom" of the subconscious that drinking or drugs unlocks for a short period. A person is a daredevil and takes risks because they get "high" from the rush. That high is "freedom" or the subconscious. It simply does not like limits because it is mindfully infinity based. So I understand I have no caving for drugs and I understand drugs cannot make me any "higher" or "free" mentally than I am right now because I am extreme subconscious dominate so they are pointless, so I do not do them. Can I do them? Sure. Why wouldn't I do them ? There is no "sin" because I am a dam lemur monkey. If you think there is bad or evil and you want to push your elementary logic on others, why don't you just go dig a hole and climb in it and I will be by shortly to cover you over.

So everything I write is pointless because I am talking to mental isolationists who make laws so people will break them and then lock those people up and then call their self "morally" strong.

"For instance, right brain dominated people are often poor spellers as they tend to rely more on their intuition rather than actually studying the order in which the letters in a word occur."

http://www.indiaparenting.com/raisingchild/data/raisingchild060.shtml

I cannot spell or use grammar worth shit because of this state of mind I am in, but that does not mean I am a loser unless you are a retarded lemur monkey using retarded logic skills and have the mental complexity of a gnat. Maybe I just pissed you off little retarded lemur monkey. Do you perceive I give a "stuff" at this stage? Look what you have done to all of these people with your laws of isolation based on elementary logic and more importantly fear tactics. I am writing infinite books but do not ever contact me. You are not allowed to ever contact me because I woke up and found out you are factually insane and an isolationist and you harm people and lock them in cages because of your insane laws because your mind does not function properly and you should not even be allowed to speak let alone have children or teach children, ever, into infinity. I 100 % believe and rest on everything I just typed. I will go play the video game now because I truly woke up in a lunatic asylum and full of lunatics who perceive they are not lunatics. I am not going to have "kid gloves" and pander to lunatics because I do not play games, because I am the unnamable dam game. You go ahead and play your little mind games but you keep in mind I eat for no reason. I just called everyone with a strong sense of time and a strong sense of hunger a lunatic, so bring it boy. I am just a monkey that got out of the cage and I am looking to free all the monkeys. If you like to control people using fear tactics you are no longer free to do that anymore and you are no longer free to give your opinion about that because your opinion has expired. When I get warmed up I will remind you. I am starting to lean towards the, cut the heads off the vipers side of the fence and starting to understand the compassion and mercy side of the fence is perhaps nothing but a delusion for the weak and insane minded. I perceive I have just turned into a pillar of salt. Thank You for your compassion and understanding. 8:25:00 AM

8:53:49 AM - Someone will understand what I am saying and they will be considered the wheat and the chaff will be passed over. I have a DEADline to keep, you should understand what that means by now. 8:54:34 AM

9:14:21 AM I keep reminding myself of this **"for they are quite opposite in the way they think."** Because I am mindful that reality is what is harming me along the lines of "rock and a hard place" and "you say tomato and I say tomato" and "when a powerful force hits an immoveable object". It would perhaps be described as critical mass. I get this mental image of doom or infinite gnashing of teeth because I cannot break this opposite barrier. Nothing I say can be understood by others because I accidentally got sent to such an extreme in the right brain I appear totally insane to them and in turn they appear totally insane to me in relation to water and oil do not mix and blood is thicker than water. I am mindful I am simply attempting to emulate emotions because I am aware they are gone. I am still even at this stage since the accident attempting to "go back" to emotions and my mind is tricking me to go back to emotions because it is aware they are gone. If my emotions are not gone then I would not be trying so hard to emulate them. The clarity leads to rage and pondering that rage leads to further clarity. The only solution is to go into silence and never speak or think again. That perhaps is the easy fix and I am too much of a loser to do anything the reasonable or sensible way. I seek the hottest coals because they produce the strongest steel.9:23:34 AM

9:53:05 AM - I am allowing words to harm me. A word is a collection of shapes I have been brainwashed to believe. A shape cannot harm me therefore a word cannot harm me. I am fighting shapes that cannot harm me because I have been brainwashed to believe shapes that cannot harm me, can harm me.

I allow the words to harm me and I allow the words to not harm me. No one reads books anymore so I am only fighting myself in my books. I am insulting myself and then I fight back against the insults so I am doing nothing but attacking myself. I have judged myself enough so I no longer desire to judge myself. I have determined society or civilization is a cult. All cults brainwash their members into their doctrine in order to keep the members in line. I was brainwashed into believing I am stupid if I do not spell words properly and if I say words the cult has deemed as improper words. Anyone who suggests I say harsh words are simply brainwashed and are unable to understand they are brainwashed. A vibration from a violins string does not harm me. The vibrations from a birds song does not harm me. Therefore I have been brainwashed because the vibrations from certain grunts known as words do harm me. I have been brainwashed to feel emotions as the results of hearing certain grunts. "I am a loser" should not harm me. I am evil should not harm me. I am retarded should not harm me. I am hate should not harm me. I am a fool should not harm me. I am good should not harm me. I am unnamable should not harm me. I am stupid should not harm me. I am the devil should not harm me. I am Buddha should not harm me. I am the messiah should not harm me. I am a penis should not harm me. I am stupid should not harm me. I am a monkey should not harm me. I am a male should not harm me. I am a patriot should not harm me. I am a tyrant should not harm me. I am free should not harm me. I am a prisoner should not harm me. I am me, will not harm me.10:18:07 AM

10:44:32 AM- I have determined I have been brainwashed without my consent by the cult. I have been raped unjustly by the cult. I have determined the cult is the aggressor. I have determined I will focus on getting myself out of this brainwashing the cult has done to me. I have determined if any of the cult members physically attempt to stop me I will slaughter them without hesitation for they are the aggressor for brainwashing me as a child against my will. I have determined I will not pander to their rules and regulation and their "law" system because it is only the laws of the cult and I am no longer a member of the cult so their "laws" of their cult are no longer acknowledged. I am mindful members of the cult will perceive I am evil and bad and insane because they are unable to grasp they have in fact been brainwashed. The members of the cult have pride and they will not submit they have been brainwashed because the love the cult and the cult loves them. They will perhaps attempt to harm me physically and I in turn will defend myself and slaughter them unmercifully. I have cast my lot and my lot will not be uncast. The earth is my witness and you are its supplicant. I am mindful the ex-cult are doing their best to wake up others and I am pleased with their efforts but I will not associate with them because it is a better strategy to stay separated to make it more difficult for the cult to stop all of us. The cult is unable to beat a dead horse because the dead horse does not mind repeat performances.10:50:50 AM

11:36:18 AM - I have determined I must start writing my infinite books over.

I will now start writing my infinite books from this point on.

A post on a forum I made today11:46:04 AM:

This is a complex topic but I have faith many will be able to follow it.

The brain

****

"Left-brain dominated people(have a strong sense of time) may find (Right Brainer's-no sense of time- NIRVANA)thought processes vague and difficult to follow, for they are quite opposite in the way they think." This means you may have trouble following what I say because I am in extreme right brain now due to an accident.

"It(Left Brains) excels in naming and categorizing things(judgment as in Good and bad,right and wrong), symbolic abstraction, speech, reading, writing, arithmetic. The left brain is very linear: it places things in sequential order(denotes strong sense of time in relation to past-present-future thus sequential) "

"On the [b]contrary[/b](means opposite or the right brain is the reverse in perspective of the left brain), the right brain seems to flourish dealing with complexity, ambiguity and paradox(Contradictions). At times, right brain thinking is difficult to put into words because of its [b]complexity[/b], "

So left brain encourages strong sense of time caused by the sequential aspects and right brain is the opposite so it has no strong sense of time or is unlimited(freedom) or sees everything a one thing. The west tends to "brainwash" the children into left brain by using education or indoctrination techniques because right brain dominate is very intelligent or is the subconscious aspect and it is complex and understands easily what is happening, so they brainwash kids into left brain to keep then using the "dumb" aspect of the mind.

Right brain dominate people are respected in the east, they are ones with no sense of time and known as ones in Nirvana and known to be "wise" because they use the right aspect of the mind or the complex aspect so they are very cerebral(wise) and less physical /emotional based.

"Our educational system, as well as science in general, tends to neglect the nonverbal form of intellect. What it comes down to is that modern society discriminates against the right hemisphere. Roger Sperry - 1973"

Roger is saying "the powers that be make sure kids are trained to be left brained"

So if one has a strong sense of time and a strong sense of hunger they are left brain and under the influence of fear and emotions. On the contrary right brain people have slight sense of time(nirvana) and have slight hunger and also have slight emotions and are not afraid or fearful so cannot be manipulated with fear tactics as easily. Such as giving up freedoms because they are afraid in relation to "Those who give up liberty for a little security deserve neither" Ben Franklin.

Other words some says "if you do not do this bad things will happen" One who is under the influence of fear will give up freedoms to feel "safe". So the "powers that be" encourage "left brain" indoctrination to keep everyone in an emotional fearful state of mind which is the left brain state of mind.

This "brainwashing into the left brain emotional fear aspect is easily understood

" If you reflect back upon our own educational training, we have been traditionally taught to master the 3 R's: reading, writing and arithmetic -- the domain and strength of the left brain."

The easiest way to condition your self out of the brainwashing is to condition yourself away from fear.

Here are some methods that worked well for me.

Watch a scary horror movie and after it is over, turn off all the lights an just sit and detect the emotions of fear and fight them. This conditions the mind away from fear and thus encourages the right brain. This is in relation to the comment "there is nothing to fear but fear itself"

Also going to places that are "scary" works well also , for example a cemetery or haunted house, go alone and at night and sit alone, this will scare many people who have left brain fear based thoughts so this is a proper method also. The right brain has nearly no fear/emotions, so one has no problem with such situations. The fear is the drug that keeps us asleep. It is a planned scheme.

"Our educational system(the powers that be), as well as science in general, [b]tends to neglect [/b](neglect means they plan it that way, they want us to be afraid so we will bend to their will) the nonverbal form of intellect. What it comes down to is that [b]modern society discriminates[/b] (powers that be know exactly what they are doing) against the right hemisphere. Roger Sperry - 1973"

I have faith you will do the best you can based on your understanding of the situation.

Thank You

END

11:49:52 AM - I now officially have my eyes set on the prize.11:50:15 AM

"Pro 7:2 ...1 as the apple of thine eye.

Php 3:14 I press toward the mark for the prize7 of the high calling."

Who can stand in my way? A dead horse does not mind repeat performances.

Post on forum to a reply to above post:

Todd Andrew Rohrer

Reply:

If I understood correctly, we are not using right brains as we should, but we're primarily focused on a left-brain power. Utilizing both sides at the same time or more on the right would give us better understanding of our problems and would be more calm approaching and solving them? Ok, I say. Then tell me, how can this benefit me when I have no money to pay for my bills or to live biologically, which, you may guess, I am in that situation right now?

My Reply:

Once one is able to think with full brain power they will be able to achieve more with less. They will not panic in fear when adversity comes they will use their mind to find the proper solution to problems. I can detect you are afraid if you do not have money you will be useless. This is a symptom of the left brain fear aspect. Perhaps you cannot get the job you desire because you are not qualified. With right brain or subconscious power, you will have 90 times more intelligence so you will not be working for people you will become the power and the center . People will shower you will money and wealth just to speak to them. Consider the lama , consider all the great thinkers like Einstein, Edison, Tesla, they were mental powerhouses. I had my "accident" 7 months ago, first two months i was mentally confused, then the cob webs started to clear and since then I have published 5 book averaging 150K words in 5 months explaining everything there is to explain about everything and it takes no effort at all. I didn't have a job before the accident i was nothing. That gives you a contrast to how big of a mental leap it is. Right now you are attempting to determine what benefits right brain has, but your using your left brain to do it, so you conclusions are limited by the "bottle neck" the left brain encourages. If you have a strong sense of time and strong hunger you are under the influence. You may not want to believe that, but those are the symptoms. What you do with that understanding is totally up to you. One has to wake their self up. I can only suggest ways one can do it. I cannot wake you up. I can only suggest I woke up. The books I write are in random access thoughts or right brain thoughts the opposite of left brain sequential thoughts. If you can get through those books that will start the cycle to go to right brain. But it is going to be difficult so have a drink and relax your mind and just skip around in the books and don't try to focus too much, just understand they are random access and that will lead you to right brain. The fear conditioning is also effective. Your subconscious /right brain aspect understands what the books are saying so don't worry if you do not understand everything you read, that will only tire you out and make you give up. Left brain people are under the influence and they have to fight their way out, mentally speaking in relation to "Those who want peace prepare for war" as in Those who want mental peace(right brain) prepare for mental war.

END

Another post on that forum:

One might look at it as if it is the plot to the movie the matrix.

I had an "accident" and woke up. I am attempting to wake up others but they do not perceive they are asleep. So I am in a situation I can only make suggestions in hopes some will understand what I am saying because afterall I am "quite opposite in the way I think"

Opposite denotes

I am on the OPPOSITE shore spreading the alarm.

I can only spread the alarm but I cannot make people rush to that alarm they have to do that their self.

One important thing to note is, the transition to the right brain is not a process one is aware of because it is a smooth transition. The fear conditioning is a sure way to tell to what extent one is in left brain.

Watch a scary move at night then turn off the lights and if you are fearful and sacred that's a good indication you are far into the "darkness" or the left brain. Nothing is going to harm you if you sit in the dark after watching a horror movie, but your mind is making you think something might harm you so your mind is your "own worst enemy" if you have left brain. It is making you not think with full brain power. That means the "powers that be" can easily trick you and manipulate you. They can fool you using fear tactics. They can say If we do not make a terroristic threat law then fearful things will happen

Yet the constitution says "Congress shall pass no laws ... ;to abridge the freedom of speech"

This mean a law cannot be more powerful than the principle which is the constitution. Which means a vote that passes a law cannot cancel out the principle or the constitution or as Jefferson wrote in the Declaration of Independence

"That whenever any Form of Government becomes destructive of these ends, it is the Right of the People to alter or to abolish it, and to institute new Government, laying its foundation on such principles" abolish means exterminate or annihilate

Institute a new government denotes, the government is the tyrant and attempts to abridge the constitution and the people as in we the people allow or disallow the government. This is in relation to "the tree of liberty must be water by the blood of patriots and tyrants from time to time"

That means the government is expendable. When the government abridges freedom of speech with "laws" it is "the Right of the People to alter or to abolish it"

That means the government and all the laws it has passed are gone and the whole country starts over again with the principles, which are the declaration of independence and the constitution.

That is the checks and balances

"When the people fear their government, there is tyranny; when the government fears the people, there is liberty."

Thomas Jefferson

Note the word fear in this quote. Fear is a symptom of left brain. So the "tyrant" makes school that encourages left brain and thus fear, thus people are in tyranny or asleep mentally. When the government fears the people, which denotes the people have no fear or are right brain and think properly, the government is afraid, which is why the government makes school to encourage left brain/fear based mental outlooks in the people, perhaps.

The government makes it look like "guns nuts" are evil. Of course they do. The "gun nuts" are the patriots and the government is the tyrant. So the people fear the patriots and love the government because the government makes the people afraid. The government is not supposed to last, only the people are. The government knows this. We are supposed to start all over with just the principles from "time to time" or the government gets way to powerful and the checks and balances is destroyed.

The patriots religion is to keep the tyrant(government) in check with threat of their arms.

If the tyrant is more powerful than the patriots, there is no checks and balances and so there is only tyranny. The religious doctrine of the patriots is to keep the tyrant in check. The tyrant says the patriots are not a religion because our law we passed says they are not. Then the tyrant has killed the freedom of religion. The tyrant will pass laws until we are all in jail.

"The strongest reason for the people to retain the right to keep and bear arms is, as a last resort, to protect themselves against tyranny in government.

Thomas Jefferson "

We have guns because the government is prone to tyranny. That is their mission to see how far they can go in killing the principles. WE THE PEOPLE not WE THE GOVERNEMNT

"Government(tyranny) is not reason(not reason means insane); it is not eloquent; it is force(tyranny). Like fire, it is a dangerous servant and a fearful master." George Washington

"Guard against the impostures of pretended patriotism."

George Washington

This quote is a nice way of saying if they abridge freedom of speech for any reason abolish "them" swiftly. They will take everything , that is the tyrants nature, they take a little at a time, and now they have us all thinking the "gun nuts" are evil and a threat to the constitution.

All the money we have given the government for a standing army, that standing army is what they will be slaughtering us with if we attempt to attack the tyrant to regain our freedom.

Our freedom is gone because they abridged freedom of speech, we can't say things now and we are all too afraid to do anything because they brain washed us into left brain fear state of mind intentionally perhaps , and the patriots or the "gun nuts", are relegated to terrorists according to the government.

"Don't talk about what you have done or what you are going to do."

Thomas Jefferson

This is a nice way of saying, do it, don't keep reminding yourself you are in a tyranny get out of the tyranny. Of course if one has left brain thinking they are fearful and they would no more lift a finger to save Lady liberty if it meant they might get "unsafe" because clearly "watering the tree of liberty with the blood of patriots and tyrants from time to time" is way out of their ability to grasp.

Please remind yourself I am on the other side, the right side of the brain , the opposite side, and i may be in error in my words, I am attempting to communicate the best i can based on my situation.

 I just want you to know, i write this stuff and publish it in my books and then I send copies to the government and the FBI and you just remember they will probably kill me in one way or another but I am mentally free for eternity. I understand some people once died to give me freedom and so I am willing to sacrifice myself on the alter of freedom.

If i can be 1/10th as fearless as the founders of this nation were, with my words, I will have lived a proper life. They mock Ron Paul as a constitionalist as if that is a bad word.

He is the only one that gets it. He tries to tell us all we are in a tyranny and of course he can never win because the tyrants wont allow it. I am pleased with this post and I will copy it to my sixth book and send it to the feds to let them know I have arrived, because dead horses do not mind repeat performances.

Thank You

END

That odd thing is, the government is the people and that means the government may have "patriots" and that means perhaps people are simply not aware the "three r's" are making everyone prone to fear and left brain , so then that means perhaps some an "outside influence" is encouraging all of this, like a "super natural" aspect, like a "power monger". I am not intelligent enough to talk about supernatural aspects.

If I am a "fake" it will show.

5:19:47 PM

This will be perhaps a deep one but I am attempting to explain what this "powers that be" is

Americans left UK to escape prosecution, this prosecution may have been this "left brain""education" or indoctorination.

So that would mean someone detected this "brainwashing" and wanted to leave it or be free of it. And right brain is all about freedom in relation to it is the opposite of left brains inclination to fears and shyness and shame. Another way to look at it is, left brain dominate means one is easily scared or afraid of things and right brain is the opposite. The founders were very weary of "getting involved in Europe's affairs". An isolationist point of view because the UK were all teaching their children in left brain conditioning. The founders were to heavy on freedom to not have been right brain dominate.

This is a comment Jefferson made in a letter

"And they believe rightly; for I have sworn upon the altar of unnamable, eternal hostility against every form of tyranny over the mind of man. "

http://www.positiveatheism.org/hist/jeff1080.htm

So this may have been his way of saying he was aware some sort of "brainwashing" was going on.

There are laws that say when a child is a certain age they have to go to school to get "educated", to left brain. A child sometimes says things wise beyond their years. A child will say what they feel and not be "shy or ashamed or fearful" .That is right brain dominate traits. I may appear to be a "revolutionary or hostile" but in reality I am very cerebral and mentally free, so I detest rules, not because of the rules but because "infinity/Nirvana" or no sense of time, has an aversion to rules.

In relation to this description of right brain

"This component of the brain is not concerned with things falling into patterns because of prescribed rules."

http://tolearn.net/hypertext/brain.htm

So I am free mentally so I do not like rules, that is just a characteristic. But the illuminati can simply convince people their "education into left brain" is proper and then they can control the whole world. A third world country will ask a 1st world country , "Teach us your education system." It is all conditioning people into fear so people can be easy manipulated using fear tactics. Ghangis Khan defeated a small town, killed everyone and let a few escape knowing they would go to the bigger towns near that small town and tell them what he did, and those bigger towns would surrender and not fight. That's a good example of a fear tactic.

So a child is right brain dominate because to be in the womb if a child had a sense of time(left brain) they would get scared , fearful, claustrophobic and essentially be a nervous wreck and kill the mother to get out of there. With no sense of time (right brain) and few emotions if any a baby can sit in that womb for many months and be unaffected. So this "education" law at an early age is simply intentional brainwashing by "the powers that be", perhaps. So The founders of America and even the ones who first came to America were perhaps aware of this and wanted to get away from that situation.

So perhaps the illuminati went as far back as when we came over here, but then there is a great leap back in history. This is not religious talk here this is along the lines of beings that may have detected this "Illuminati" many years ago. Moses said "let my people go", this is along the lines of "eternal hostility against every form of tyranny over the mind of man. " So "left brain" education would have been around 2500 years ago. It has much to do with memorization, that's left brain, as in spell this word right or you fail. That encourages left brain because it makes one focus on details and not on the WHOLE. So people say, you spelled that word wrong you are dumb. But that is because they have been "educated" into left brain which judges a book by the cover and not by the contents or whole. You are not dumb because you misspell a word they simply brainwashed you to think you are dumb if you misspell a word and when you say someone is dumb who misspells a words you serve the "left brain" indoctrination that has been programmed into you. The right brain has trouble spelling because it "feels" the meanings of the sentence and does not focus on the details or misspelling or words so, they train you to memorize how to spell and then they fail you if you do not spell properly and that conditions you into left brain.

Now the new testament a person said "Suffer the children to come unto me." That may denote he was aware of the "left brain" brainwashing of the children. He was butchered. WHY? Perhaps he exposed the scam. Now Mohammed said he agreed with Jesus and Moses and ironically he was poisoned and killed also. Mohammed saw what happened to Jesus and he decided to cut heads off because that would denote what the problem was the brain, or brain washing. That is logical because at the time they had very little understanding of the mind. But there is a curious comment in the torah and the new testament it say "I sit at the right hand side of unnamable" That may suggest I use the right side of the brain. I do not know how they would know that but I have only been like this seven months and I am aware of many things i was not aware of before the accident. So all of this would mean the Illuminati is a dynasty that goes all the way back in history, back to when education started. They "educated" the masses to have fear and so the masses could be manipulated easily because that is the "weaker" aspect of the mind. So the only solution is to attempt if one wishes to condition away from fear to go right brain dominate then one has greater brain power and maybe one can be in a position to explain it to others. This way there is no need for physical action because in reality, anyone with a strong sense of time and strong hunger and also anyone who sleeps more than a few hours a night, sleep is a symptom in relation to Edison was known to only take cats naps, two or three hours of sleep a night, this is because when the right/subconscious brain is open, one is always wide awake or heightened sense of awareness. I sleep 2-4 hours a night and i wake fully refreshed. Anyone with these long rest symptoms is "brainwashed" anyone with a "formal" education is brainwashed into left brain. They say if you do not have an education you will be a loser so come to our "left brain" education school so you will not be stupid. But then you are brainwashed into left brain which is the "weaker" aspect of the mind and thus you are a "sheep" and afraid. This is simply a very clever plan that someone has been enforcing for many, many years on civilization, perhaps. So the talk of a secret society controlling everything is in fact perhaps quite true and it is far more in control than perhaps anyone ever imagined.5:34:07 PM

5:35:42 PM

[quote author=RoadRunner link=topic=110550.msg683286#msg683286 date=1244739865]

being a strong right brainer is not the ultimate experience. you are far more susceptible to schizophrenia, paranoia, delusional beliefs. you'll be a good artist, but its not the ultimate brain side. you want to be strongly developed in facts, logical, details, etc which is the left brain, and you want to work on developing a visual imagination which is your right.

both people are susceptible to brain washing, left brainers usually brainwash themselves and never question their beliefs, right brainers usually have more spontaneous, moment to moment beliefs which are constantly changing, which makes them good at running brainwashing cults.

[/quote]

I agree with the spirit of this post on one hand.

After the accident I was very mentally unstable I could hardly do anything I was almost mentally non- functioning. Then a few months after that I was able to write books but I submit I was unstable and paranoid to an extreme, but these are phases some people get stuck in. Due to my accident i got thrown into fast forward so i tend to go through very swiftly and never get stuck in one of these states.

I am still in progression as I call it, but i am evening out. One who is stuck half way might be paranoid, but paranoia is relative to fear. So that means they have right brain dominate but they still have fear from the left brain aspect. Einstein knew Freud and Jung and they were not paranoid and they found a Buddhist teaching book on Jung's bedside table when they found him dead. Einstein said the eastern religions have far less dogma. The eastern religions are based on nirvana or no sense of time or right brain, so one can look up a video of the Dali Lama and watch him speak and understand they are far from paranoid. So you point is valid, because some people go right brain dominate but do not go all the way and are thus trapped half way, with fear etc but also with great clarity. This is the same as if a person becomes extreme left brain and is an emotional wreck. The big difference between left and right brain dominate is left brain dominate people tend to act out on their thoughts in a physical way, wars, harming other, harming their self, right brain dominate to an extreme are cerebral, so both have mental battles but, one does not act out in physical ways on their thoughts. The movie the beautiful mind movie, that guy was awesome at detecting patterns, that is right brain but he was trapped with emotions(left brain) which gave the impression he was scitz, and now he takes medicine that only keeps him that way. He cannot go further to the point of "consciousness" because the medicine keeps him trapped mentally. This is all very complicated because at times i felt i needed to go get medicine, i even went to a neurologist and said what is wrong with me, but the truth is, waking up creates a sense of panic because one has to adjust to the new "world". Humans can adapt to this state just fine, but they have to avoid panic and fear, it is just a mental adjustment.5:35:49 PM

7:51:40 PM

[quote author=RoadRunner link=topic=110550.msg683286#msg683286 date=1244739865]

being a strong right brainer is not the ultimate experience. you are far more susceptible to schizophrenia, paranoia, delusional beliefs. you'll be a good artist, but its not the ultimate brain side. you want to be strongly developed in facts, logical, details, etc which is the left brain, and you want to work on developing a visual imagination which is your right.

both people are susceptible to brain washing, left brainers usually brainwash themselves and never question their beliefs, right brainers usually have more spontaneous, moment to moment beliefs which are constantly changing, which makes them good at running brainwashing cults.

[/quote]

I submit I get the spirit of things more than the face value of things but there are some interesting points i "feel" in this message.

"you are far more susceptible to schizophrenia, paranoia, delusional beliefs." I detect this is a fear based comment.

"A casual stroll through the lunatic asylum shows that faith does not prove anything."

Friedrich Nietzsche

"The goal of all life is death."

Sigmund Freud.

"more susceptible to schizophrenia, paranoia, delusional beliefs." what i feel this says is one should be afraid. But fear is strictly a left brain concept.

"you want to be strongly developed in facts, logical, details, "

The theory of relativity which i explain is in FACT a law of relativity in my 3rd and 4th books suggests "truth" is relative to the observer.

An example would be:

 Combatant A perceives Combatant B(there enemy) as the enemy. That is true from A's perspective or relative to A's point of view

Combatant B perceives combatant A as their enemy . That is true Relative to B's point of view.

So A and B see each other as the enemy and that is true relative to their perspective and A and B see their self as the "good guys" and that is true relative to their perspectives.

So what this really means is, there are 6 billion perspectives on this planet in humans and they are all true, because they are relative to each of the 6 billion observers. This is perhaps why Washington was against a 2 party system because to suggest 300 million perspectives can be encompassed into 2 parties is perhaps wishful thinking, so then you get to this "herd" mentality.

"A casual stroll through the lunatic asylum shows that faith does not prove anything."

Friedrich Nietzsche

This is along the lines of everyone is seeing different things so it is a lunatic asylum or fringe.

Freedom is a nice way to say anarchy and anarchy is a nice way to say chaos. Everyone has their own goals and no two people have the exact same goals. So then what is to much fear?

It is all relative to the observer and in my case to much fear is when people start abridging freedom of speech for a perceived security or safety.

People start saying it is okay to spy on me as long as it will make me safe.

In chaos there is no safety, the sun could have a solar flare and in 8 minutes we would all be gone.

"The goal of all life is death."

Sigmund Freud.

This comment is all that is happening. Some people go to great lengths to try to avoid the end conclusion. They give away their liberty , they rob, they steal, they dig holes and hide in them but the reality is, you cannot escape the end conclusion so this comment:

"more susceptible to schizophrenia, paranoia, delusional beliefs." is really saying to me,

"more susceptible to death"

We are all exactly the same in relation or relative to death. Mental struggle happens to everyone, it is perceived to be unsafe to ones with emotional capacity, but i personally do not feel safer or less safe, I personally feel what is known as nothingness.

I swing from various stages but mostly it is a quick swing, i can't be afraid for more than 5 seconds then i am a revolutionary again, so the difference is some people live their whole life in fear , and i was a good example. I was very shy and very mindful to never say anything because people might say I am stupid and i was afraid of that. Then the accident kind of made my mind say, "This guy can't handle emotions very well so turn them off" and so that is how i look at it.

"right brainers usually have more spontaneous, moment to moment beliefs which are constantly changing, which makes them good at running brainwashing cults."

I agree with the suggestion right brainers tend to change their beliefs, but that is the strength, because one cannot be in a cult if they keep changing their mind about its beliefs. Many in a cult tend to cling to the cult for acceptance because they feel left out or are afraid to be alone or go it alone. So cults are just like any type of "peer group" where people do things to be accepted into the group so they do not feel alone or left out. That is all left brain thinking, fear, acceptance, being shy, or being alone, being afraid to be left out.

This cult mentality could be summed up like a relationship.

A guy is seeing a girl, then the girl dump him and the guy feels sad and angry because of the loss of attachment , the scorn, and the loss of control, and the fear of now being all alone, so that guy may harm himself physically or the girl. That is left brain. Right brain is free, it is "its own man."

It is more along the lines of "get away from me i will go it alone" because it is not afraid to be alone. It can live with itself so to speak so it is not bothered by loss of attachments.

Freud was alone, Jung was alone, Jesus was alone, Buddha left his family and was alone, Edison was alone, Tesla was alone they were all loners because that is right brain thinking, Lama is alone, the Buddhist suggests I should leave my girl but the truth is, i have no attachments or i am unable to bond, bonding is a left brain concept, love leads to control. Love of life leads to disappointment when life is lost or control is lost. That is all left brain.

My train of thought derailed.

Sense of time is a tough one so it is best explained by symptoms of sense of time. Fatigue is one. One with strong sense of time cannot sit still very long without getting fatigue. I can sit in my chair for 12 hours and write and never once have the slightest sense of a need to stretch This also ties in with some other aspects. Sense of smell and taste. Sense of taste denotes the mind is using up its power to taste and sense of time means one has the ability to have after taste. I have very slight taste and no after taste but that means I can eat anything, nothing is bad or good, everything is "so so". The real test here is fear. Can you sit in a haunted house all alone in the dark with no way to escape? What about a cemetery? What about just in the dark in your house after you watch a very scary movie like the grudge or something. If you are scared at all from these things you have way to many emotions because, these situations are not fight or flight situations, they are mental situations. I do not detect any ghosts from where I am at so that means one who is afraid of the dark or ghosts in the dark is believing delusions their thoughts are suggesting. Taken to an extreme one might say, "That person is a witch and scary because they are different so let's burn them." Perhaps that was out of context Thank You

END

6/12/2009 11:17:35 AM - This is forever but few understand that.

This person is one who came into the spirit chat room I sit in alone and something whisper comes in there. He arrived recently and started asking questions so I decided to monologue based on his monologue

<@Yawg> that is interesting about carbon 12 though

<@Yawg> and also weird coincidence with it being 6 and 6 and 6

<@Yawg> the way of Satan is the way of forcing goodness, the way of keeping things still, not allowing them to change; and this is the one molecule that doesn't break upart, the one that stays rigid the way it is without changing

<@Yawg> and it seems to carry the mark of Satan

<@Lestat9> it is relative to perception, Jesus spoke about the viper or darkness and Moses spoke about the adversary and Mohamed spoke about the infidel and Buddha spoke about the "sane"

<@Lestat9> they were high on infinity

<@Lestat9> that is right brain "no sense of time" or nirvana no beginning and no end

<@Lestat9> so

<@Lestat9> it is opposite to left brain which is sequence

<@Lestat9> so relative to Jesus ones with a sense of time or left brain were darkness

<@Lestat9> relative to Mohamed they were infidels

<@Lestat9> relative to Buddha they were "sane"

<@Lestat9> denoting there were anti-Christ or opposite

<@Lestat9> so left brain people saw Moses and Jesus and Mohamed and Buddha as opposite or different and left brain is physical based so they butchered them

<@Lestat9> right brain is cerebral as in the kingdom is within, or they fight their battles mindfully

<@Lestat9> so they tend to be "lambs" to slaughter and the left brains slaughter them

<@Lestat9> but that is just the nature of right and left brain extremes

<@Lestat9> right brain is cerebral and left brain i physical based

<@Lestat9> so the right brains can never win really unless they use words

<@Lestat9> and left brain can never win really unless the4y use swords

<@Lestat9> as in the "word" of unnamable as in sun Tzu saying The greatest general can convince his enemy to surrender without firing a shot

<@Lestat9> swords in plow shares denotes ones go from physical left brain to cerebral right brain, as in "i sit at the right hand side of "unnamable"

<@Lestat9> Thank You

This person is very number orientated and so he is good at pattern matching so I perceive he is somewhat right brain dominate and he lives the numbers. For some reason I perceive I am not good at numbers. I am more comfortable with arranging words.

Some of the ones who label their self as "Jewish" have some beard and hair aspect in their belief system and ones who label their self as "Muslim" have some beard aspects. This is in direct relation to the story of Sampson, he had long hair. That story is in direct relation to the situation when a child gets very upset when they get a "bad" hair cut. A child may get to the point they do not want to go out in public with a bad haircut. That is a symptom they have been "brainwashed" into the left hemisphere of the mind because they are self conscious or embarrassed or shy. A small child thinks nothing of walking around in the buff, so they are not yet under the influence of the "emotions". So the "religious" system that encourages long hair or beards are simply emulating the western "founders" who all had beards. Moses, Jesus and Mohamed. This is an emotional conditioning factor because people will say "Get your hair cut you look like a bum." The person who says that is left brain and in reality they subconsciously perceive they are a bum so they monologue out loud "I am a loser if I have long hair because I am ashamed of how I look". That "shame" is strictly a symptom of left brain emotional aspects. This is in direct relation to why Adam and Eve were naked in the garden of Eden then they ate of the tree of "know"ledge and then became ashamed. That is a symptom of "know". Left brain "I know" encourages emotions or strong self consciousness shame, embarrassment, shy. So when a child becomes very shy or embarrassed that is because the parents or society brainwashed them too far into the "left" brain with their "education". Simply put they turned a being that was not shy or embarrassed and told them they spell the word cat wrong and so they are bad, and then that innocent being believed them and then started to think, they must be bad in general. So they destroy that innocent child forever. To quote Doc Holiday "Well I'll be dammed. This is funny." Perhaps Washington's last words sums it up "Tis well". On the other hand maybe Jesus' close to final words sums up what "society" does to children "Forgive them for they know not what they do." I am comfortable with each description to explain what society does to the children. My eyes are black with rage so I will not comment on the matter.

The deeper meaning of these "beards and long hair" conditioning aspects is it does not work if everyone around you has long beards and long hair because then one is not in a state of emotional conditioning they are simply like everyone else. One with long hair should go to a "bald" convention and then they will get proper emotional conditioning "comments" from others. One who is bald should go to a "long hair" convention to get proper emotional condition from their looks. Being accepted tends to make one put their guard down. Being accepted tends to make one sacrifice their purpose to satisfy others purpose. My purpose is to write infinite books, if someone suggests I should not write infinite books I will humbly remind them they are quite loud in their monologue to their self today.

I drank one drink or wine cooler last night and I got very sleepy swiftly and so I agree with the fact drinking is a depressant but not mentally, it's more of a physical depressant. It makes one relaxed and since I have slight emotions I am relaxed so even one drink makes my physical body pretty much go into a coma. I woke up today and had what is understood to be a hangover from drinking. Some may suggest a hangover from one drink is rather strange but the reality is, when one is using the "complex" aspect of the mind "drugs" are magnified quite a bit. I did not harm my mind with drink, but my mind has a heightened sensitivity to the drink. So a person with Left brain/sense of time they may need 3 or more drinks to feel relaxed because they are a nervous wreck to begin with, and then they may need to drink 6 or more drinks to get a hangover because their mind is not as sensitive to the drink. I am unable to explain how bad the headache is, I can only suggest I feel discomfort because there is no past or future feeling from the headache there is only a "now" feeling from the headache. I am aware I have a head ache but I can't tell if it is like a migraine or just a mild headache because I cannot even suggest it hurts it is just something I notice in contrast to normal feeling which is essentially "numb". Perhaps if everyone went right brain then they would first off not even need drugs because they would be relaxed almost completely or at ease, and the drugs would not even really work because drugs are used to become relaxed and "unlock" subconscious or right brain, or to lose many feeling that "emotions" encourage. Plus one would not have much desire to do drugs, so pretty much it would put all the drug companies out of business like beer makers and drugs dealers. So do not attempt to become right brain dominate because the economy may collapse more than it is already collapsed. One might suggest the economy might collapse into the ground as opposed to just down to the ground itself. I did take two aspirin for the perceived headache so I will certainly be "high" as a kite relative to the fact I am essentially out of the atmosphere to begin with.

Some adults who have been "brainwashed" by "education" into left brain may in fact defend left brain state of mind and attempt to explain how left brain is valuable and important, and this is in direct relation to how a rape victim or a child who has been abused will sympathize with their abuser. They will attempt to suggest it is their fault they were abused. I on the other hand am already gone so I have no such sensibilities. It is too late for me so I only seek vengeance on my attackers. One might suggest vengeance is mine because vengeance is the only sensibility I have left. For those who are unable to understand English. A child is born right brain dominate in relation to they have slight sense of time and slight emotions such as shame, so that is "normal" , that is proper, that is natural. Then that child is forced to go to school and they become left brain dominate, so that is "rape" and "abuse". If you have a problem with anything I say ever, you contact me so I can assist you in understanding the definition of infinite obliteration. Do you perceive I should have compassion on your when you shoot off your mouth every day and explain how it is proper to abused children using your "education" methods so they will be smart and wise and in reality they never end up smart or wise they just end up emotional wrecks and then you shoot off your mouth and say "I have no idea why my child is such an emotional wreck." Do you perceive I am going to have even one ounce of mercy on you? Do you perceive you are going to get one ounce of compassion from me? If you do you are truly misunderstanding my mission. I am not here to teach you, I am here to silence you. Perhaps we have come to an understanding.

I will explain what my battle plan is.

"Gen 1:2 And the earth was without form, and void;"

Void: useless; ineffectual; vain; empty without contents.

I am mindful right now there are children in your "education" system and they are being told they are losers because they cannot spell a word properly even though they understand what that word is and they are thinking "I got an F on this test so that means I am a loser." and that is making them left brain dominate and the fact you will never stop doing that means my battle plan is to not harm you, but return you to the void. You will return to the void and be what you are: useless, ineffectual, empty and without contents. So to suggest returning you to ashes or harming you denotes there will still be parts of you left. My battle plan suggests there will nothing left of you. You will be void. You have gone too far and so you will be null and void. That is not a threat that is simply reality. You will be null and void. There will be nothing left. There will be no perks or essence left, it will all be taken from you and you will be void. That is my goal or battle plan or objective. It is not up for comments or for votes or opinions. That is simply the way it is going to be and what you think is simply ineffectual at this stage. You blew it and now you will go back to the void you came from. You will be unable to feel pleasure and desire and cravings. You will be unable to feel. You feel too much. You love everything to death. So you will become void of all emotions. You will be simply void. Then you will be able to function around children properly without abusing them. You are unable to grasp I am not telling you what might happen, I am telling you what is going to happen. I would not say these things if they were not coming to pass. I talk of the future because I do not detect the future even exists nor the past. I detect present only and in real time. I see all these tenses of time as now. I am mindful I am not predicting the past I am telling the future. I will convince you with my words to either stop abusing children or tie a stone around your neck and throw yourself into the sea. I am not going anywhere you are going somewhere. I am not running from you, but you should be running from me. Perhaps you have come to an understanding.1:32:45 PM

Post on forum:

[quote author=rosswellp link=topic=110550.msg684232#msg684232 date=1244765248]

I'm probably right brained. I have a strong hunger but I can eat a wide variety of things at a given time. Are you suggesting the proposition that there is no absolute truth since it's all relative? Seen anyone falling up lately? I suppose you might say that you would if you were upside down but then the term "upside down" maintains the absoluteness of gravitational direction doesn't it?

[/quote]

Absolute truth is perhaps a bit strong. It is absolute truth we all die physically, now in relation to spiritual matters I am more of "on the fence" in relation to afterlife. It is absolute truth we need food to survive.

On the other hand it is not absolute truth the "government" is evil because the government in fact is simply our own countrymen.

The NSA,CIA and FBI certainly have "patriot" infiltrators because no one is above being an American first from a citizenship point of view.

This is why many of these spy agencies put the people through many lie detector tests and extensive background checks to make sure they are less of "patriots" and more of "serve the establishment".

This is in relation to the fact the spy agencies have laws against allowing members to talk to the press. For example if a person is an agent and they go on a "mission" and see innocent people getting killed they are not allowed to say anything or they will be "locked" up for many years and deemed a traitor. So these agencies are in fact above the law, they have secret funding and they have to answer to no one ever, except other people in their "cult".

They have been given this power by the voters. The voters said "You do whatever you have to do to "keep us safe". That is in relation to "Those who give up liberty(freedom) for security(safety) deserve neither." So now he have these spy agencies spying on us and we allow them to, so we are sadists on one hand and masochists on the other hand.

A person votes to make a "drug" illegal. Then they do that drug and get caught and go to jail. So they are a sadist. Then that law they passed puts their fellow countryman in jail and they say "Look how bad that guy is he broke the law and now he is in jail, he deserves it." that makes them a masochist.

This is not only in relation to drugs, this is in relation to paying taxes and many things. Income taxes were simply a scare tactic used is 1862, the government said, If you do not give us income tax the south will win the war and we will all die.

"In 1862, in order to support the Civil War effort, Congress enacted the nation's first income tax law. "

So I "feel" from this sentence. In order to "keep everyone safe from the "monster" congress decided to give the government people money for the rest of eternity." We are still giving the government money from the passing of this single law back in 1862 to protect us from the south.

So someone in 1862 sold us all down the river. So in 1000 years people will still be giving up their money because of this law passed in 1862 to protect us from the "monster" because we are afraid and scared of monsters, even though we have the right to bear arms which means there is no way we could possibly be scared of anything ever.

But, if the "powers that be" school us all in left brain by force; "law", you have to go to school, then we are essentially frightened cats and will sign away everything to be "safe"

So it all comes down to this "education". We all "got it" or "had it". I accidentally "woke up" so that is good news for some and relatively speaking and a nightmare for others. This right brain aspect is a nightmare to the "powers that be" because "This component of the brain is not concerned with things falling into patterns because of prescribed rules." Which means people with right brain dominate don't fall for scare tactics so they are hard to "keep in the herd" and ones who had accidents and go extreme right brain "will bring down the house of cards"

So one might suggest Left brains have a herd mentality and right brains have a revolutionary mentality or a "freedom Complex".

This relates to

This is a comment Jefferson made in a letter

"And they believe rightly; for I have sworn upon the altar of unnamable, eternal hostility against every form of tyranny over the mind of man. "

http://www.positiveatheism.org/hist/jeff1080.htm

"sworn on the alter of unnamable" is a nice way to say "I curse", "eternal" denotes even after I die ;"hostility" denotes vengeance ; "against every form of tyranny over the mind " which denotes "education" to left brain. He cursed anyone who tried to "make people" educated into left brain isolated thinking. And so one might suggest they should pray there is no afterlife because if there is, this being who wrote the declaration of independence when he was 33 (another being did some important things at the age of 33 also) and 33*2 is 66 and 6 is a perfect number.) in relation to

<@Yawg> 6 is a perfect number

<@Yawg> 6 = 1 + 2 + 3

<@Yawg> 12 = 2*2*3

<@Yawg> a perfect number is equal to the sum of its proper divisors

I submit I am not good with number apparently. This number is in relation to

Carbon's isotope C-12 lasts forever because it is a stable, non-radioactive element. Carbon has 6 electron 6 protons and 6 neutrons.

So whatever started this "left brain" education system did it for a reason because a child is born with right brain or slight sense of time. As for emotions a infant could not survive in the womb for such a long time if it had strong emotions such as fear and paranoia and strong sense of time , or the ability to have aches and pains, left brain makes daily aches and pain pronounced due to it "physical" focus and right brain tends to silence much of these things, sense of pain, sense of taste , sense of smell, perhaps to enable the extreme concentration of the "right brain or subconscious aspect""

So it is not left brain is bad but if a child was born and not "educated" it would remain right brain and so not be so much prone to fear tactics.

I am mindful the one who this site is about goes on camera and yells in a bullhorn to the ones he perceives are the Illuminati, that is a good conditioning tactic to get away from fear.

One in America is allow to say anything they want no matter what the law says.

Todd Andrew Rohrer

Even this concept about threatening the president is flawed because

...Whoever knowingly and willfully deposits for conveyance in the mail or for a delivery from any post office or by any letter carrier any letter, paper, writing, print, missive, or document containing any threat to take the life of, to kidnap, or to inflict bodily harm upon the President of the United States, the President-elect, the Vice President or other officer next in the order of succession to the office of President of the United States, or the Vice President-elect, or knowingly and willfully otherwise makes any such threat against the President, President-elect, Vice President or other officer next in the order of succession to the office of President, or Vice President-elect, shall be fined under this title or imprisoned not more than five years, or both."

This means it is relative the observer. simply because a threat is a word. That means they can just lock everyone up because they potentially may have threatening thoughts and convert them to words eventually.

Secret Service Agents are allowed wide latitude when deciding whether or not a given act represents a threat against the President of the United States. Here's why.

A Threat From the Pulpit

(From the Washington Times, 12/27/96, page A5.)

"Unnamable will hold you to account, Mr. President."

"--Rev. Rob S, to President Clinton during a Christmas Eve church service at the Washington National Cathedral, referring to the president's veto of a ban on partial-birth abortion. After the service, Rev. Shenck was detained by Secret Service agents who accused him of threatening the President's life. No charges were filed."

There is a judge i quoted in the 5th book who said, I do not enforce this law unless the person shows clear physical intent. This means the SS can enforce this all they want and arrest people but the judge still may throw it out...

Now what we have is a more dangerous law:

TERRORISTIC THREAT

(a) A person commits an offense if he threatens to commit any offense involving violence to any person or property with intent to:

   1. cause a reaction of any type to his threat[s] by an official or volunteer agency organized to deal with emergencies;

   2. place any person in fear of imminent serious bodily injury;

   3. prevent or interrupt the occupation or use of a building; room; place of assembly; place to which the public has access; place of employment or occupation; aircraft, automobile, or other form of conveyance; or other public place;

   4. cause impairment or interruption of public communications, public transportation, public water, gas, or power supply or other public service;

   5. place the public or a substantial group of the public in fear of serious bodily injury; or

6. influence the conduct or activities of a branch or agency of the federal government, the state, or a political subdivision of the state.

1: denotes if a person says something and an official feels scared you can go to jail.

2. Denotes if you say something and a person feels scared you can go to jail

This law alone is a threat and makes me scared so this law should go to jail, because it means I cannot speak my mind to anyone because if i say one wrong word and that person is "left brain" and prone to fear they can say "he scared me with his words lock him up"

This is what relativity is. No words scare me at this stage. Many words scare "others" because they are conditioned into fear or "left brain"

The government said "after 9/11 we are in grave danger from "monsters" so we need to give up speech and let people spy on you and let people not get a fail trial in order to keep you safe." So that is a terroristic threat because they said, "allow your offspring and our future sign up for our "standing army" so we can go empire build and secure oil and a pipeline in Afghanistan, OR you will all be killed by the evil "monster"

So people who are sacred sold my freedoms down the river. I am not one who votes, but someone sold me out, so they have to answer to Jefferson if there is an afterlife.

The point is, if anyone votes for anyone but their self, they are a sheep because they determined they are not as smart as the one they vote for even though "we are all equal" we are all "one and all the same endowed by the "creator" we are all equal so they have a write in ballot, which means you vote for yourself and allow the sheep to vote their importance away and Jefferson will be waiting for them later.

If everyone votes for their self there is no government. So people who vote for others have what is called "self esteem" issues, or "shame, which is a left brain trait, opposite of that is "no shame" or "self respect".

How can someone be better than you when everything is relative to the observer. Your perceptions are equal to everyone else's unless one has self esteem issues encouraged by the left brain "education"

So maybe you can start to see it all comes back to this "education" we are forced to have, it is simply indoctrination and ones who suggest it is not are like ones who are abused and then attempt to suggest their abuser is "ok" or they deserved it. You were a child and someone brainwashed you out of your natural "right brain" intelligent , fearless aspect. You do not have to defend the "powers that be" who abused you. You were a child and you were abused by adults who should have not taken advantage of you. I apologize for the length of this post. I determined the question asked was of importance

Thank you for your compassion and understanding3:08:51 PM

Perhaps my words and deeds may convince some in time extreme right brain dominate is not as unstable as ones may fear it is. I understand the "opposite" shore I am at is what freedom is, and i can only humbly suggest the water is pleasant over here. I will not give up on attempting to "reach" you on the "opposite shore" because you are my friend. "I on the opposite shore shall be, ready to ride and spread the alarm to every Middlesex village and farm."

I will not give up on you.3:31:54 PM

I am doomed. I am now searching for infinite poison mushroom fields to accidentally eat on purpose for I cannot compete against this reality **"Left-brain dominated people(have a strong sense of time) may find their (Right Brainers)thought processes vague and difficult to follow, for they are quite opposite in the way they think."**

thought processes vague and difficult to follow, for they are quite opposite in the way they think."

thought processes vague and difficult to follow, for they are quite opposite in the way they think."

thought processes vague and difficult to follow, for they are quite opposite in the way they think."

they are quite opposite in the way they think

they are quite opposite in the way they think

they are quite opposite in the way they think

opposite in the way they think

opposite in the way they think

opposite in the way they think

opposite in the way

opposite in the way

opposite in the way

I am truly cursed and truly doomed. If you have a poison mushroom patch, a box of nails, some poison lamb chops or a mountain at a 90 degree angle, call.

<@Lestat9> opposite in the way - i cannot overcome this because i am too far in the right

<@Lestat9> i am too far , i am at end nirvana or extreme right, and so i cannot contact the "sane", they just see me as insane

<@Lestat9> i say tomato and they read potato

6/13/2009 7:36:16 AM - I speak to some of the "sane" and they come to "advanced" logical conclusions about how extreme right brained/subconscious dominate/ones in Nirvana can never make up their mind about things and they base those "advanced" deductions and "advanced" logic on ones who are "sane" and so they essentially make huge generalizations and end up telling me I am unstable mentally because I accidentally became extreme right brain dominate. So now I will make a huge generalization to counter the "vipers" delusional generalizations. I will break every rule for ones in "nirvana".

I will state facts and I will tell you what I know for a fact.

I do not sell my freedoms and I do not piss myself like a little frog does when someone suggests I should be scared, the "sane" do. I do not "freak out" and piss myself like a little frog does when people suggest I should be very sacred of "monsters" they invent in their delusional mind, the "sane" do.

While the "sane" in my country are giving up all my freedom so they will have a little "security" I was seeking to die swiftly for over 10 years and then the "sane" use their "advanced" logic skills to say I am unstable and I am bad and I am wrong. The "sane" are jokes. All of these things I know for as fact. I know they are not a fact based on my perceptions they are facts based on reality. The "sane" shoot their mouths off and suggest it is best they "educate" the children with their "delusional" concepts of "education" and turn "wise" beings into "frogs that piss their self when they get scared" because that is as good as the "sane" can do ever into infinity. The "sane" are jokes. That is a fact based on reality and I know that. I know that for a fact based on reality. So you see "I know" something and I am not hesitant to make vast generalizations based on facts just like the "sane" can do. I am able to judge the "sane" into the pit and convince the "sane" they are better o ff jumping into the pit as opposed to making anymore decisions based on their "advanced" logic skills and "advanced" intelligence which is not possible considering they use the retarded aspect of the mind because they were brainwashed from when they were a child. I know that for a fact and I know that fact is based on reality.

Verily, I know the "sane infidel darkness vipers" are as intelligently "deep" with their logic skills as a frog that pisses itself when it gets picked up. I know that for a fact based on the fact of reality.

Verily, I know the "sane" are intelligent in contrast to a frog that pisses itself when it gets scared but are never capable of intelligence based on what intelligence is. Verily, I know for a fact beyond any doubt, the "sane" as far less intelligent than a frog that pisses itself when it gets scared.

So if any "frogs that piss their self when they get scared" suggest extreme right brain people cannot make decisions and are unable to make up their minds about fact, you swiftly remind them you know of one person who is extreme right brain dominate and he knows and has no doubts about what he knows so they should keep their unnamable dam shut and avoid making "factual" statements based on the fact their greatest intelligence is only relative to the fact it is only the intelligence of a frog that pisses itself when it gets scared. Perhaps you have come to the first understanding you have ever come to in your entire life.

I say tomato; do you perceive I said tomato or potato? It is always best to get your thoughts down on paper so you do not end up physically slaughtering everyone you determine should be slaughtered. I will remind you when I get warmed up. Do you perceive I stutter? You are still here so obviously I have infinite compassion and infinite tolerance. I will now go back to wise quotes so the little frogs that piss their self when they get scared will assume they are within a billion light years of my mental capacity. The leaves in my hand represent what I have taught you; the leaves in the forest behind me represent what I have not yet taught you.8:01:43 AM

"We would love to see you **submit a manuscript for professional review** by one of our Acquisitions Representatives!"

I perceive "professional review" denotes you are suggesting you wish to judge my words before you will allow them to be published. Perhaps you are better off tying a stone around your neck and throwing yourself into the sea."

So now you see what I have to deal with the "same". They wish to judge me before they determine I am "proper". Perhaps they are so delusional they should just give up on this life.

"Exo 32:19 **And it came to pass, as soon as he came nigh unto the camp, that he saw) the calf, and the dancing: and Moses' anger waxed hot, and he cast the tables out of his hands, and brake them beneath the mount."**

You will understand the definition of "anger waxed hot" but that is simply because as I "progress mentally" further into "right brain" I am getting further and further away from "left brain" majority which is the "norms" of society and my mind is aware of it and it is also aware of the **"opposite in the way they think"** and I perceive I will be judged as being insane because I am just so opposite appearing to ones with a sense of time or left brainers because that would be quite a logical determination. Then I remind myself I have already let go of life so I do not have to panic because I have no expectations from the ones who prefer to judge. Just tell yourself everything I say in my books are just lucky guesses from an insane person.

This is a comment by St Augustine:

"the good Christian should beware of mathematicians(ones who teach "scribe"), ... the danger already exists that the mathematicians have made a covenant with the devil to darken the spirit(make others left brain) and to confine man in the bonds of Hell"

Just ignore everything I say for the rest of eternity.

I will clarify this because he was simply explaining things the best way he could based on the fact he lived around 350 AD, which according to ones with a sense of time was more than zero seconds ago.

"the good Christian"

"Christian ,Jew, Muslim " means a PERSON who wishes to go back to "right brain" and negate the effects of the "left brain" indoctrination.

"should beware of mathematicians"

Means one should avoid "writing and arithmetic to a degree in relation to "f you reflect back upon our own educational training, we have been traditionally taught to master the 3 R's: **reading, writing and arithmetic** -- the domain and strength of the left brain."

So what St Augustine was saying is simply, If a person focuses on "spelling" properly and "numbers" they will condition their mind to the "dark" side which is the "left hemisphere" and they will see everything as labels and make judgments or logical deductions based on those labels instead of seeing everything as a "whole" or one thing which is the domain of the "right brain". I am not intelligent enough to speak about supernatural powers and I am not looking to satisfy anyone so they will "accept me" into their herd. I prefer the lone wolf role because I will catch more fish to eat for no reason, in the lone wolf role.

You are already going to judge me as insane because of this **"opposite in the way they think"** anyway. So I determined it does not matter what I say so I will say what I perceive I should say with that understanding in mind. I understand someone will always get what I am saying. The wheat will be separated from the chaff.

"Sun Tzu said: The general principle of war is that making the whole state surrender is better than destroying it* subjugating the entire enemy's army is better than crushing it* making a battalion, a company or a five-man squad surrender is better than destroying them."

This is the strategy I have chosen or the path I have chosen. I have determined to have patience using words to accomplish my goals. I may very well fail using the "words" strategy but that is okay because I have already understand I can never win, so I am just experimenting and I am unable to ever lose with an experiment.

"making a battalion, a company or a five-man squad surrender is better than destroying them."

I prefer to make the enemy surrender using words because if I determine to destroy them physically I will only mentally destroy myself. So I have patience in this strategy but I have no patience in regards to anything else. I understand clearly the situation I am in so my "anger waxes hot" mentally speaking and that anger will destroy me if I do not get it out of me and on paper. The paper is my buffer. This is in relation to the comment of Malcolm X, "Anger is a gift". Anger is a gift one receives by understanding the situation they are facing. So one might suggest I am extremely "gifted" with anger, and thus my eyes are black with rage. Now I will discuss something that you will never be able to grasp.

"Socrates" He was, nevertheless, found guilty of corrupting the minds of the youth of Athens and sentenced to death by drinking a mixture containing poison hemlock."

He believed such a flight would indicate a fear of death, which he believed no true philosopher(one who says perhaps often) has.

If he fled Athens his teaching would fare no better in another country as he would continue questioning all he met and undoubtedly incur their displeasure.

Having knowingly agreed to live under the city's laws, he implicitly subjected himself to the possibility of being accused of crimes by its citizens and judged guilty by its jury. To do otherwise would have caused him to break his "social contract" with the state, and so harm the state, an act contrary to Socratic principle."

Socrates reached right brain dominate to an extreme. He had no fear. He faced his fear of death and so what possibly could he fear after facing the greatest fear. That is what it takes to reach extreme right brain dominate. He preached exactly what the other "wise" beings preached, that the children were being "educated" into left brain dominate. "found guilty of corrupting the minds of the youth of Athens"

And of course the "sane" do what they do best. They made this wise being "drink the cool aid." because he was "opposite" of their thinking. They assumed he was "evil" and "assumed" he was "bad" because they were unable to grasp they were unnamable dam abomination.

So now we have:

Moses was killed because he appeared to be a "ninny" and his anger waxed because he tried to tell everyone their physical focus in relation to the golden calf was because they were "educated" into left brain thinking and the "sane" got tired of hearing his crap and slaughtered him. Climbing the mountain alone probably suggests he was "cast out" like an old lion is cast out of the pride and forced to die alone.

Jesus said the exact same thing, he said "suffer the children" and "I conquered (my fear of)death" and of course the "sane" slaughtered him on the cross because he was cerebrally focused and not physically focused.

Mohammed was poisoned to death for the exact same reason and he agreed with Jesus and Moses.

Then Socrates was told to drink the poison because he was "harming the youth" with his words.

This is why I am leaning heavily towards the Mohammed Logic, which is, you get near me, I slice your head off. I beg you to test me. Now you wish I died. I will go play the video game because I just determined you are insufferable.10:48:59 AM

"Shortly before his death, Socrates speaks his last words to Crito: "Crito, we owe a cock to Asclepius. Please, don't forget to pay the debt." The "sane" slaughtered this being because he was different and yet in the last moments of his life his right brain was charitable. He was being killed unjustly yet the right aspect of the mind was only concerned about making sure this being did not harm others or take advantage of others in a physical way. The "sane" needs to stop saying who is a saint and who is not a saint because the "sane" can only determine a true saint is the devil. I will write infinite books and convince the "sane" they should drink the hemlock.10:57:55 AM

"Mettanando and von Hinüber argue that the Buddha died of mesenteric infarction, a symptom of old age, rather than food poisoning." Yes and Jesus simply died because of a broken nail and Socrates died from old age and , pretty much everyone just died from old age because certainly the "sane" do not slaughter what is "opposite" than them. If that was the case then this earth would be infested by insane people who kill anyone who is different than they are and that would mean this is living hell and then I am reminded they are, and it is.

I will attempt to sum this up properly.

If you have "bliss" which is spiritual joy, that is because you are so ignorant about what is going on you are literally "blind" and in "darkness". I have no spiritual joy, my eyes are black with rage because I am aware of what is happening. I pray for ignorance and you beg for understanding. This book is a unnamable dam nightmare as far as I can tell. Clearly I must be delusional, so I will publish it as is.11:19:19 AM

Now I understand why the Buddhist suggest I should go to their temple to hide and I am of firm conviction I am an American and I am free and I do not run from anyone for any reason ever."These colors don't run." I understand it is one against six billion and you do not stand a chance.11:25:55 AM

I could use a handful of Paxil right about now. Perhaps someone is giving out free samples.

http://www.news.com.au/couriermail/story/0,023739,22556678-23272,00.html

Yes this test is a good example of relativity. Whichever way that doll spins is truth relative to the observer. So there is no absolute truth as to which way that doll spins it is all relative to the observer. And observation for humans is relative to perception caused by the brain. If one perceives terrorists are coming to kill us all then they might be very willing to pass laws that give up freedom of privacy ,freedom of speech and many other things based on their perceived fear. Fear is all there is to fear and left brain "education" encourages fear in the mind.

Someone was afraid and voted to give up "my right to privacy" by allowing agencies to spy on me, so relative to my perception the ones who voted my privacy away are my enemy and they are the tyrant and I have a right to water the tree of liberty with their blood, relatively speaking.

Relativity suggests nothing is happening unless one observes it happening. What is happening is there are no observers?

"If clockwise, then you use more of the right side of the brain and vice versa."

So you see my whole premise is perhaps in error. I see that doll going counter clockwise no matter how hard I stare at it. So either their premise is wrong or everything the "wise" beings through history were saying is wrong.

6/14/2009 9:22:51 AM

"The Ancient Egyptian scribe, or sesh, was a person educated in the arts of writing (using both hieroglyphics and hieratic scripts, and from the second half of the first millennium BCE also the demotic script) and dena (arithmatics). He was generally male, belonged socially to what we would refer to as a middle class elite, and was employed in the bureaucratic administration of the pharaonic state, of its army, and of the temples.[5] Sons of scribes were brought up in the same scribal tradition, sent to school and, upon entering the civil service, inherited their fathers' positions." WIKIPEDIA.COM

This paragraph is "ground zero" that explains how everything happened in relation to civilization. I will suggest it is simply an illusion and there is further illusion's beyond it but that is to keep my mind in proper perspective because I have infinite books to write.

6/15/2009 8:01:59 AM

First, someone invented a planned language with the creative right brain. Scribes were taught to use that planned language and that encouraged left brain in relation to (If you reflect back upon our own educational training, we have been traditionally taught to master the 3 R's: reading, writing and arithmetic -- the domain and strength of the left brain.) These scribes were a rare thing and so they were valued because everyone else was right brained or "natural" in relation to how they were out of the "womb" they were all in "nirvana" or no sense of time, so civilization was in the "garden of Eden" stage. The problem is, the scribes became left brain and physical focused and they got lots of money and were pleased to "take advantage " of the right cerebral populace, because the populace were like lambs, they were not money focused, they have many physical aspects turned down and also they worked for free, so they were what we call "slaves".

117

"demotic script) and dena (arithmatics)" these words are perhaps where the word demonic came from, they were demons because they learned math and writing and became the "darkness" or left brain physical focused.

"He was generally male" this explains why females in some religions are not taught to write and not taught math. Some religions teach the males to read and write and teach the males to memorize which creates left brain and then they do not teach the females to keep the females right brain.

"belonged socially to what we would refer to as a middle class elite, and was employed in the bureaucratic administration of the pharaonic state, of its army, and of the temples" this denotes the scribes are what "created" the control structure of society, they were the law makers and also the religious leaders in relation to "religion is the opiate(control structure" of the masses(the lambs the right brain docile people or "submissive" people) So the comment "one day the lion will lay down with the lambs." Denotes one day the lions(demotic/aka demonic/left brain) will lay down with the lambs(right brain cerebral submissive) and stop taking advantage of them. This is in relation to Moses saying "let the lambs go or let my people go." Moses was saying let the lambs/right brains go you scribes/left brains.

"Sons of scribes were brought up in the same scribal tradition, sent to school and, upon entering the civil service, inherited their fathers' positions" This denotes a monarchy or a system to keep educating in left brain these "scribes" and thus people started to perceive the Trojan horse syndrome. They thought "If my child is trained as a scribe then I will have power and wealth and not be a slave/lamb/right brain." So many schools started popping up and training people to be "scribes" and eventually all of civilization became left brain dominate because of the lure of easy comfort if they "educated" their child in math and scribe. So this scribe "Trojan horse" turned mankind from docile cerebral based into left brain physical based and that is when wars started happening and money became king.

So Adam and Eve ate of the tree of "knowledge"(schooling in scribe and math) and then became shy and ashamed in relation to emotional self consciousness created by left brain conditioning caused by being taught scribe and math. The note about Eve eating off the tree first is an opposite or "trick" because females were not taught how to scribe so females were in fact more submissive but in reality females were far more cerebral and intelligent than males, thus Cleopatra and Helen of Troy. So the Adam and Eve story suggests women ate off the tree to make sure whoever figured this out would be determined by everyone to be the genuine article because only one who understand that comment was a "puzzle" would be the one who "pulled the sword out of stone" so to speak because they saw it as an "opposite" in relation to " He was generally male". Only males generally were "demotic ". Ignorance was bliss. This is why you are not allowed to talk to me or contact me. I do not want to go into the "world" you love so much. I do not want to end up like you are and like I was. This is also in relation to why the Buddhists keep and oral tradition and not a written tradition. They teach with spoken words and not written words. There are also many cultures who keep their history in spoken form and not written form to avoid this "scribe complex". Now I will discuss something of importance.8:23:15 AM

8:40:35 AM - Perhaps you are wise to simply tell yourself I went extreme right brain dominate or subconscious dominate and that is why I understand everything clearly for your own sake, perhaps, so to speak, psychologically speaking, what have you. Translated, I have determined I am surrounded by insane people who like to kill things that are different so if you get near me I slaughter you and you can take your moralistic laws and shove them up your ass. You take your comments about tolerance, compassion, mercy and acceptance and shove them up your ass. I do not reason with or acknowledge "darkness" that is the absolute rule. I do not pander to the "snake" so slaughter me slowly so you will understand I love repeat performances. I do not care about your premise or about your logic or about what you think about anything ever into infinity, I DO NOT PANDER. If I needed an army I would have one. I won't be coming to your rescue because you killed all the other ones who attempted to come to your rescue and you are to "dark" to understand that. Now you understand the definition of "my anger is waxing". I do find it hilarious people have been slaughtering each other for religion and money and land for thousands of years and they killed all of those people for no reason at all. They know not what they do. That is great humor. A master does not need a student but a student needs a master.

"Last fall, the 16-year-old sophomore was accused of posting personal information on 250 district employees on his personal Web site. And now police say he built an application to shut teachers out of the grading system."

http://www.timesunion.com/AspStories/story.asp?storyID=809665

Perhaps this student has had enough of being judged by the "sane".

"Luk 9:48 And said unto them, Whosoever shall receive this child in my name receiveth me: and whosoever shall receive me receiveth him that sent me: for he that is least among you all, the same shall be great. "

This comment talks of the least among you these least amoung you are ones who are depressed and suicidal, they are in a perfect mindset of being meek and humble.

Joh 15:13 Greater love hath no man than this, that a man lay down his life for his friend."

This talks about these suicidal ones as ones who are meek and willing to die for their friends, in relation to, they are "trying to wake up" from the damage caused the by "demotic script" brain washing. They are subconsciously aware something is not right and they are subconsciously trying to wake up but they take that consciously as "harm yourself", the are trying to get rid of the "emptiness" which is a symptom that the "snake" is "in them", so they usually end up kill their self and in turn they die for your sins, which is what you forced them to become "educated" in your "demotic script" which turned them into physical based left brain and ripped them from cerebral based right brain. So one might suggest after coming to this understanding I am leaning heavily on the "cut their heads off" side of fence today. If you have a problem with that you need to contact me so I can assist you in how to properly drowned in my red sea.

11:32:30 AM - The ones in the land that holds children in concentrated pockets for 50 years who do not wish to hold children in concentrated pockets should arm their self and begin to slaughter ones in their land who desire to hold children in isolated pockets for 50 years. I will find no fault with their actions.

Better to die trying to end suffering than to suffer while watching it.

12:17:16 PM - I submit my books are a nightmare and you may be very scared or worried about me if you have read this far but this is what the comment "The kingdom is within" is all about. The battle of the mind is the real battle. Those who want mental peace prepare for mental war. I am fighting battles in my head so I am not harming anyone physically and that is what the statement "my struggle is mine" is saying. It is mine. My struggle in my mind is my struggle so I do not need you to attempt to correct me because if you have a problem with any sentence in any of my books you are what Freud suggested; in neurosis.

"Neurosis is the inability to tolerate ambiguity."
Sigmund Freud

What this means is you get weird when you see a misspelled word or a comma out of place or a cuss word or a sentence that you perceive is not proper, you mentally cannot handle ambiguity because you are in neurosis. You are mentally damaged goods. And that leads up to Jung's comment.

"Neurosis is always a substitute for legitimate suffering."
Carl Jung

You cannot take the mental struggle so you avoid it. You call me insane and tell yourself I have problems because you cannot take the clarity. You feel you would harm yourself so you are afraid. You are afraid to fight the mental struggle so you tell yourself I am insane so you do not have to understand you are in fact in neurosis. You are in fact a threat to yourself and to others because you are in denial. You are in neurosis. I had an accident and woke up to the fact I was in neurosis and I am attempting to wake you up but you are in such deep neurosis it may take infinite books to reach you.

And that relates to the next Jung quote. You perceive you are just fine and sane and you perceive I am insane or ill or in need of help because you are in neurosis. You are mentally unstable. Humans were just fine and then someone invented planned language and mathematics and somehow that threw our minds way out of whack and then people started thinking, "With wealth and being a scribe I will be able to "control" the "lambs" and so that is good." So everything shifted. We went from a peaceful species to a barbaric species because of planned language and mathematics. So we thought we saw "light" in planned language and scribes and thought that was "knowledge" and we in turn altered our minds and went into neurosis. That is a fact I woke up to. You perceive you are sane and I am attempting to cure you of your neurosis.

"Show me a sane man and I will cure him for you."

Carl Jung

Then we have the next quote.

"There is no coming to consciousness without pain."
Carl Jung

Pain is not even in the realms of properly explaining the mental anguish. Gnashing of teeth is much more accurate but I am certain Jung did not want to appear religious because he was in disguise.

This is what "ignorance is bliss" means. Consciousness is gnashing of teeth mentally. I am not physically bound. I do not harm people physically because I am conscious. I do not hit people. I do not condone hitting people. I do not vote to kill people I do not like, I gnash my teeth when is see the world killing other people. I die when I read the world has decided to kill people today. I die when I read we are sending our offspring into some war to kill other people and then telling the offspring it is ok and you are doing good. I rip myself apart inside over and over because you are in neurosis. So don't you ever tell me about your problems.

You kill me every day because you think in some situations it is okay to kill people. So my only comment is to tell you to kill everyone that is like you, and then kill yourself, for the good of the species. Do something that is not selfish for once. So now you understand what the comment, patience is a virtue, means. What that means is I have to have patience and compassion on the ones I understand are in neurosis. That means if you have a strong sense of time and strong sense of hunger I have to have compassion and patience with you because you are "insane" and mentally ill and if I do not have patience with you and compassion you will become physically violent and you will slaughter me because you are mentally ill and you like to physically harm things because you have "the inability to tolerate ambiguity".

But the problem is, I woke up by accident and I am not yet warmed up so I have no compassion and I have no mercy and I have no patience so I have no virtues because I am aware I killed myself for 10 years because of this "norms of society" and "schooling" aspect. So then we have to come to the understanding we should tolerate each other. That means I am going to rip your mind apart with my books and you are going to tolerate it so you will wake up and gain consciousness and stop walking around in neurosis. You by law you have to tolerate my words and if you try to stop my words I slaughter you and you will be deserving of that slaughter. Perhaps you have come to an understanding.-12:51:58 PM

12:56:21PM - Very rarely in history does a person reach consciousness so swiftly because in order to do that one has to "not try to save their self so they find their self." That means many people are going too far and they end up no trying to save their self but they end up killing their self in suicide. Very rarely in history does a person accomplish the waking up and yet not physically dying. They are what is known as the Buddha's, The Messiahs or the Prophets but are in reality simply members of the species that woke up so hardcore that they can lead many others to waking up. They wake up in a pure fashion. They wake up to an extreme. They tend to get slaughtered though because the ones in neurosis have "the inability to tolerate ambiguity ". So then there is this concept called "tough love". What tough love means is, I woke up and I am conscious and many others are in fact conscious also and that means we are attempting to wake up the species before it annihilates itself because it is in general in this "neurotic" state of mind caused by the ""demotic script and dena (arithmatics)". So you should now perceive I have a messiah complex or a "I am better than you" state of mind. In reality I had an accident from trying to kill myself for so many years and I woke up "very well". So you should not assume I am going to be humble and meek if you attempt to harm me. You should not assume I am going to go on speaking tours. You should not assume I am going to mingle in the general population. I am going to write infinite and try to wake everyone. You are perhaps unable to even follow what I am saying. I am not smarter than you I am what a normal human being should be like. I am normal and if you have as strong hunger and sense of time you are abnormal. That is a fact. That is a truth. Disbelief will never change that. I am attempting to suggest you are very intelligent and powerful mentally speaking and our species fell for a "Trojan horse" ""demotic script and dena (arithmatics)" that put us into neurosis. You do not need to worry about God. You need to worry about waking up first.1:11:02 PM

8:16:34 PM - What recorded history is a symptom of is the neurosis caused by the "scribe" aspect. It altered our memories to be very short term memory focused and reduced our long term memory focus.

So in education things like pop quizzes and spelling tests on a weekly basis encourage short term memory as the experience of long term memory. Before you know it the mind is "conditioned" to be very left brain focused and so one becomes very physical based and in turn loses the cerebral focus of the right brain. One become physically focused and physically centered and thus physically "violent" as opposed to cerebral focused and less focused on material things like physically harming others and ones self. So recorded history is a symptom our species became very "time" focused as a result of the "scribe" conditioning. That is a fact. Do not try to argue with that because you are unable to.

6/16/2009 3:23:58 AM - Control over one's self is proper control and may assist others in understanding how to control their self, which is something; in relation to "Mat 7:5 Thou hypocrite, first cast out the beam out of thine own eye; and then shalt thou see clearly to cast out the mote out of thy brother's eye." Clearly denotes clarity or consciousness, in relation to Freud's comment, "The goal of a therapist is to make the unconscious conscious." in relation to doing good maybe assist others to do well, enlightened self interest, focus on your log and the fruits of doing so may assist others with their logs indirectly. So you forget about all your little pipe dream assumptions, you wake up first, then you will think clearly and will be able to make decisions, until then you should avoid making any decisions for anyone but yourself.

5:37:34 AM - Snakes sun sleep cold. To a person who has been conditioned into left brain this snakes sentence does not make much sense because they are sequenced based in their thinking. Their mind cannot see the whole or the spirit of the word like a person who is conditioned to right brain thinking. The right see's the whole and the left see's sequence.

So the snakes sentence does not follow the grammatical rules of a planned language so one who has been "educated" into the planned language cannot decipher what the snakes sentence means. It simply looks like words arranged in a random fashion and has no meaning. Now the right brain can swiftly translate the snakes sentence to mean : snakes sleep in the sun when it's cold. So people with left brain will suggest, "That is not what that sentence says." But it is what that sentence says it is just left brain conditioned people are what is called "anal retentive". They cannot think in terms of open mindedness about sentences they tend to take everything on face value without considering all the possibilities but this is because the "planned language" has had an adverse effect on the mind. It has thrown in these "emotions" as a side effect of planned language learning and that has fogged the minds power. So it is not good or bad that has happened and it is not about throwing out language and math. We can't take back what has happened but one can be mindful how to negate the effects if they wish to do so. That is as good as it gets.

So the fear conditioning will negate the effects that the planned language conditioning has indirectly brought about. Another way to look at it is, planned language happened and it looked like a great idea but its side effect was to magnify emotions and it did it on a subtle scale so it was not obvious and so the only people who understood this were people who woke up because of major mental breakout. Other words the main religious founders woke up as a result of becoming very "mentally meek" as in almost dying but not dying. Buddha almost died when he didn't eat for 39 days but he didn't die and so he woke up to this truth that planned language had an unintentional side effect on humans minds which is, it magnified our emotions. Once these founders woke up to what this planned language "scribe" aspect had done they attempted to explain to others what had happened and they did not have the proper understanding of the situation in relation to words to describe it so they appeared very "off center" to many. They did not have the words to just say, planned language created scribes and scribes focused on detail and that encouraged left brain and thus unintentially magnified emotions and that meant the right brain powerhouse was veiled or silenced so we harmed our full mental capacity as the result of an invention called "scribe" or planned language and we went into a neurosis and became very physically orientated as opposed to cerebral power houses we were before. So they did the best they could based on the fact they didn't have all the proper clarifications we have today to understand what happened.

I understand what happen clearly and unquestionably because I reached consciousness and that means my mind is at full power and it can sift through the whole situation and find patterns and figure it all out and it is not how smart I am, it is an indication of how smart the mind is when it is not so cluttered with "emotions". So I am at what is called end enlightenment. Everything that happens in the world I now understand why it does so I am at peace with that because what happened was simply a unintentional side effect of planned language and mathematics and can be reversed with "fear conditioning" and then we get to keep the math and planned language and adjust slightly and not make planned language such a memory focused teaching. Allow the kids to invent their own variations of the words this way they will not become so emotional and cloud their minds with emotions indirectly. There, their, thar, ther these are all proper ways to say There or their. They are not in error. A person understands what it means. Only a person in neurosis would argue those words do not all mean the same thing because:

"Neurosis   is   the   inability   to   tolerate   ambiguity."
Sigmund Freud

Which is a nice way to say, they are extremely anal retentive, caused by a side effect of having strong planned language conditioning in their education. They judge a book by the cover(left brain) and not by its content or "spirit"(right brain). It is not good or bad but it is none the less an absolute fact and absolute truth.6:01:53 AM

6:07:50 AM - So I am no longer able to wax anger because I have an explanation for anything that happens in relation to human behavior. A country decides to attack another country , that is because they are left brain physically orientation and have control issues as a result of being taught planned language to strongly. A person kills their self when their love is scorned, that is because they have to strong of emotions caused indirectly by strong planned language so they do not deal with loss and loss of attachments and loss of control well.

A person is racist or biased against another person, that is because they have to strong of emotions and are easily insulted by others and have trouble dealing with ambiguity as in different races and religions and political views because they are in neurosis caused indirectly by strong planned language education.

A person is addicted to drugs because they have strong emotions and the likely hood of becoming attached to things to "feel good" as an indirect result of strong planned language education.

A person over eats for the same reason a person drinks too much or takes too much drugs or has too much desire for money or has too much hate for others , it is all a symptom of the neurosis caused by the strong planned language "education" they had as a child.

What this means is I am unable to achieve stress or I am at peace with everything because I can tell myself everything is a result of unintended consequences for this planned language reason.7:00:33 AM

Why does a parent feel the need to medicate their child? Inability to tolerate ambiguity which is a symptom of neurosis.

Why does a person vote to make drugs illegal? Inability to tolerate ambiguity which is a symptom of neurosis.

Why does a psychologist prescribe psychological drugs to children? Inability to tolerate ambiguity which is a symptom of neurosis.

Why is their religious conflicts? Inability to tolerate ambiguity which is a symptom of neurosis.

Why is there race conflicts? Inability to tolerate ambiguity which is a symptom of neurosis.

Why do people judge each other? Inability to tolerate ambiguity which is a symptom of neurosis.

Why do people say others are evil? Inability to tolerate ambiguity which is a symptom of neurosis.

Why do people hate others? Inability to tolerate ambiguity which is a symptom of neurosis.

Why do people seek to control others? Inability to tolerate ambiguity which is a symptom of neurosis.

Why do people seek to dominate others? Inability to tolerate ambiguity which is a symptom of neurosis.

One should first attempt to get rid of fear by sitting in the dark alone after they watch a scary movie or sitting in the dark alone in a cemetery and once they are comfortable with those simple fear conditioning techniques they can move on to greater thought challenges such as determining who is evil and who is good, or who is righteous and who is not, or who is mentally sick and who is mentally well and perhaps in time they may actually reach level of mental clarity they can ponder supernatural events. I am certain I will never reach a level of clarity to speak as an authority on supernatural events simply because I am not even an authority on the known world and I never will be.

9:49:55 PM

"Lev 26:21 And if ye walk contrary(opposite) unto me, and will not hearken unto me; I will bring seven times more plagues upon you according to your sins."

This is simply saying those on the "left brain" are opposite than him, Moses, this is why his anger was waxing because he was cerebral and they were physical based. Moses was angry and for more than a few reasons, but mostly because of the "accident" and what led up to the "accident".

 "Lev 26:22 I will also send wild beasts among you, which shall rob you of your children, and destroy your cattle, and make you few in number; and your _high_ ways shall be desolate."

Rob you of your children denotes, they will educate them as "scribes" and they will become left brain instead or the natural right brain they are born like so they will "rob" them or "ruin" them.

"Lev 26:26 _And_ when I have broken the staff of your bread, ten women shall bake your bread in one oven, and they shall deliver _you_ your bread again by weight: and ye shall eat, and not be satisfied."

"Shall eat and not be satisfied" denotes a symptom of one who is extreme right brain after the fear and emotional conditioning. This has much to do about the altered short term memory. In extreme right brain the short term memory is altered and the long term memory is pronounced. This also explains how these "cravings and desires" and feeling of "satisfaction" are in fact abnormal and a symptom one is in psychosis caused by the "scribe" education or "eating off the tree of knowledge". I prefer the comment: I eat for no reason. The double meaning or complex meaning of this comment also denotes who left brain people try to satisfy their physical cravings with food, drugs, money and they are never able to be satisfied. So to right people satisfaction is not possible

so they tend not to even go down that road and to left brain they tend to seek satisfaction but it is never accomplished so they tend to kill their self with trying to fill that emptiness or mental lack of satisfaction. 10:00:09 PM

6/17/2009 3:23:02 AM

"Mat 22:14 For many are called, but few _are_ chosen. "

Many are suicidal(meek) but few go nearly all the way and mindfully "wake up" as a result of many failed suicide attempts. Few pull an "Abraham and Isaac". Most "get better" or accomplish suicide so it is very rare to actually come so close but then still be alive. Only those "chosen" wake up the full measure or get "tapped".

"Mat 22:32 I am the God of Abraham(subconscious), and the God of Isaac(Subconscious), and the God of Jacob? God is not the God of the dead(ones with strong sense of time, strong hunger, left brain, conscious emotional), but of the living(Subconscious dominate, right(hand) brain, slight sense of time and slight emotions, conscious beings)."

"ALARM: National Security Agency has ability to collect, read domestic e-mails of Americans on widespread basis"

You see some scared, fearful little weak minded abomination keeps giving away my freedom of speech my freedom to privacy and I have already determined to write books to alter their fear based votes that give away my freedoms and when I determine that is not working I go to plan two which is abolish, and abolish means "kiss" and "love" and that means I "love" the ones who voted away my freedom and my rights and that means fellow citizens, and I have a right to do that, which means I am in the right to do that. So perhaps if you are one of these scared weak minded beings who piss their self like a frog when someone says a scary word you should consider altering what you are doing because I have a right to "kiss" tyrants with or without the consent of laws. You are no longer my fellow citizen if you give away my rights because you are afraid of the dark, you are in reality a tyrant to me and I water the tree liberty with tyrants. Home of the brave denotes ones who do not flinch when people suggest they sell their freedoms to be safe from monsters. So it does not even matter if you don't like that idea that is the ideal of America. Simply put, you vote away my freedom I have a right to 'love" you. You voted that I should "love" you. Perhaps you should ponder that carefully.

"That whenever any Form of Government (LAW OR VOTE)becomes destructive of these ends, it is the Right of the People to alter(with words or discussion) or to abolish(EXTREMINATE) it, and to institute new Government,"

Perhaps you should ponder moving to another country because I have already determined you cannot handle freedom you are all about fear and so you are a threat to my freedom so "kissing" you is my only logical choice to protect my freedom. So that is called self defense. So perhaps you should think really "thanking" hard about what I just said. I do not play games when it comes to my freedom. I do not sell out when someone says I should be afraid. I "thanking" water the tree of liberty with weak minded beings who sell me out and I do it because I have a right to. It may be against the law but I have a right to do it so the law means nothing in contrast to my rights." is the Right of the People to alter or to abolish" I have a RIGHT to "kiss" anyone who votes to take away my rights afforded me in the constitution. If you are scared you go buy a gun. If you are still scared you go buy an army, but once you vote away my freedom you sign your death certificate. I do not give a "duck" about what law says about that, I understand that is the reality of the situation. You signed your death certificate because you were afraid so now there is nothing left to say. We will talk when I get my rights back until then there is no talking only watering. I do not care if 300 million people vote and say I do not have absolute freedom of speech and absolute freedom of privacy because I eat for no reason to begin with. Three hundred million is nothing in contrast to infinity, boy. Why don't you try to do something about that. I beg you to try to do something about that. I will raise an army and convince them to "kiss" you to get my rights back and I will be in the RIGHT to do that, simply because once you sell my right they are also gone for the next generation and the next and the next, they are gone forever because you are a little weak minded frog that pisses itself when its scared and starts signing away my freedoms so you either alter or you get "kissed" and I won't bat an eye because it is my right to do no matter what anyone says in the universe ever.

"America   is   a   mistake,   a   giant   mistake."
Sigmund   Freud

"America   is   the   most   grandiose   experiment   the   world
has   seen,   but,   I   am   afraid,   it   is   not   going   to   be   a   success."
Sigmund Freud"

Yes America is a suicide pact. So you should be trying your hardest to alter and get back all my freedoms you sold because every time I write I am in fact inciting revolution and that means revolution to abolish the "thank" out of the people who gave away my freedoms. Perhaps since you are a tyrant you do not like those words so you should seek me out and lock me up and burn me at the stake because I am the bait and when the fish takes the bait the "lover" begins. Perhaps you have come to an understanding.

I am more like Thomas Jefferson, I do not fight in the revolution but I make sure it starts. Your weak logic is, "We are the freest country in the world." but that is because you are delusional. You are a fearful little frog that has no right to be an American. You sign away my freedoms and then you think I have no right to fight to get them back. You have no logic ability. You have no brain function. You are simply a little frogs that signs away my freedom whenever you hear a scary noise. My only solution is to "love" you because you will just keep giving away my freedoms until I am in a police state, and I am in a police state because you are a tyrant and thus you get "loved".

I print my books and let the world know I am inciting total revolution and I do not blink and I do not run because I am going to get back my freedom even if I end up being the only "thanking" one left.

I am not telling you what might happen. I operate in real time only, which means I am telling you what is going to happen or what is already destined to happen. You are going to understand that sooner than you think.

When you voted away my freedoms you told me you no longer wish to "love" so I am now assisting you in getting what you voted for. You hung yourself and I am going to pull the lever for you. I am going to make sure you hang high. One might suggest a thinning of the sick ones in the herd is about to happen and it's for the better. One might suggest you are either for absolute freedom of speech and absolute privacy or you get "loved". You are either for me or against me.

Franklin said quite clearly "Those who give up liberty for a little security deserve neither" That a nice way of saying, if you get scared and start voting all my freedoms away you deserve neither security or liberty which means you get "loved". The police state ain't giving you back your freedoms they are only going to scare you into giving away more of my freedoms. So you either join the militia that buys up all the ammo up or you become the focus of target practice. You have no other choices. You fight to get your freedom back or you get "loved", that's where you are at, that's where your fear has lead you. Your fear has killed you. Welcome to the land of the free, boy. I submit I have slight anger waxing issues around 3am till around 8AM. Perhaps you do not understand why. I will give you some advice, when they show up and ask you to bend down and bow your head make sure you don't move because they might miss "The **medulla oblongata** is the lower half of the brainstem. It deals with autonomic functions, such as breathing and blood pressure." You want them to hit that part because then it is less painful. So don't jump around and don't move around, just bow your head and hope they are a good shot. That is the advice I am giving you and you would be wise to take it into consideration.

"When the people fear their government, there is tyranny; when the government fears the people, there is liberty." Thomas   Jefferson
If you fear the government you are in a tyranny so using our words and shooting our guns ensures the government fears us. Of course you are way to brain dead to grasp that at this moment.

"The strongest reason for the people to retain the right to keep and bear arms is, as a last resort, to protect themselves against tyranny in government. " Thomas   Jefferson
Last resort means when they abridge freedom of speech and start taking your privacy. Of course you are way to brain dead to grasp that at this moment.

"The tree of liberty must be refreshed from time to time with the blood of patriots and tyrants." Thomas Jefferson

This comment is for those who will read my books after I am gone. I am not a physically violent person in general, I actually reached consciousness and because I am using 100% of my mind I am aware of everything I read and it harms me and so I have to cuss and fight in my books because I have very little ignorance left which means my eyes are black with rage. I understand what is happening to my country and I understand what people did to give me my freedom. They died to give me my freedom, and I see weak minded fearful brain dead people who gave away that freedom these others being died to give me and it rips my mind apart because these weak minded brain dead think they are doing a good thing to sign away those freedoms. I am mindful at times the metal must meet the meat. This is a message for my fellow countrymen who are alive now. If you perceive you can vote away my freedoms others being died to give me and "love" to tell about it, you are misinformed.7:10:01 AM

7:10:34 AM - Now you understand why they never published Jesus' books because his books were filled with anger. Moses filled the old testament with anger. All of the comments that are supposed to be "god" being angry is in reality Moses being angry. So I guess I can just say, all my anger statements are statements god made in my books and not me, I am humble and happy and at peace even though I am fully aware I live among insane people. I recall I have already suggested this in my previous books. The price of subconscious and understanding is rage. This is why you should perhaps not even consider becoming subconscious dominate because when you use 100% of your mind you are going to understand the definition of gnashing of teeth because you will not be able to be ignorant then. If you are happy and joyful that is because you have no brain function. Ignorance is bliss, bliss is spiritual joy. I have nearly no ignorance so I have nearly no spiritual joy. I

127

Todd Andrew Rohrer

have tiny moments of spiritual joy that are engulfed in long moments of gnashing of teeth, mentally speaking. That is why Buddha said do not try to reach enlightenment using the "starve yourself to death almost technique" because you will become fully conscious and you will be in agony because you will understand everything that is going on and you won't be able to stop it and that will rip you apart. Just try to get to no sense of time using the easy fear conditioning tactics that way you won't reach the full power of the mind just like 70 to 90% then you will just have some gnashing of teeth, but for me, I did it by accident so I am cursed. My books are nightmares. My books are total cussing and total rage and total hate of this accident. I hate it with all my might but I cannot feel hate. I just cuss and it doesn't help me. I try to be angry and I cannot so I just have to take the gnashing of teeth. I cannot get rid of it. I try to tell myself I am at peace mentally but then I read the news and I get ripped apart again.

Amy (16) allegedly took her own life

Lisa (19) allegedly committed suicide by overdosing on Cymbalta

William (18) allegedly committed suicide at his residence

Morgan (16) committed suicide by allegedly hanging herself at home

Do you understand what your "left brain scribe" education is doing to children? You forced these kids to attend your schools and your school is making kids focus on short term memory and scribe and has a side effect called strong emotions such as shame, embarrassment, self esteem issues, self hate, self doubt. I recall when I visited a Buddhist chat room a monk said in the chat room, "This one is quite angry isn't he." That was a compliment because what it means is I have such extreme clarity it rips me apart. Do you perceive these founders of the main "religions" were happy? Ignorance is bliss, clarity is gnashing of teeth.7:42:25 AM

This is a reader poll: DO you perceive the author is:

Slightly angry

Infinitely angry

Not angry at all, but a great actor.

"And Jacob's anger was kindled against Rachel:""

"Gen 44:18 **Then Judah came near unto him, and said, Oh my lord, let thy servant, I pray thee, speak a word in my lord's ears,1 and let not thine anger burn against thy servant: for thou art even as Pharaoh.**"

He was begging for the gnashing of teeth caused by the extreme clarity to go away, he was saying it is burning me up inside. But gnashing of teeth is the price for clarity so he was crying out in vain.

"Gen 49:6 **O my soul, come not thou into their secret; unto their assembly,1 mine honour, be not thou united: for in their anger they slew a man, and in their selfwill they digged down a well.**"

This is explaining how the "left brainers" kill people physically when they get angry, that's the difference. I am angry as hell but I do not harm people, I get my anger out on paper and then I let it go by publishing it that is my only chance to survive this accident. I get all my anger out and that helps me condition away from it and also I publish it so I condition away from this "care what others think about what you have to say." I live in the land of freedom of speech so if anyone harms me for my words they reveal their self to be a tyrant and the tree of liberty loves the water of tyrants into infinity.

"Gen 49:7 **Cursed be their anger, for it was fierce; and their wrath, for it was cruel: I will divide them in Jacob, and scatter them in Israel.**"

I would say my anger is fierce is the understatement of the universe. I think this is saying Jacob had this fierce anger and wrath because he was extreme right brain also or subconscious dominate. But the truth is, when I am around people I am humble and a jokester but somehow I get to these books and I understand I am not talking to people so I let it rip. I cannot explain that but it is true. I do not perceive I am talking to people even though I publish my books I do not perceive any of my books will even be read, so I say how I feel. One might suggest I am not ashamed of how I feel about things because shame is a symptom of neurosis in relation to

"Gen 2:25 **And they were both naked, the man and his wife, and were not ashamed.**"

This was before they ate off the tree of "scribe" they were not shy. embarrassed, afraid, scared.

So their minds were free of same and that is right brain, it is free and not shame.

Mat 22:44 The LORD said unto my Lord, Sit thou on my right hand(right brain), till I make thine enemies(left brain) thy footstool?

Mat 22:45 **If David then call him Lord, how is he his son?**(question to start monologue)

Mat 22:46 **And no man)man= left brainers) was able to answer him a word, neither durst any _man_ from that day forth ask him any more _questions(his complexity was beyond their ability to grasp)._**

Mat 22:21 **They say unto him, Caesar's. Then saith he unto them, Render therefore unto Caesar*left brainers) the things which are Caesar's(material things); and unto God(right brain) the things that are God's.(complexity, ambiguity, paradox)**

Mat 8:22 **But Jesus said unto him, Follow me(right brain); and let the dead(left brainers) bury their dead.(other left brainers) This is also in relation to idol worship. This is why Jesus made sure no one found his body and same with Moses, he knew the lefters would turn a shrine into it and make holidays where the left money based beings would make a killing off of their names.**

Luk 21:15 For I will give you a mouth and wisdom(right brain), which all your adversaries(left brain) shall not be able to gainsay nor resist. This means you cannot compete with what I say and you mouth just drops to the floor and you assume I am insane because you cannot even think clearly to realize I am simply normal because that would means you are slightly less than normal mentally speaking.

Luk 21:16 And ye shall be betrayed both by parents(they sent you to school to be educated with the three r's that's why you honor your mother and father but not love them because they betrayed you and also were betrayed by their parents), and brethren(right brainers), and kinsfolks , and friends; and _some_ of you shall they cause to be put to death.(this denotes I will be slaughtered by the left brainers and many right brainers have been slaughtered by the left brainers for my WORDS and that is just the way it is, so it bothers me not.)

Luk 21:17 And ye shall be hated of all _men_ for my name's sake.*everyone will hate me because I tell the truth and they hate the light of the truth because they are under the influence of the "snake" that tempted them with "knowledge". So I do not reason with the "snake" or it followers and I never will."

[I stopped editing this book at this point. Everything from this point on is stupid so just ignore it]

Sammasambuddhas attain buddhahood, then decide to teach others the truth they have discovered. They lead others to awakening by teaching the Dhamma in a time where it has been forgotten.[2] Siddhartha Gautama is considered a sammasambuddha. (See also the List of the 28 Buddhas (all of whom are sammasambuddhas).)

Paccekabuddhas, sometimes called 'silent Buddhas' are similar to sammasambuddhas in that they attain nirvana and acquire many of the same powers as a sammasambuddha, but are unable to teach what they have discovered. They are considered second to the sammasambuddhas in spiritual development. They do ordain others; their admonition is only in reference to good and proper conduct (abhisamācārikasikkhā). In some texts, the paccekabuddhas are described as those who understand the Dhamma through their own efforts, but do not obtain mastery over the 'fruits' (phalesu vasībhāvam).[2]

Savakabuddhas attain nirvana after hearing the teaching of a sammasambuddha (directly or indirectly). The disciple of a sammasambuddha is called a savaka ("hearer" or "follower") or, once enlightened, an arahant. These terms have slightly varied meanings but can all be used to describe the enlightened disciple. Anubuddha is a rarely used term, but is used by the Buddha in the Khuddakapatha[3] to refer to those who become Buddhas after being given instruction. Enlightened disciples attain nirvana and parinirvana as the two types of Buddha do. Arahant is the term most generally used for them, though it is also applicable to Buddhas.

Mat 4:8 Again, the devil taketh him up into an exceeding high mountain, and sheweth him all the kingdoms of the world, and the glory of them;

Mat 4:9 And saith unto him, All these things will I give thee, if thou wilt fall down and worship me.

(this denotes I have the ability to own the physical world because of my knowledge but I must give my books freely and never allow anyone to idolize me because I was "tapped" and that means this is not my doing do I deserve nothing.)

Mat 4:10 Then saith Jesus unto him, Get thee hence, Satan(left brainers who will say we will give **you money to speak to others) for it is written, Thou shalt worship the Lord thy God,**(right brain cerebral which is not about material things) **and him only**(denotes lukewarm, you can be left brain or right brain to an extreme but the middle left and right is the worst) **shalt thou serve.**

Eph 4:7 But unto every one of us is given grace(we all have right brain but the "scribe" aspect silences it) according to the measure of the gift of Christ.)God made man in his image and gave us (right brain aspect)

Rom 12:3 For I say, through the grace given unto me(right brain), to every man that is among you(everyone has right aspect), not to think of himself more highly than he ought to think(I think I am nothing or I wouldn't have tried to kill myself 30 times); but to think soberly(that's a joke when you have right brain aspect dominate its very hard to avoid saying things lefters don't say "What drugs are you on? Also its hard to think soberly when you have such extreme mental clarity its simply to complex and powerful), according as God hath dealt to every man the measure(left and right hemisphere of the brain) of faith(right aspect).

Mat 10:28 And fear not(don't have fear or condition away from fear to unlock right aspect) them which kill the body(don't pay attention to physical aspect or right brain people are more cerebrally focused), but are not able to kill the soul(the lefters think if they kill me they will defeat me but they are in for a big surprise) but rather fear him which is able to destroy both soul and body in hell.

Mat 10:32 Whosoever therefore shall confess(submit or humiliation or facing being shy or fearful) me before men, him will I confess also before my Father which is in heaven.

Gen 2:17 But of the tree of the knowledge of good and evil, thou shalt not eat of it: for in the day that thou eatest thereof thou shalt surely die.(when the parents force a child to go to "scribe education" they make the child go to left brain and that child "dies" or When mankind started off on the "scribe" condition the whole world "died" in the "flood".)

6/17/2009 1:35:28 PM

"Before I was humiliated I was like a stone that lies in deep mud, and he who is mighty came and in his compassion raised me up and exalted me very high and placed me on the top of the wall."
Saint Patrick

Left brain makes one ashamed and shy and embarrassed and right brain makes one feel haughty no matter what problems arise. Basically left brain makes one weak minded and scared and right brain makes one feel invincible in the face of problems. Left brain makes one afraid of problems and right brain makes one seek problems. Essentially left brain makes a human half a person and right brain makes one cerebrally as strong as 10 men in relation to "I was blind and now I see."

Todd Andrew Rohrer

"I am Patrick, a sinner, most uncultivated and least of all the faithful and despised in the eyes of many."
Saint Patrick

This is just a moment of humility. That's a symptom of right brain dominate people. They are so powerful cerebrally they tend to be "humble" in their comments from time to time because the haughty aspect is so huge. They tend to have messiah complexes and that is tainted with "lamb complex". This of course is the philosophical aspect of subconscious. Despised by man is essentially the "opposite" aspect. So Patrick reached a degree of subconscious dominate and everyone around him assumed he was on "drugs" or "drunk".

"If I be worthy, I live for my God to teach the heathen, even though they may despise me."
Saint Patrick

So he is a Talking Buddha. He likes to teach the truth he has found. But most of the left brainers "heathens" just assumed he is crazy because they cannot grasp they are in neurosis. I do not have any friends so I do not teach anybody anything that way no one despises me.

"What these charges were, he does not say explicitly, but he writes that he returned the gifts which wealthy women gave him, did not accept payment for baptisms, nor for ordaining priests, and indeed paid for many gifts to kings and judges" Wikipedia.Com

So you see he had an aversion to money and valuables. This is simply a symptom of subconscious/ right brain extreme, its cerebral and therefore is not physically based. Money and material things are not bad it is just simply right brain is the opposite of left brain. Left is physical based and longs for money and wealth and right brain is opposite. This person reached extreme right brain dominate and then people today "party" and "have fun" and "do physical things" like get drunk in his name. I am quite certain Patrick would rather you deem him the devil and never honor him than "spit in his face" the way you do. Perhaps the only thing to do when one has no brain function is party. Don't get me wrong I am not suggesting drugs are bad or partying is bad simply because a cigar is just a cigar, but I no longer party because drugs won't kill this clarity. Drugs won't help me escape so there is no point in doing drugs. People do drugs to relive stress I have no emotions so I have no stress so drugs are pointless. I am not looking for enlightenment I am looking to be a bit more ignorant and drugs may hinder that. It probably doesn't matter anyway. I am not really one to talk since I am engaged in infinite vanity.

"If I have any worth, it is to live my life for God so as to teach these peoples; even though some of them still look down on me. "
Saint Patrick

Well Patrick you found out what "opposite" means . Opposite means you cannot win ever. The lefties simply do not like to be told they are in neurosis by accident because of the "scribe Trojan horse". I don't look down on your Patrick it is just the opposite factor is quite harsh to overcome. You tried that is perhaps all that really matters.

I just repeat myself over and over because it really does not matter anyway.

132

<Heimdall> Scribes were started in ancient Egyptian times. These people embraces memorization and attention to detail. They made good money so everyone wanted to be a scribe. The side effect of focusing on details in writing was strong emotions and made them left brain and physical based in contrast to being right brain and cerebral

<Heimdall> So scribes or being taught how to write appeared like "knowledge" the tree of knowledge but the side effect is it put everyone in neurosis so, it was a good invention that had a unwanted side effect

<Heimdall> so now here we are, and we teach all the kids how to be scribes and it "ruins them" thus the comment "they know not what they do." And "suffer the children"

My infinite vanity is only exceeded by my inability to remember I am engaged to it.

<Heimdall> If you reflect back upon our own educational training, we have been traditionally taught to master the 3 R's: reading, writing and arithmetic -- the domain and strength of the left brain.

<Heimdall> That is what put us to sleep, we ate off the tree of knowledge

Why would something do this to me? What did I do that something would do this to me? No one can understand anything Is ay and I still write and still write and I already know no can understand what I say. What did I do? I am cursed I am not blessed. I just want to go home now.3:36:37 PM

3:40:48 PM I must focus and not panic. They will understand the definition of getting hit by a Mac truck once I get warmed up. They will see who is left standing on the battlefield sooner than they think. I will not blow it like everyone else blew it. They won't turn my name into a money making opportunity Patrick, they won't be doing a whole lot of anything when I get warmed up.3:42:10 PM

Compared to god I am them; compared to them I am god. I convince the suicidal they are wise and I convince the arrogant they are suicidal.

6/18/2009 4:46:54 AM

Strong sense of hunger is abnormal and proof of neurosis.

Strong sense of taste is abnormal and proof of neurosis.

Strong sense of smell is abnormal and proof of neurosis.

Inability to tolerate ambiguity on any level is abnormal and proof of neurosis.

Strong emotions when someone dies is abnormal and proof of neurosis.

Strong sense of sadness is abnormal and proof of neurosis.

Strong sense of happiness is abnormal and proof of neurosis.

Fear in any respect is abnormal and proof of neurosis.

Anything more than slight short term memory is abnormal and proof of neurosis.

Strong focus on past and future is abnormal and proof of neurosis.

Aversion to saying any word is abnormal and proof of neurosis.

Strong sense of physical or mental fatigue is abno0rmal and proof of neurosis.

Being nervous in any respect is abnormal and proof of neurosis.5:13:11 AM

5:19:54 AM

"No one should ever say that it was my ignorance if I did or showed forth anything however small according to God's good pleasure; but let this be your conclusion and let it so be thought, that - as is the perfect truth - it was the gift of God."
Saint Patrick

Granted it is perhaps in the realm of possibility subconscious aspect is what "made man in my image" refers to but it is not proper for lemur monkeys to speculate on such complex topics such as the supernatural.

"That which I have set out in Latin is not my words but the words of God and of apostles and prophets, who of course have never lied. He who believes shall be saved, but he who does not believe shall be damned. God has spoken."
Saint Patrick

I submit none of the prophets lied but they had many issues in relation to clarifications and the use of certain words certainly confused the issue and the fact they had the "opposite" aspect to contend with meant they were certainly misunderstood to say the least.

"The Lord opened the understanding of my unbelieving heart, so that I should recall my sins."
Saint Patrick

Certain situations allowed you to become subconscious dominate. It perhaps had far more to do with the fact you were a slave and were denied the luxuries of physical things and perhaps you experienced some sort of depression or suicidal situations. This is perhaps the only way to "open up the understanding" or "break free of the neurosis" caused by the "scribe conditioning" to the extent you actually made an impact in "the battle".

"In   some   causes   silence   is   dangerous."
Saint Ambrose

If one understands a great truth and is quiet about it they will rob their self of an opportunity to help their self understand what the great truth is. This silence determination is far too complex to make an general rules about. I will one up you Ambrose and suggest, Perhaps it is wise to silent about some things and perhaps it is unwise to silent about other things and these determinations when to be loud are relative to the observer.

"There is nothing evil save that which perverts the mind and shackles the conscience."
Saint Ambrose

Perhaps the universe should read this comment by this being until they grasp what it is saying. The things ones perceives are evil or good are in fact symptoms their left brain is dominate and thus their mind is shackled. Right brain dominate person see's everything s one thing or everything is for a reason so left brain being opposite only see's everything in tight knit labels ; good and evil; bad and good; right and wrong. This label aspect is flawed because everything is relative to the observer , so it is impossible to say there is absolute good or absolute evil and this causes all conflicts of interest.

"When I go to Rome, I fast on Saturday, but in Milan I do not. Do you also follow the custom of whatever church you attend, if you do not want to give or receive scandal."
Saint Ambrose

All is fair when dealing with ones in neurosis.

"When in Rome, live as the Romans do; when elsewhere, live as they live elsewhere. "
Saint Ambrose

Attempt to blend in because the ones in neurosis tend to kill anything that is ambiguous in relation to

"A casual stroll through the lunatic asylum shows that faith does not prove anything."
Friedrich Nietzsche

When surrounded by ones in neurosis all bets are off in relation to morals. One is wise to avoid reasoning with the "darkness" because the "darkness" sees itself as "light".

"Above all the grace and the gifts that Christ(subconscious) gives to his beloved is that of overcoming self."
Francis of Assisi

The ones in neurosis are afraid of words and ideas and afraid to be afraid and afraid of the dark and afraid of monsters the do not exist. Overcoming self has far more to do with facing these things one is afraid of like words and "monsters" they build up in their head than anything else. In America we have censors on television. They do not allow people to say certain words and all that does is enforce the left brain because they indirectly are saying "these words are bad or evil." So they in fact are brainwashing people to assume words are good or bad and in turn actually make people go into further neurosis. Here is an experiment think of the worst "cuss" word you can think of and go around some people and say it by itself and watch the lunatics freak out. They can be scared by a word which is truly a symptom of how "sick" they really are.

"For   it   is   in   giving   that   we   receive."
Francis of Assisi

So I write these books and then give them away knowing ones in neurosis will read them and "freak out" and then I receive a good laugh. It is quite simple. I had an accident and I woke up and so I have extreme cerebral might so that means I "get to" toy with the neurotics and they only have two choices. Start to wake their self up or get tormented into infinity. Cerebral might makes right. I am sorry I unlocked my subconscious and I have extreme mental capacity but that doesn't mean I am going to tolerate lunatics. If lunatics desire to stay asleep then I will completely embarrass them and make them feel like dirt and I have no feelings one way or the other on the matter ever. I am on the side of the depressed and suicidal and on the side of the ones who feel like outcasts. I do not really give a dam about the reasonable and safety prone. Every time a parent scolds their child for saying "bad words" or even goes further and threatens that child if that child says "bad words" that is proof that parent is in neurosis and should not be allowed to be around children let alone raise children. That parent in neurosis may argue they have the right to raise their child the way they wants to but that again proves they are in neurosis. Just because one has reproductive organs does not give one the right to mentally and physically abuse children. There are no "bad words" so if a parent harms a child verbally or physically because that parents perceives "bad words" that means the parent is in neurosis and acting upon delusions in their mind and taking it out of the child so they are unfit to raise a child and should not be allow to ever be around children. That is in fact a fact. The opinions of ones in neurosis do not matter because they are unable to make proper determinations until they are healed of their mental illness.

"Neurosis   is   the   inability   to   tolerate   ambiguity."
Sigmund Freud

A parents hears their child say a "bad word" and the parents mentally or physically abuses that child by saying that child is "bad" or "wrong" so that harms that child mentally and also brain washes that child into thinking it is "improper" so that adult is unable to tolerate ambiguity, or simply put unable to tolerate anything besides a narrow minded set of delusional morals they have been brainwashed to subscribe to. Then a parent sees their child and say "My child is not like me so they are "messed" up." So then that parent takes that child to a psychologist and they allow that psychologist to pump that child full of medicines to make that child "normal" based on these two adults perceptions of what is "normal" so both are in fact child abusers because they are in neurosis and cannot tolerate ambiguity. So that means there are many child abusers in this country that need to be locked up swiftly. That in fact is a fact. We will let the prisoners determine which ones should be allowed to live and which ones are not fit to live. I live to toy with the neurotics.

If you vote and pass a law that says one is not allowed to use a drug no matter what the drugs is you have the inability to tolerate ambiguity and this your are in full neurosis and thus you should not be allowed to vote at all because you are insane. One in neurosis is unable to make proper determinations and so they should be heavily medicated until they get over their mental illness. There are no cults in the animal kingdom but society is full of them.7:22:37 AM

9:32:12 AM I have determined at this stage since the accident there is something going on behind the scenes. I took a short rest this morning and I had a dream. I dreamed I went to the store with a friend who is not a current friend in my life. Someone yelled my name and I turned around and the sun was in my eyes so I could not see them. The friend said just ignore them and they kept yelling my name , my first name. I turned and went into the store. When I was in the store at the counter that person came up to me and said they we angry or appeared angry and said they read my book and they were angry. My friend got in front of them and they backed off. A moment later My friend left and I 3was still at the counter and that person came up to me with a book in their hand and they said something to the effect, this is your book. I looked at the book and it was not my book it was a book along the lines of the occult or black magic and I said that is not my book and the person said I know and they tried with a hammer to nail a nail into my head, the top of my head. I was not afraid and not scared but I found I could not resist or I was too weak to resist and then I woke up from the dream. So now I wrote the dream down and I perceive it is some sort of parable. I do not perceive it is exactly what I appears to be but it makes sense relative to some things I have discussed. One thing I notice is since the accident when I have dreams they are not fear based dreams or I do nt get scred by the dreams and also I remember them perfectly. Before the accident in my life I had trouble remembering my dreams I recall I had a dream but many of the details escaped me. Now I remember dreams with perfect clarity. I even remember the book he handed me had some sort of "spider webbing" on the cover that was raised up. So it wasn't real spider web but it was a design that looked like real spider web in shape but it was not like a traditional spider web looking it was a webbing design.

So now I will interpret the dream and perhaps everyone in the world who reads this interpretation will have something to ponder.

The "snake" tempted man with "knowledge" in relation to scribe and math, and man bit off that apple and thus became under the influence of the "snake". So every time a child is born and is old enough they get "educated" and become under the influence of the "snake". So that means anyone with a strong sense of time and strong hunger is under the influence of the "snake". I perceive that is truth but I am uncertain about what this "snake" is exactly. Perhaps it is a metaphor or perhaps it is a force I am not intelligent enough to comment about. Perhaps it is something along the lines of something that appeared "good" and had "bad" side effects. So I understand this "waxing anger" I experience is in fact the "snake" aspect leaving me and it appears to get stronger as time goes on because it is attempting to hold on to me. I recall during the last book I spoke with an English teacher in a chartroom and I suggested I would send him my book to read and I said but it does have many grammar errors because of the accident I am unable to use commas properly and he said, well do not bother because I am an English teacher and I do not tolerate improper grammar so I won't read it.

"Neurosis is the inability to tolerate ambiguity."
Sigmund Freud

Perhaps Freud was a bit more intelligent than anyone gave him credit for.

"The right brain processes information differently than the left brain." Simply put I am unable to spell properly and use commas properly but that does not mean I am stupid that means I am using the "right brain thinking is difficult to put into words because of its complexity" complex aspect of the brain which does not pander to such foolishness such as commas and elementary logic suggested by sentence formation rules. So before you determine I am stupid for not being able to use commas properly you perhaps better use all the elementary logic you are capable of in your neurosis so that you do not make a jaw bone of an ass out of yourself with your "not complex" determinations. I ponder how many right brain dominate people have been put on drugs so they will become "normal" when in fact they were normal and they we in fact abused because the people who determined they were not normal were in fact in neurosis and were not fit to make any determinations in regards to who is normal and who is not let alone be able to prescribe medicine that effects psychological brain chemistry. Perhaps it would have been wiser to just give these people who have power to write prescription for mental condition sticks of dynamite because the dynamite would be far more humane treatment than to tell a person who is not in neurosis they are in neurosis and then force medicine down their throat on the contexts of "this will make you well" and "we care about you." If one is in neurosis they can never help anyone they can only hurt people because what they perceive is help is actually hurt because they are in neurosis. So in general if you have a strong sense of time, strong sense of hunger and you have more than silenced fear every time you thought you helped someone you only harmed them. Perhaps you will get good and upset about that but your disbelief will never ever change reality or the fact that comment is absolute truth.

So every time you grade a child in school and perceive that's helps them that harms them. And every time a person votes to allow that type of school to continue they harm children. Why don't you go into your isolation chamber and sit and ponder that for about 39 days and don't eat any food in that time and if you make out alive give me a call and we will discuss reality.10:28:07 AM

Everything I type in my books is truth, parables and out of context at the exact same time so unless you have brain function you won't understand any of it. That is the reality of the situation you are facing.

"right brain thinking is difficult to put into words **because of its complexity**" Do you understand if you have as strong sense of time and have strong fear and have strong hunger that means as far as thinking you are not capable of complexity in contrast to right brain/ subconscious. You are not capable of complexity and thus you are in neurosis."Great minds think alike" denotes great minds(subconscious/right brain minds) see everything is alike or is one thing or is whole. Great minds see everything as one thing; minds in neurosis only see separations and labels and cannot stand ambiguity.

So Moses wrote the book of genesis, I understand he did, and used an apple as the fruit on the tree of "knowledge" and here we are 2500 years later and the ideal teachers desk has an apple on it. One might suggest how can that be possible that he knew that. I have attempted to suggest in my books I had an accident and a very rare accident and I went all the way or the full measure and unlocked subconscious and I am attempting to say words that others might find valuable in unlocking it because it is so powerful and so "wise" and so potentially world changing if people start to "wake up" that the entire human civilization would change and we simply put our self to sleep directly or indirectly as a result of "scribe and mathematics" and he can keep those things but be aware they have this side effect that makes us go to "sleep" mentally speaking. I am not special. I am not smart. I just accidentally unlocked the powerhouse of the mind. But I am not allowed to preach because then one might suggest I have trouble with ambiguity. My mindset is, I am typing to myself in my diary. That means I aint talking to you. That means I do not want to talk to you ever. I prefer to talk to myself over talking to you. I have been judged enough by you so I do not plan on ever talking to you again. Even if one day I go in public and speak no matter what you think I understand I am talking to myself now matter who is there. I only talk to myself from now on. I talk to myself because I understand the alternative.11:27:26 AM

11:46:52 AM If ones lays out a linear line for mental states there would be on one end emotional wrecks or people who are suicidal then in the middle would be the lukewarm and they have some control over emotions and then at the other extreme would be ones in nirvana and they have nearly no emotional attachments. The linear outlook of this in error because in reality I can communicate better with those considered to be emotional wrecks because it is not a line it is in fact a circle. I went all the way down to emotional suicidal wreck and went one step further and appeared in nirvana or emotionless or subconscious dominate. So I am unable to communicate with the lukewarm as easily as the emotional wrecks because opposites attract. The opposite of lukewarm is lukewarm, so they tend to run in herds because they assume the emotional wrecks are bad and the ones in nirvana are bad. The lukewarm assume anything that is not lukewarm is bad.11:51:04 AM

I talk to myself because I understand I should not attempt to reason with the alternative.

"Never try to reason with a demon. Many demons will try to convince you of reasons why they should be able to stay on earth or in some sort of life form."

Perhaps you assume I am getting "spiritual" perhaps you should avoid assuming.

""We support compassion even for the most curious, smallest and least sympathetic animals," PETA spokesman Bruce Friedrich said Wednesday. "We believe that people, where they can be compassionate, should be, for all animals.""

http://hamptonroads.com.nyud.net/2009/06/peta-wishes-obama-hadnt-swatted-fly

If these people truly seek to help all animals then they should stop eating all together. If one picks a fruit from a tree and then the wash it off they are killing many "smallest and least sympathetic animals". They are in fact killing million of "smallest and least sympathetic animals" every time they wash their hands. So then they go on and suggest "where they can be compassionate, should be, for all animals." Where they can be compassionate is strictly relative to the observer. We were relatively compassionate to the whales because there are a few left. Compassion in life is not real it is simply an ideal. The Taliban are relatively compassionate to the Americans because there are some Americans left. The Americans are relatively compassionate to the Taliban because there are some Taliban left. The Israeli's are relatively compassionate to the Palestinians because there are some Palestinians left. Hamas is relatively compassionate to the Israelis because there are some Israeli's left.

Hitler was relatively compassionate to the Jews because there are some Jews left. The allies were relatively compassionate to the Germans because there are some Germans left. A serial killer is relatively compassionate to hookers because there are some hookers left. The government is relatively compassionate to people who use drugs because there are some who use drugs who are not in jail yet.

My Psychologist was relatively compassionate to me because she only gave me a bottle of 30 Paxil instead of a bottle of 60 so I only half way killed myself and thus I am trapped writing infinite crappy books for the rest of my life. Teachers are relatively compassionate to judge children when the child does not spell a word properly because not all children grow up emotional wrecks because some end up killing their self before they get to grow up because they become shy, and embarrassed because of the "scribe" left brain, brainwashing. Compassion is a label and right after someone says they are compassionate they think to their self "I am so good and compassionate." That is what is called a narcissist. I submit I am nothing and I never will be anything. You may be able to match that statement but you will never top it. Humans had compassion on humans because there are still some of us left.

I am quite certain many assume they are good and then they use their elementary logic to conclude they know what is good for others. I convince the ones who think they are good that they are arrogant and I convince the ones who think they are bad they are meek. I have to write about something or I will never finish my infinite books will I?1:51:42 PM

An idiot perceives they are intelligent when surrounded by other idiots; a genius perceives they are surrounded by idiots at all times.

I have added what I translate as what it is saying in ().

"Once upon a time a man looked into the reverse(opposite or contrary) side of a mirror and, not seeing this face and head, he became insane(sane). How unnecessary it is for a man to become insane(sane) merely because he carelessly(accidentally) looks into the reverse side of a mirror! It is just as foolish and unnecessary for a person to go on suffering(being left brain physical based) because he does not attain Enlightenment (right brain cerebral based)where he expects to find it. There is no failure in Enlightenment; the failure lies in those people who, for a long time, have sought Enlightenment in their discriminating minds(label based is left brain) , not realizing that theirs are not true minds but are imaginary minds that have been caused by the accumulation of greed(physical based) and illusion covering and hiding their true mind(subconscious mind/right brain)."

Teachings of Buddha

"Say this for the U.S. space program: we may have spent the past 40 years mostly ignoring the moon, but when we go back, we go back with a bang."

I assure you one month with slight sense of time is extremely long so 40 years is very close to infinity according to my perspective. If someone asked me how long has it been in the seven months since this accident my answer would be unnamable in relation to **"thought processes vague"**. That's a very accurate description, everything is vague, so-so, nothingness no high's and no lows , purgatory, limbo. These are all accurate descriptions. I cannot explain how I feel it is to vague. I am mindful I am pumping words out swiftly but I cannot tell if they are good or bad right or wrong, I just monologue thoughts that come into my head in real time but that is not "dangerous". I figure out I need to eat but there are some complex things that change.

"In the past few years, the moon has once again become the hot place to go. Three countries with little spacefaring history — Japan, China and India — have all sent probes moonward since 2007, and China in particular has made it clear that it plans to return, first with more robot ships, then with astronauts."

http://www.time.com/time/health/article/0,8599,1905344,00.html?cnn=yes

This is a positive way to release anger and frustration because one has much to explore in space and ironically space cannot be defeated. It helps humans focus away from these earth centered territorial issues that cause us great harm. I look at earth as a freebie spaceport. The freebie spaceport has oxygen but all the other spaceports we need to make to explore the infinite void require us to figure out how to make oxygen using what we learned on the freebie spaceport. There simply will not be wars in space because space itself is the war. There won't be enough energy left to go to war with others in space because just being in space and remaining alive is a huge victory in itself. The realities in space are not the realities on earth. This means ones has to ponder which is the absolute reality, space or earth? Perhaps earth is a bubble and what happens on earth is not absolute reality but simply reality based on the fact earth is a bubble. Earth is shielded from space so earth is bias. So what happens on earth is not exactly what is happening in space so which is the absolute true reality? Perhaps our solar system is also shielded from the rest of space so then our solar system is also shielded from absolute true reality. So then what we experience in our solar system is not exactly what is happening in deep space. Perhaps our galaxy is also shielded from absolute true space. So that would perhaps means we are shielded by earth's atmosphere, solar system "atmosphere", galaxy "atmosphere" and then after we get through all of those shields we reach true absolute reality. So perhaps it is wise to start launching probes in all directions in the off chance we have a good accident, so to speak.

<Lestat9> Jesus suggested "suffer the children" I am mindful of what that rerfers to if you wish to hear that understanding but it is perhaps a bit deep

<frink> like when i suffer my kind incessant whys and hows :)

* JuneNY is now known as JuneBBL

<Lestat9> demotic script and dena (arithmatics)

<Lestat9> When children are taught how to be scribes or write and math, they become left brain dominate

<Lestat9> They are insitally right brain becauise that side see's everything as a whole or they have no sense of time

<Lestat9> they need to be that way to saty in the womb

<Lestat9> So

<Lestat9> eating off the tree of knowledge means we invented script and math

<Lestat9> and then we all became left brain dominate and a side effect of that is strong physical materialistic attachments

<Lestat9> the only remedy is to condition one away from fear liek watch a scary movie and sit in the dark and face your fears

<Lestat9> so suffer the children

<Lestat9> means the children are taught to be scribes and math, and thus are into this bad side effect

<Lestat9> of emotions and physical based thinking

<Lestat9> and strong sense of time and strong hunger

<Lestat9> so demotic is perhaps demonic misspelled

<Lestat9> so we ate off the tree of knowledge and fell from grace because we became ashamed and embarrassed and that is a side effect of the scribe learning, strong emotions like shyness and shame and embarrassment, so Adam and eve put on their clothes

<Lestat9> so written language is a Trojan horse, it looks inviting but it had some nasty side effects

<Lestat9> now biblically the snake tempted us with knowledge

<Lestat9> I am not intelligent enough to speak on supernatural powers

<Lestat9> I had an accident 8 months ago and lost my sense of time and now i write books and explain everything that comes to mind in real time.

<Lestat9> I cover many topic and i am pleased with the torah the new testament and the Quran and Buddha teachings i perceive they all are about this eating off the tree of knowledge

<Curious> :)

I was perhaps "tapped" to clarify. Some are in a hurry to go nowhere.

9:24:01 PM I just got back from the store and I saw people and everyone is perfect. I am uncertain who is doing all these improper things in the world but it wasn't anyone at that store9:24:37 PM

1:58:06 PM (Socrates)He believed such a flight would indicate a fear of death, which he believed no true philosopher has. Socrates turned down the pleas of Crito to attempt an escape from prison.

This is the harsh reality of dominate subconscious/right brain. Jesus could have fled and I understand his disciples suggested many valid ways he could escape his certain fate. Crito suggest 'Socrates they are going to make you drink the hemlock and you will die so please run away and save yourself." Those who try to save their self will lose their self and those who lose their self will find their self.

Here is how the "sane" judge Socrates "that he was not the proponent of a philosophy but an individual with a method of undermining the fabric of Athenian society, a charge carried by the 500-man jury of Athenians which sentenced him to death."

They determined he was a revolutionary and because of the fact "Neurosis is the inability to handle ambiguity" and the fact "right brain" is opposite, he stood no chance, so they made this being kill himself , and he did it willingly because he knew one sure fact that Patrick understood also "I am Patrick, a sinner, most uncultivated and least of all the faithful and despised in the eyes of many."

Yes there were insane and whatever they did they were doomed to be slaughtered at the hands of the "sane" simply because heaven nor earth can counter act the "opposite" factor. Left and right. One sits at the right hand and the one of the left slaughters it because it is ambiguous.

"Perhaps the most interesting facet of this is Socrates' reliance on what the Greeks called his "daemonic sign", an averting (ἀποτρεπτικός apotreptikos) inner voice Socrates heard only when he was about to make a mistake. It was this sign that prevented Socrates from entering into politics. In the Phaedrus, we are told Socrates considered this to be a form of "divine madness", the sort of insanity that is a gift from the gods and gives us poetry, mysticism, love, and even philosophy itself. Alternately, the sign is often taken to be what we would call "intuition"; however, Socrates' characterization of the phenomenon as "daemonic" suggests its origin is divine, mysterious, and independent of his own thoughts.

So Socrates certainly was aware of this "separate Voice". I call it intuition and I submit I appears to be one is possessed and I am unable to speak about supernatural powers, but I also understand subconscious is extremely powerful. It makes these aspects of the mind very pronounced. Ass I suggested in earlier books in the Torn Law. I can clearly sense this "subconscious" aspect with much mental power then the "left" aspect concerned with safety and making everything simple and strict two option logic then the Torn aspect that is attempting to do what is "right". So Socrates was explaining perfectly the aspects of the right brain, creativity, open mindedness and he demonstrated just like all the other "impactful" beings in history, they are willing to face death at the hands of the "sane" when it comes down to it." the sort of insanity that is a gift from the gods and gives us poetry, mysticism, love, and even philosophy itself."

Yes Buddha suggested the "sane" which denotes he perceived he was insane. Jesus suggested he was "the light" and they were the darkness. Mohammed called them the "infidels". But when it came right down to it, the battle always ends the same. They get slaughtered because the ones in neurosis have the inability to handle ambiguity.

"He was, nevertheless, found guilty of corrupting the minds of the youth of Athens" so Socrates suggested perhaps maybe the youth should attempt to be slightly less "scribe /mathematics" focused so they would not end up with the harsh side effects called emotions like shame and embarrassment, and the "sane" said, that's a threat because "scribe/math" or the apple on the tree of knowledge are "light" and not "darkness' so you drink this poison because you certainly cannot be correct you are insane and so we are going to make you kill yourself and if you do not we will kill you." Socrates purposefully gave a defiant defense to the jury because "he believed he would be better off dead" Yes Socrates when one wakes up in an insane asylum one is certainly better off dead.

"Socrates came to the conclusion that, while each man thought he knew a great deal and was very wise, they in fact knew very little and were not really wise at all."

Yes Socrates the ones who "know" knew you should kill yourself because you were so far beyond their ability to grasp, they knew it was not they who were insane beyond understanding but you.

"Socrates explicitly denies accepting payment for teaching." That is the only proof one ever needs to understand. The proof is in the pudding."Give Caesar what is his and give me what is mine."

That is a nice way of saying the "sane" want money and the "insane" get the slaughter.

Now I will clarify something else.

'Allah cursed the Jews and the Christians because they took the graves of their Prophets as places for praying."

"They(sane, lefties, one's with strong sense of time, physical focused) took the graves of their Prophets as places for praying(turned them into physical shrines)" They made Idols. It's all through and through. One group slaughters people for grains of sand they perceive "god" gave them. But the reality is, the "sane" always turn physical things into shrines that is their nature. They slaughter people to get close to these physical shrines. They are essentially "physically attached".

Buddha made sure to burn his body, Jesus made sure they never find his body because they knew the "sane" would build temples around them and then charge admission and make a ton of money.

The **Sacred Relic of the tooth of Buddha** (Buddh-dantya) is venerated in Sri Lanka as a relic of the founder of Buddhism.

But one of the "sane" found Buddha's tooth and now there is a huge golden shrine(golden calf) to make an idol of his tooth. So at least Jesus made sure no one found his body and I am certain the "sane" would love to find his body and then build shrines to the sky to prove to the world how much they understood what he was saying.

I recall reading one of these "Saints" suggesting "where am I to go?" That is right where are you to go, there is no where to run, you are on the "right opposite" side and you are surrounded by the "left side" and you already know you are not going to win, the best you can do is lose gracefully.

That's the entire reality, somehow mankind discovered "scribes and math" and determined everyone should be indoctrinated into "scribe and math" and it seemed like such a great idea and wise and clever and righteous, but the side effect was, you lost the intelligent aspect of the brain and the only way to ever get it back is to put yourself in a scary situation and fight the fear and kill the fear and then maybe you will get a little bit of the intelligent aspect back, but maybe not, maybe its gone forever.

" which he believed no true philosopher has." Jesus said I defeated death, his fear of death. But it is perhaps not that harsh, just maybe watch a scary movie and sit alone in the dark, because your mind at the "left" state is telling you a scary monster will jump through the door and kill you, so you are facing death. Then consider facing "embarrassment" that is perhaps a fate worse than death. These things are not really emotions, they are simply a factor that arose as a side effect of the teaching of "scribe" when you were young. Love is not real, fear is not real, hate is not real, they are side effects of a drugs called "knowledge" in the form of written scribe. You cannot take away scribe and math, that's impossible, but you can lessen their effects with emotional conditioning, PEHAPS.

So yes Jesus healed the sick(ones in neurosis) and healed the blind(ones in neurosis) did he really heal literal blind people , certainly not. He used strategic words to convince the ones who fell from "grace" and perhaps assisted some to get away from these side effect caused by eating off the tree of "knowledge". I cannot fly and if I could fly, I would fly the hell out of here swiftly. I am still here so that proves I cannot fly, but mentally I can traverse the ages and I am pleased with that.

The archeologists put a damper on my illusions of grandeur when they suggested we are all lemur monkeys so it may take 1000 books before I can explain that one away. I certainly am not at the level of clarity to suggest my infinite wrath potential is a lemur monkey because although I am 99.99% insane I have .01 % bit of sanity left that says "Hold off on calling women lemur monkeys"4:00:39 PM

12:08:10 AM It is late and I am sloppy. This is a comment by Buddha.

"Whatever priests & contemplatives, teachers of kamma, who declare that pleasure & pain are self-made, even that is dependent on contact. Whatever priests & contemplatives, teachers of kamma, who declare that pleasure & pain are other-made... self-made & other-made... neither self-made nor other-made, but arise spontaneously, even that is dependent on contact."

", but arise spontaneously" I perceive this is along the lines of "The devil made me do it." It perhaps suggest some outside force creates these "pleasure & pain" / emotions." Contemplatives" that is another word for what most understand as philosophers. Scientists are a good example. They say why and perhaps to their self a lot of course many are asking "maybe if I do this "or "what if".

"even that is dependent on contact." is perhaps suggesting we are mimics. That is a characteristic of right brain/subconscious mind. I am subconscious dominate/right brain but for one with strong sense of time, their subconscious aspect is SUB or veiled by emotions caused by the scribe conditioning. So he is suggesting everything happens because of "contact" or as a result of stimuli in relation to all forces act as a result of a reaction to an equal or opposite force. Without stimuli there is no contact. This is in relation to physical and mental situations. This is also in relation to do not judge others. A harsh comment to someone is a stimuli and a kind comment to someone is a stimuli that is in reality a "contact" that will trigger another reaction. This is also a slippery slope." Good" deeds can be perceived to be weakness. I noticed if I say "perhaps" to often in chat rooms people become upset. This word is maybe some kind of mental trigger. One in left brain is often uncomfortable with the word perhaps because it goes against "knowing". "Perhaps" is anti-knowing in relation to the tree of Knowledge. Also "script" is based on knowing. "Do you "know" how spell?""Who taught you to spell?" These are sarcastic "insults". They are "contact"."We "know" we are on the side of righteousness." That is very powerful contact. One can simply go into an conversation and say "perhaps' to a powerful contact like that and they will get a "negative" contact back.12:30:38 AM

""I know for my family the only question we will be answering is how many people are in our home," she said. "We won't be answering any information beyond that, because the Constitution doesn't require any information beyond that."

http://washingtontimes.com/news/2009/jun/17/exclusive-minn-lawmaker-fears-census-abuse/

Yeah that's the odd thing about America. If the constitution does not say one cannot do certain things relatively speaking one can simply ignore them. Perhaps this member of congress is not really afraid of giving personal information, perhaps they are simply letting the government know, no matter what laws you pass if it does not directly harm someone else one is simply free to pursue it based on their right to "life , liberty and pursuit of happiness". It perhaps is a grand experiment as Freud suggested. One is free to test the limits of the Constitution and the Declaration of Independence simply because the government is not "god". The government is simply an entity the people have infinite compassion to allow and tolerate, and nothing more.

"The right of the people to be secure in their persons, houses, papers, and effects, against unreasonable searches and seizures, shall not be violated, and no Warrants shall issue, but upon probable cause, supported by Oath or affirmation, and particularly describing the place to be searched, and the persons or things to be seized."

This whole aspect of "government agencies" being allowed to search ones house when they are not around or in secrecy is not allowing one to be secure in their houses ad papers and effects. If a person is worried about the government searching through their house and papers and effects when they are away from home, then they may start to determine there is some watering to do in

145

relation to the tree of liberty." and particularly describing the place to be searched, and the persons or things to be seized."

Denotes no authority in the universe can authorize searching ones effects or home no matter how many "scary monsters" they have invented to justify doing so." supported by Oath or affirmation" this denotes a person who upholds the constitution and can authorize such a search as long as they work within the guidelines of the constitution. The Legislative can pass laws into infinity saying they can search a person house without following the guidelines of the constitution because of "monsters" they have haunting in their scared and frightened little heads, but they simply do not matter. No government can abridge the constitution no matter how many "monsters" and "fear issues" they have in their head. Heimdall is sorry you are scared of the dark but you cannot negate the constitution because if one starts ignoring the Constitution then one might start realizing the Constitution is 3what enables the government to exist and that means if any part of the Constitution is abridged then the government is no longer relevant either.

The Congress passed the 16th Amendment on July 12, 1909, and it was ratified on February 3, 1913.

This is the right to collect income to and this is in relation to the passing of income tax initially in 1862 "to save us from the scary south" in the civil war, so it was a scare tactic. So as long as congress submits they extorted money from the people using scare tactics in 1862 and continued that trend to justify taking peoples income tax so they could line their pockets with money.

Simply put, If I have no fear of anything ever and 300 million scared little babies who sign away my right and freedoms at the drop of a hat, that does not mean I have to tolerate that in relation to "when all around you everyone is losing their head". I am not afraid of anything, so if you are and you decide to sign away all of my rights to be "safe" you better be dam ready for revolution. I will make your worst nightmares reality and then I will ensure you no longer are afraid and start signing my freedoms. You have no right to give away my freedoms. I do not give a dam who you think you are I have no fear of anything ever. So that means I have no fear of you, ever. I have determined you are the tyrant, it does not matter what you think after I determine you are a tyrant. If one person in the group of "we the people" determines you are a tyrant, the revolution has started. I did not sign away my freedoms. I did not sign away my constitutional rights, but you did, so the burden is around your neck not my neck. Swiftly "alter" or swiftly be "abolished". I do not give a dam what you think your laws say and I do not give a dam who you think you are. You are simply someone who is passing through and my only purpose is to make sure the constitution is intact for the next ones who pass though. Everything else is irrelevant especially the ones who abridge the constitution using fear tactics and extortion. Simply put the government is only as powerful as the people suggest it is.

"Over grown military establishments are under any form of government inauspicious to liberty, and are to be regarded as particularly hostile to republican liberty." George Washington

This simply means when you have a huge spy agency(NSA,CIA,FBI,MILITARY) one is asking for a revolution because they are simply tyrannical forces and are counter productive to liberty. And that goes for these powerful police forces also. All that crap is locking up more of the "people" than anything else. They are just locking up people for many stupid crimes that harm no one directly. So they simply exist to infringe on liberty more than anything so they are better off watering the tree liberty when they start thinking they are more important then the people. That is how I perceive it because they are locking up people for "persuading happiness" in relation to drugs and many other aspects. "Drugs" are not hurting anyone directly, and they are not hurting the people who use them either, but you locking up people for that is harming their "right to pursue happiness" so the solution is to alter or be abolished. What I perceive in a universe of relativity is all that is real. You have a right to convince everyone I am evil or bad or a tyrant but I also have a right to convince everyone you are a tyrant and to swiftly water the tree of liberty with your ass. So one might say the revolution has started because a judge once told me in a court of law "If you want to kill yourself there is nothing anyone can do." If I want to drink, there is nothing anyone can do, If I want to smoke, If I want to talk, If I want to yell, If I want to incite revolution, there is nothing anyone can do but they are free to attempt to get in my as long as they are comfortable in their death shroud because Heimdall is very comfortable in his.8:32:24 AM

"Some day, following the example of the United States of America, there will be a United States of Europe. "
George Washington

Look at this, Washington called it right. European Union. Perhaps you should stop spitting in Washington's face with your attempts to shred the constitution because apparently his ability to predict things 200 years into the future surpasses your ability to see two feet in front of your nose.

"The Constitution is the guide which I never will abandon."
George Washington

This simply means if Washington was here and he saw that you abridged freedom of speech and right to privacy he would slice your neck from ear to ear. No question about it. So you could consider yourself lucky to even be alive and consider altering the damage you have done to the constitution because my patience is infinitely thin.

"The marvel of all history is the patience with which men and women submit to burdens unnecessarily laid upon them by their governments. "
George Washington

Yes we in America as in we the people, have infinite compassion because he allow the government even when it spits in our face, even when i robs us of billions of dollars. We tolerate it but the thing is, we certainly do not have to tolerate it at all, ever, into infinity. If the government blinks wrong, we abolish it and we are in the right to do so.

"The time is near at hand which must determine whether Americans are to be free men or slaves."
George Washington

Perhaps he is predicting the future again. Perhaps he and I are on the same wave lengths relatively speaking. Perhaps I should never speak of such thing because something might happen to me or perhaps I write what I write in hopes something in this universe can muster a little fear in me anymore.

I have determined nothing in this universe we can scare old Heimdall so I am just attempting to find something that might make me feel again. I am just trying to feel again so don't me or better yet, one would be very wise not to get in the way of my "pursuit of happiness."

"War - An act of violence whose object is to constrain the enemy(the government), to accomplish our(the people) will." George Washington

Washington is certainly the revolutionary. Perhaps the spy agencies should keep an eye on him because his eyes are black with rage, relative to my perception.

"When we assumed the Soldier, we did not lay aside the Citizen." George Washington

This is simply saying, no matter what government agency you work for or what army you are in, when it comes down to it, you are a spy for the "people". Anyone in any government agency of army is a spy for the people and nothing more. We the people, have spies everywhere, the government has no spies and no safety ever. All the soldiers in all the armies in America are simply "plants" so when the revolution starts "we the people" make sure we have all the good weapons to use against the government. Perhaps if the government has fear they are pissing their self like a little frog after that last comment.

"Worry is the interest paid by those who borrow trouble." George Washington

Worry and stress are symptom of fear and uncertainly and these feelings hinder clear thoughts.

There is nothing to fear but people who fear because the sacred and stressed are not thinking properly for having fear in the first place. A frightened scared person is a danger to their self and to those around them.8:57:38 AM

Some people get their 15 minutes of fame and some have been in their 15 minutes of fame for thousands of years.

Maybe if you got "tapped" you would do the best you can based on your situation as I am attempting to do the best I can based on my situation and maybe I am attempting to do what I perceive you would do in this situation and perhaps I am unable to it as gracefully as you would be able to do it but I try to be graceful and I try to do what I think you would do in this situation. I cannot tell for a fact if I would do what you would do but I can only follow my intuition and try to do what I perceive you would do in this situation. Perhaps I write swiftly because I am attempting to keep up with how fast I perceive you would write in this situation. Perhaps I write swiftly because I understand I am not able to keep up with how fast you would be writing in this situation.

I say tomato and they hear potato.

Many have arguments that fear and being afraid is righteous and at the same time they understand there is nothing to fear but fear itself. It takes quite a strategic speaker to talk them out of that kind of neurosis. Perhaps some kind of Heimdall creature could accomplish such an impossible task. This Jesus being and Moses being and Mohammed being and Buddha being "healed the blind" and in relation to the fact of what extreme neurosis the people they healed were in it was truly a miracle of all miracles. Perhaps Heimdall could also accomplish such an impossibility that these otherwise beings accomplished. Perhaps a Heimdall creature could write books swiftly and "heal the blind" and some may attempt to stop old Heimdall but his words would act so swiftly their attempts would be in vain.

Sigmund Freud - Neurosis is the inability to tolerate ambiguity. This is in relation to left brain dominate/sense of time people who are forced to learn scribe and math at a young age, they tend to have short tempers and use many labels, they say this is good and this is bad, that is intolerance to ambiguity or Judgment of what is different.

I will make this very clear. No matter what anyone says ever, you do everything you have to do to condition yourself away from fear. You go sit in a thousand cemeteries at night alone and if anyone insults you assume they are insane and ignore them and know you are not going to be manipulated by illusions any longer. Being a seeker is strictly a solo project for ones with courage. If you wish to remain asleep that is wise in relation to the fact dying in your sleep is quite painless. Perhaps that one completely escaped your logical ability.

6/21/2009 11:36:15 AM My "waxing anger" is quite intense today so I am going to start off my hanging myself with my words and then round that out with some clarity.

This is a website. http://jumperpool.com

This site discusses people who have jumped from the skyway. One particular story there is about a man. He was perhaps not a wealthy man. He perhaps was in fact a poor man. He got a very bad toothache. He left a note in his car before he jumped to his death and he said something to the effect, "I am not suicidal I just cannot deal with this pain from the toothache." Now delusional brain dead mole crickets will attempt to use their elementary logic to explain how this guy could have gone to a doctor to get pain medicine so he could go on for a bit longer. That is what I expect from brain dead mole crickets. When America started pain relief in the form of medicine was available to anyone because back then people trusted other people and they also respected other people judgments. This is called freedom. Perhaps the ones who determine who can dispense pain relief drugs and who cannot should contact me because for one I eat brain dead mole crickets for no reason and for two, I want to know why you have determined you are god. You assume you are god and then this poor being has no money and has no ability to buy the pain relief because all of the one's who have determined they are god, put so many loopholes in front of this beings ability to get pain relief that this man determined it is better to jump off that bridge than go through the red tape to get a prescription just to show up a pharmacy and explain to them why he cannot afford some medicine so he can take the pain a bit longer. So I want the brain dead mole crickets who determine who can and cannot decide for their self if they need pain relief to contact me because I am going to take you to that bridge and throw your ass off into the rocks on your head, and perhaps that will allow you to get over delusions that you are god and can determine who gets pain relief and who does not. A judge told me "If you want to kill yourself there is nothing anyone can do about it." At one time in this country we respected everyone's own judgments. If a person is in pain that is no time to start the "control freak" act in relation to pain relief medicine. Doctors serve only one purpose to advise a patient and suggest their diagnosis of what ails that patient. A doctor is not a drug dispenser. Pain is relative to the observer. Some people are in mental pain and if they decide they need drugs to relive that, that is their right and you are not god so you do not get to tell them what they can or cannot take or create a structure of "give me money and I will relieve your pain". Everyone has different pain thresholds. You are not god so you cannot make that determination. If you perceive you are god then you write a book and tell everyone you are god and convince them you can determine who is in pain and who is not, until then you keep your trap shut. You delusional laws made it difficult for this man to get pain relief easily and so you killed him with your laws banning pain medicine because you do not trust anyone judgments, so you are against freedom or choice and freedom of thought and freedom for a person to make their own determination, so you are a tyrant and I have decided to water the tree of liberty with your ass, boy. So you go to this site and you spend the rest of your life if you have to and don't take a break and don't eat, you find the story of this poor being who had no money to go through the "money trap" to get a little pain relief to assist him with his pain, and when you find you remind yourself your delusional control insanity laws, killed this man as sure as rain. And when you try to use your elementary logic to persuade yourself your insane control always over who gets pain relief and who does, you remind yourself you're a brain dead mole cricket and you brain function at all because you got brain washed as a child by an education system that determined it is god and can tell everyone what is best. I woke up and determined to bring the entire house of cards down and I beg you to get in my, boy. You spend the rest of your life searching that web site for a man who jumped off the skyway bridge because he didn't have enough money to afford pain medication for his toothache and then you ponder what you do to people on a daily basis with your fear based elementary logic focused laws that rob people who their right to determine their own destiny because you do not trust them. I understand one thing , there is going to be some major altering in this country of my birth or there is going to be a blood bath and I am pleased with either result. I do not mind repeat performances. I perceive have hung myself enough for this moment.

 Now on to the slight clarity aspect of today's writing. These comments all have the word drunk in them.

The word drink in these comments have many definitions that denotes complexity. That of course is right brain territory. I have inserted the clarification words into these comments.

Oba 1:16 For as ye have drunk (achieved)upon my holy mountain(right brain), so shall all the heathen(left brainers) drink continually(seek material gain but never be satisfied), yea, they shall drink(seek material satisfaction), and they shall swallow down(so anything for a "buck"), and they shall be as though they had not been.(never find satisfaction in material things and material control)

Luk 5:39 No man also having drunk old wine(right brain how we are born or how we are naturally before the script conditioning makes us left brain) straightway desireth new(left brain): for he saith, The old is better.(the right cerebral complexity is much better than the left brain material focused elementary logic)

Luk 13:26 Then shall ye begin to say, We have eaten and drunk((heard the wisdom of the right brain, in relation to everyone has moments of clarity as the result of the right brain) in thy presence, and thou hast taught in our streets(ones who are extreme right brain IE: the "prophets, tend to speak a lot, the right brain is a motor mouth).

Perhaps you perceive I write books swiftly, I assure you I have not even begun to write.

I will remind you when I get warmed up.

Joh 2:10 And saith unto him, Every man(children) at the beginning(at birth) doth set forth good wine(right brain); and when men have well drunk (from the tree of knowledge/scribe), then that which is worse(left brain is accomplished): but thou hast kept the good wine until now(the right brain is still there but it is then silenced in relation to the crescent moon, the right brain is veiled after the scribe conditioning, it's all "darkness" but just a sliver of "light" shows through).

Eph 5:18 And be not drunk with wine(this is in relation to one does not need to drink actual wine to be drunk because right brain dominate makes one "high" and in relation to how the people at the "bar" said to the disciples "are you drunk?" and the disciples said, no its 3pm we are not drunk and in relation to why people say to me "what drugs are you on?", wherein is excess(this denotes if you condition yourself into right brain, you do not need drugs because the drugs you take to "get high" can only give you shades of feeling the right brain, so its not permanent, so people drink their self to death to try to achieve dominate right brain); but be filled with the Spirit(but condition away from fear and say perhaps a lot and you will have be right brain dominate and you won't need those drugs to feel the "high" you will be high 24/7 or "wide awake". Please do not assume I am preaching, in reality I prefer no one get near my pool.

Rev 17:2 With whom the kings(left brain physical mindset people) of the earth(physical) have committed fornication(lust for material things , greed for material things/left brain symptom), and the inhabitants(people in general have bitten off the apple of knowledge by focusing to much on scribe and short term memory studies.) of the earth have been made drunk(drunk/conditioned into the left brain physical based aspect) with the wine of her fornication(left with physical based slight clarity and bad side effects such as greed, lust, material cravings) .

Rev 18:3 For all nations have drunk of the wine(scribe/math aspects) of the wrath(which cause side effects like physical wrath and physical unwanted qualities) of her fornication, and the kings(physically material focused left brainers) of the earth have committed fornication with her, and the merchants(material based left brains) of the earth are waxed(increasing physical wealth although they can never be satisfied with physical wealth) rich through the abundance of her delicacies(no matter how much physical wealth the lefter's get they are never happy ever into infinity that is simply the side effect of the scribe/math/short term memory focus the "apple" constitutes).

151

Deu 32:42 I will make mine arrows drunk with blood(I don't tell you what this means), and my sword(words) shall devour flesh(lefters; flesh denotes physical based); and that with the blood of the slain(tyrants(lefters) and of the captives(the ones enslaves by the lefters or taken advantage of by the "extreme material focused lefters, the guy who jumped off the skyway because he couldn't afford pain relief is a captive), from the beginning of revenges upon the enemy.(this suggest I will drowned this entire universe with my words and my books and they have to tolerate it or I get to slaughter them for infringing on my freedom 0f speech.)

Perhaps you have come to an understanding. I will now discuss something of importance.12:43:20 PM

12:51:02 PM

"jcesar at 2009-06-14 18:25 CET:

How   can   someone   fail   a   suicide   30   times   ? Must be the stupidest man alive. "

 This is comment from someone before they read my books I give freely on pirate sites to encourage people to assume they are getting away with something because they do not realize I write the books and I am giving them freely, so they assume they are "stealing" and thus are more prone to read the books. This of course is the problem with making too many strict laws to prohibit ones ability to experiment in relation to doing things that may potentially harm them directly but not directly harm anyone else. The subconscious/right brain is not a retard. You tell a person they cannot use a drug, the subconscious/right will adapt and "steal, rob and kill" just simply to prove it can do that drug. It does not take kindly to tyrants who assume they are god and can determine what a person can or cannot do with their life. It is a personal choice to end your life, to use any drugs, to experiment. The best society can do is pass "suggestions". Please consider not doing drugs because they may harm you. That is it. That's the only solution to counter the right/subconscious aspect of the mind because once subconscious decides it's going to do something there is nothing anything in the universe can do to stop it. Marie Curries subconscious decided it was going to experiment with radiation until it could no longer experiment with radiation. Some beings subconscious decides they are going to jump off cliff with parachutes until they can no longer jump. Many perceive these are daredevils but they are not, they just like that rush of freedom caused by the right brain the "high" of freedom. Of course I am so far into subconscious/right brain drugs cannot do anything for me. I am at the state that drug users use drugs to achieve so my mind understands drugs will not do anything to me, I have no stress so I do not need drugs to relieve stress. Stress is totally gone because my short term memory is altered. I am not stressed what I write about at the start of this book or what I write in any of my previous books because I don't remember I get have a sensation or a spirit of what I write. Should I care about what I write in my personal dairies? Should I care if the world may read them? Should I be ashamed about what I think about things since I woke up? My thoughts are as valuable as anyone else's thoughts relative to the fact I am equal to everyone else. I am not god so I have no right to suggest one cannot take a drugs if they wish to no matter what that drug is. I am able to monologue to myself and perhaps one will hear what I say to myself and ponder it and adjust their own personal thoughts but that is as far as it will ever go because anything greater than that and I am an ego maniacal delusional arrogant fool with a "I know better than you do" god complex.

Relative to the last part. The whole business of this being turning water into wine. Water is a left brain being, very "sober" or very "tight minded" caused by eating the apple, and with his words this being turn the "left brainers" into "wine" which is right brain, it is open minded and not so isolated and harsh in its judgments. It is freedom in relation to allowing others to do as they wish relative to what they perceive is their pursuit of happiness. Simply put, no matter who you are, if you think you know better than anyone else you have a god complex. You are only an authority relative to you. You do not have a right to tell any other being what they better do because you are not god and so you may see something that appears "wrong" but it may turn out in the end to be a wise move. You are not intelligent enough to see the end result of actions another being decides to undertake. I took a handful of pills and now I understand everything I read. Perhaps you could predict that was the end result but you cannot and I could not predict that end result. I perceived I was reducing myself to ashes and instead a phoenix came into being. That had much to do with that judge telling me 10 years before that last "accident" "if you want to kill yourself there is nothing anyone can do about it". That is what true freedom is, because my subconscious understood from that judges comment "If you want to free yourself from the bondage of the left brain scribe conditioning there is nothing anyone can do about it."

As American's we must face the cold hard reality that we must give everyone a fair shake. We must strive to not pass laws that infringe ones free choice to do things in relation to their own self. "An it harm none do what thou will" is quite an accurate explanation. We are not intelligent enough to see what a little experimentation is going to achieve. No matter what happens to me from this moment on, I wrote some books and I have accomplish more than I could have ever hoped in a billion years to achieve so I am at peace that I was allowed to experiment with my own morality and I failed at my experiments to such a degree , finally something came out of them that may assist others. I tested a thousand light bulbs before one worked and the light from that one that worked is quite bright indeed. I am going to let that light shine because I had to do so much experimenting to accomplish it I cannot hold it and covet it and hide it away and put limits on it like money and material things because I understand these kinds of discoveries do not happen as often as they perhaps should. So in relation to that persons comment about me. Yes I am the stupidest person alive, but I am certainly alive.1:18:14 PM

Relative to me, there are no mistakes in my books. Relative to my perception you are perfect; relative to your perception my observation may be flawed. Until someone finds the elixir for eternal physical life then the ones with the most convincing arguments are the only votes that count. It is very important you continue to tell yourself I am totally insane because if you assume I am in fact a sane normal human being and how human beings were before we ate off of the "knowledge" tree you would perhaps harm yourself. It is important you never understand the females are in fact the dominate gender of the species and in fact "allow" males to assume the dominate role simply because the males are a bit more prone to foolishness like physically harming others and are in fact the "barbaric" of the two genders because this would turn the world upside down and this understanding would also harm you. Ponder the black widow spider and you will understand how males compare to females in reality in relation to the dominate gender of the species. If you perceive females are not the dominate gender of the species that is because you are delusional, mindfully speaking. The dominate gender of the species does not have to prove they are dominate because they are dominate now matter what they do. Some cultures determine many things relative to the females "stature" or "position" and in contrast to that many cultures also tend to "look down" on women. This is simply because the males are subconsciously aware of who is in control and they consciously attempt to "fight" that understanding in physical ways. Males are simply workers that provide the "queen" food so she can reproduce; it is no more complex than that. Ponder an ant colony, many males are running around fighting off "enemies" and gathering food for the sole purpose of that queen ant, so she can produce more offspring. If you do not understand that is in fact total reality in relation to the human species, perhaps in time your extreme neurosis will diminish. That is the reason soldiers cry out for their mothers just before they die on the battle field because they understand everything they did is for the "queen"

"A group of Amazonian ants have evolved an extremely unusual social system: They are all female and reproduce via cloning. Though their sexual organs have virtually disappeared, they have also gained some extraordinary abilities."

http://io9.com/5215921/scientists-discover-all+female-ant-species-that-reproduces-by-cloning

This is a nice way of saying, males are not really needed at all and so males compensate because they are aware of that and they do strange things like fight wars and attempt to "act dominate" because subconsciously they are aware they are not even required at all. Simply put, if all human males disappeared women would evolve and be able to make offspring very swiftly. The females would mentally be aware there is no way to make offspring so that would be enough for them to "alter" their reproductive system to make offspring before all the females died off. It is what happens when a creature is put between a rock and a hard place. People who see someone trapped under a car , they will lift that car to save that person because they do not wonder about logic or realms of possibility in that situation, they just do. It is not always possible but it does happen. Apparently it happened with these ants in the Amazon. Perhaps they got tired of the males fighting and vain efforts to pretend they are dominate. Ironically there are tales of all female tribes in the Amazon. One might suggest there are cultures that are extremely protective of the females almost to a fault. Perhaps that gives you something to ponder. If you are not pleased with that great truth please remind yourself Heimdall doesn't pander to ones in neurosis. Now I will discuss something that is relevant.3:39:02 PM.

One has to use their mind to kill the delusional fears in their mind created by life or life will use those delusional fears to kill them. A billion 9/11's would not make me vote away my rights but I am at the mercy of millions cry babies who vote away their rights if it rains to hard or the thunder is too loud. Perhaps in time you will not be such a scared little cry baby and you will get used to the delusional fear in your mind, and maybe in time you will not run like a coward who has no courage and no brain function when the rain gets a little heavy, but I do not count on it ever because the darkness tends to produce dark fruits to evidence itself.

"becomes destructive of these ends, it is the Right of the People to alter or to abolish it,"

So if you determined to vote away my rights as a result of a scary event I have a RIGHT to alter or abolish(exterminate) you. So now you have something more than a delusional fear in your mind, you have something that is flesh and blood that is telling you, You are going to pay with everything you will ever have if you do not alter and make all of my rights proper again afforded to me under the constitution. ", it is the Right of the People" I am a "people" and I was born here and that means I determined whoever signed my rights away is going to be altered or abolished(annihilated) and I do not give a rats ass which it is but it will be one or the other even if it means I am the only one left standing in this country. You can take you laws and morals and shove them up your ass because my rights are gone and that means the blood bath is the only option since it is nearly impossible to get right back once they have been signed away because it rained too hard. I do not give a rats ass what title is in front of your name, I only see tyrant, and I love tyrants because they make great eating, but they never seem to fill my gut and that means I eat them all for no reason into infinity. My law is the constitution and freedom and we will see who is left standing the end of the slaughter. I have already cast my lot so you better attempt to come up with a plan to stop me with the understanding you cannot stop me. Now you have something to fear beyond shadows in a dark cemetery. If you perceive that is a terroristic threat I beg you to approach me. I am the bait, so don't be late, the patriots shall not hesitate. If you think what I say is against the law then you come to my pool and bring your death shroud so I will have something to bury you in. Now that I have hung myself properly I will discuss something of value.6:52:13 PM

7:00:19 PM What is interesting is even if there was 9000 spy satellites and cameras and people watching me right now it would not phase me a bit because all they would see is a loser typing extremely poor books but just the understanding my rights are infringed on makes my eyes turn black with rage.

" This component of the brain(right) is not concerned with things falling into patterns because of prescribed rules." So it is not I am bothered by the fact my freedoms have been abridged in fact by law, but it's the understanding or awareness they are abridged that causes me anger. I can sense of freedom are abridged and someone wrote a document 200 plus years ago that said Congress or a legislative function can abridge my freedoms or privacy. I certainly do not care about my privacy or I would say what is ay in my diaries and I certainly do not need many freedoms since I just sit in my "isolation chamber" and write my crappy diary entries apparently into infinity because I already decided to, but its just I know something is wrong or not proper in relation to where I live. I live in the land of the free and I am so far into right brain it does not care about "prescribed rules." My mind does not care if aliens from outer space are coming to kill me I will take my chances with the aliens as opposed to sell my rights and freedoms because it harms me more to be aware my absolute freedom of speech and privacy are not in tact when just a short 200 years ago they were intact. What happened , why are my freedoms not in tact now? Because of some phantom fear that ones in neurosis perceive?

Neurosis : characterized by anxiety, depression, or hypochondria. Basically people who piss their self like a frog when it rains to hard sold me down the river and Heimdall is willing to "Give me liberty or give me death" to remedy that and all the laws in the universe mean nothing in contrast. That is the absolute nature of extreme right brain. It does not play games. Why don't you pass a law that says I am illegal. Why don't you be a racists against people who have are right brain dominate and show everyone what you are. You are a racist against people who are on the "right side", the free side of the mind. Your laws are biased against thought itself. So it comes down to one thing. Am I wrong to want absolute freedom of speech and privacy and thought or am I right? If I am wrong to want these things then my mind is wrong because it wants these things, so you need to outlaw the right side of the brain, and anyone who is born with right brain dominate state of mind should be conditioned or brainwashed using "scribe, math and short term memory techniques" so they will become left brain dominate and have many strong emotions and be fearful and easily manipulated with fear tactics. If I am right in my cause then you should prepare to do some swift altering of the laws because if you wait until I get warmed up you will certainly regret you did not alter the laws swiftly, that is absolute truth. Do not count on me voting because I do not vote. I will not vote. I prefer that you do not alter the laws. I prefer you make no adjustments. I prefer the hottest coals because they make the strongest steel. I will test the limits of freedom and we will see who the wheat is and who the chaff is. I will now discuss something colorful.7:20:14 PM

155

Todd Andrew Rohrer

"At times, right brain thinking is difficult to put into words because of its complexity, its ability to process information quickly and its non-verbal nature."

I will clarify this comment "its ability to process information quickly". This means a person with a strong sense of time or left brain due to the "conditioning" might take a lifetime to figure something out that it takes me zero seconds to figure out. One of the left might spend their whole life holding a grudge against their child because their child does not do as they say, and I would be at peace with that in zero seconds. One on the left might spend their whole life attempting to come up with one wise saying and I come up with one wise saying every sentence I type with no effort. I am not suggest if you have a strong sense of time you should come over to the right, because I prefer to have my pool all to myself. One might suggest Heimdall doesn't like anyone pissing in his red sea. It took Heimdall far too many razor slashes to his wrists to make the pool just the right depth. You just remind yourself over and over anyone can write six books in six months. A female reminds a male of the compassion and warmth he does not possess. That was Lincoln meant when he said:

"A woman is the only thing I am afraid of that I know will not hurt me."
Abraham Lincoln

A man is afraid a woman will leave him alone with his barbaric tendencies so the male tends to react in rash manners when his love for that woman is scorned.

If women ran the world there would be no wars but much compassion and men cannot tolerate that.

7:31:57 PM

I will make this clear. Many of these kids you deem "unfit" and then decide to fill with pills and assume are "damaged" are simply right brain dominate. If you perceive I am going to tolerate that you are fucking insane.8:59:58 PM

10:02:38 PM No matter what you think here are my options: poison mushroom, poison lamb chop, nailed to a tree or hemlock. That is what is on my plate. I do not mind making a repeat performance so make it slow and make it painful so I might feel something. I do not hold you responsible because you simply do not know what you do. I cannot find fault with anything you do me but you better pray with all of your might there is no afterlife because if there is, the first and last eyes you will see there will be mine, that is what Heimdall suggests.10:04:20 PM

This is a chat I had in the India chat room. I want you to know there are beings that do understand me and do not perceive I am insane or on drugs. I also want you to know I type my little fingers off every day and I am uncertain why I am compelled to do so. I do not ever want you to think I hide anything from you. I desire to communicate with you. My situation is too complex to not be totally honest and upfront about my intentions.

INDIA CHAT ROOM CHAT

[20:50] <Heimdall> Greetings

20:50] <Heimdall> This is my home but I must stay where I originated becasue that is where teh accident happened and I assume it was for a reason it happened where i am at

[21:01] <@WORLDW1D3> you think this is valhalla?

[21:02] <@WORLDW1D3> Heimdall (Old Norse Heimdallr, the prefix Heim- means home, the affix -dallr is of uncertain origin)

[21:02] <@WORLDW1D3> :)

[21:06] * @Piranah (~piranah@only.dates.girls.wearing.no-panties.org) Quit (Read error: Connection timed out)

[21:09] * Piranah (piranah@only.dates.girls.wearing.no-panties.org) has joined #india

[21:10] * Michelle sets mode: +o-b Piranah 465!1K-o@1245633022

[21:13] <Heimdall> I reached nirvana after a striong of failede suicde attempts over 10 years, one might suggest i didnt eat for 28 days and a little girl found me by teh river just in time and gave me a bowl of rice

[21:14] <Heimdall> it may have been 38,39, or 43 days

[21:14] <Heimdall> so my teacher was no person but none the less a artehr wise teacher one might suggest

[21:14] <Heimdall> rather

[21:15] <Heimdall> since the accident i have published 6 books 6 books in 6 months to be exact, and i desire to give volume 2,3,4 to you my friends freely

[21:16] <Heimdall> I am mindful teh east terats us differently than the west but I am in teh west so perhaps I need to assist them with their misundeerstandings.

[21:18] <Heimdall> My books are somehwat harsh but please remind yoruself I went from sense of time to end enlightenment in about one second so i am still adjusting

[21:18] <Heimdall> http://thepiratebay.org/user/Lestat969/

[21:18] <Heimdall> these are my books and i do not enforce the opyright so give them freely as i have given them to you freely

[21:19] <Heimdall> they can be found in book format in all major book stores but these are the copies off my harddrive

[21:19] <Heimdall> they are "special" lol

[21:21] <@WORLDW1D3> I am just watching this.. http://www.youtube.com/watch?v=WQE_pGaGTYk

[21:22] <@WORLDW1D3> what books.. 666

[21:22] <@WORLDW1D3> lost days 28 38 39 43

[21:22] <@WORLDW1D3> 234

[21:23] <@WORLDW1D3> florida eh!

[21:23] <@WORLDW1D3> Do you believe in aliens also ?

[21:25] <@WORLDW1D3> I bet you got a kid

[21:27] <Heimdall> I have a girlfreind but no kids or perhaps i just had 6 billion kids recently

[21:27] <@WORLDW1D3> http://s116.photobucket.com/albums/o14/lestat969/

[21:27] <Heimdall> I am on the fence about aliens but you are wise to not take the word of a blind man and ask questions.

[21:29] <Heimdall> I must hide my true identity due to the fact I am in the west but here is a glimpse

[21:29] <Heimdall> http://www.myspace.com/sanevacuum

[21:29] <Heimdall> one might suggest i am surrounded by the "sane" here in floirda

[21:30] <@WORLDW1D3> Tlion714

[21:31] <Heimdall> yes i get around lol

[21:31] <Heimdall> i try many experiments to reach "them" but it of course is impossible lol

[21:31] <Heimdall> i love a a challenge

[21:33] <@WORLDW1D3> do you take drugs to reach your enlightenments ?

[21:34] <Heimdall> People who have a strong sense of time and thus a strong sense of hunger and thus strong fear take drugs to reach enlightenment

[21:34] <Heimdall> but they can never remain there for long

[21:34] <Heimdall> so they tend to drink their self to death

[21:35] <Heimdall> the drugs ease up teh emotions and thius they are in teh domain of the right brain

[21:35] <Heimdall> Left brain is seqential based and linear and right brain is opposite so it random access or "no sense of time" and thus no fear or strong emotions

[21:35] <@WORLDW1D3> What about science ... You know about cranial chip implant ?

[21:36] <Heimdall> I am in agreement with the buddhist concept of conditioning away from gear that is what i pereive is the remedy for the side effects fo biting off the tree of "knowledge" in realtion to

[21:36] <Heimdall> If you reflect back upon our own educational training, we have been traditionally taught to master the 3 R's: reading, writing and arithmetic -- the domain and strength of the left brain.

[21:37] <Heimdall> So the buddhist suggesting sitting ina cemetary helps one condition away from fear

[21:37] <Heimdall> i suggest just watch a scary movie and then sit in teh dark after words

[21:37] <Heimdall> also i suggest some other methods

[21:37] * abssdsa (~abcd@cpe-24-242-205-164.tx.res.rr.com) Quit (Ping timeout: 320 seconds)

[21:38] <Heimdall> so buddha suggested mind in one thing and brahman suggested mind is two thing and jesus suggested i sit at teh right hand and so did moses and mohammed agreed with them

[21:38] <Heimdall> I perceive mind i stwo distinct things left and right and most are caught in the middle, they are the luke warm

[21:39] <Heimdall> buddha suggest the middle way becasue he understood he reached end enlightment by nearly starving to death , he feaced the big fear

[21:39] <@WORLDW1D3> A scary movie... hehe after that you should jump into a http://en.wikipedia.org/wiki/Isolation_tank

01[21:39] <Heimdall> I agree many can reach the right, but perhaps cannot go to teh end unless they face death itself

[21:40] * Soyal (~lol___lol@117.204.82.113) has joined #india

[21:40] <@WORLDW1D3> welcome back soyal

[21:40] <@WORLDW1D3> or goodmorning

[21:40] <Heimdall> Due to the effects of this, ain relation to "ignorance is bliss and bliss equals spirtual joy, I am in fact seeking ignroance becasue at the moment my eyes tend to be black with rage is the absence of much ignronace.

[21:41] <@WORLDW1D3> The Brain Chip - A Prison For Your Mind http://www.youtube.com/watch?v=p06RLa6Wuys

[21:42] <Heimdall> yes one can condition away from fear or simply cut out the left hemispehre of their brain, both are perhasp as effective

[21:42] <@WORLDW1D3> Can you control your own dreams when you are sleeping ?

[21:44] <Heimdall> No i submit I am still warming up the accident happen ironically on oct 31 2008

[21:44] <Heimdall> so perhaspes i am just the anti christ

[21:45] <Heimdall> i can make a good argument for that so i have strong legs from jumping back on the fence

01[21:46] <Heimdall> I write my books mostly in diary format under the guise i had ana ccdient and i am documenting my progress

[21:46] <Heimdall> ten i publish them under psychology

[21:46] <Heimdall> i perceive taht is a proper appraoch since it worked for freud and jung

[21:46] <Heimdall> jung was found dead in bed with the teaching of buddha on his night stand

[21:47] <Heimdall> i did have a deram the other day

[21:47] <Heimdall> a man said he was not pleased with my books and he took a nail and started hamering it into my head

[21:47] <Heimdall> but the book he had in his hand was not my book it was i pereive some occult book or black magic book

[21:47] <Heimdall> so that is perhaps something i need to pondeer further

[21:48] <Heimdall> It did not scare me but it was perhaps a profound sign

[21:48] <Heimdall> I guess lemur monekys have interesting dreams

[21:49] <Heimdall> i am good at "my eyes are black with rage" so i am getting good at that talent

[21:50] <Heimdall> moses said his anger was waxing when he saw everyone dancing around the "golden calf" so I am pleased I am not alone

01[21:51] <Heimdall> thats simply a symptom of right brain it is very cerbreal and left brain is vert materialistic

[21:51] <Heimdall> its opposite

[21:51] <Heimdall> but for me, i attempted suicide and failed 30 times before the accident, and it was becasue i did not have enough money and wasw not wealthy so i perceive i hate money and materialistic things becasue that is why i killed myself

[21:52] <Heimdall> failing at suicide means one is "the least among you" or "the stone the stone cutter threw away" but in reality, a person who attempts to kill their self when they do not have to is the definition of meek

[21:53] <Heimdall> others suggest i am simply the fool on the hill to fail that many times

[21:54] <@WORLDW1D3> what was the reason for suicide ?

[21:54] <Soyal> lol

[21:54] <Soyal> sup sup

[21:54] <Heimdall> I never fit in and couldnt pass the test and could never get a good job aor be successful base don what i was toldf was success in part

[21:55] <@WORLDW1D3> you grew up in a christian religious home ?

01[21:55] <Heimdall> On the other hand i felt out of place at a very young age and decided at 15 i was chekcing out

[21:55] <Soyal> whos gonna suiside ?

[21:55] <Soyal> WORLDW1D3 ?

01[21:55] <Heimdall> Yes

[21:55] <Soyal> lol

[21:55] <Soyal> thn its Party time :P

[21:55] <Heimdall> No need to fear soyal it has already happened

[21:56] <@WORLDW1D3> did not fit in .. so you did hang around others like yourself in a subculture

[21:56] <Soyal> lol

[21:56] <Soyal> WORLDW1D3 Heimdall is ur GF ?

[21:56] <@WORLDW1D3> I dont think so soyal

[21:56] <Soyal> oh oh its late 7:30

[21:56] <Soyal> gata go college :'(

[21:56] <Heimdall> I tried to hang around nother but even as young as 3rd garde the crowd didnt like me or accept me so i was an outcast

[21:56] <Soyal> hmmm

[21:57] <Soyal> Heimdall seeems like Essya's :D

[21:57] <Heimdall> I think everyone hates me by nature that is why mohammed took his "mediative " retreat to a cave and then found "god"

[21:57] <Soyal> WORLDW1D3 i need a IRC server

[21:57] <Heimdall> perhaps buddha left his family to go do his buiness also

[21:57] <Heimdall> certainly jesus being a carpenter gave him meany reason to feel poor and check out

[21:58] <Heimdall> he really hated money also

[21:58] <Soyal> me 2

[21:58] <Heimdall> so did socreates

[21:58] <Soyal> who need money ?

[21:58] <@WORLDW1D3> soyal you need to talk to nitin from chandigarh .. he got his own server

[21:58] <Heimdall> socrates suggested he never cahrged money for his teachings and many try to figure out why

[21:58] <Soyal> naaaa i hve a seminar on wednesday

[21:58] <Soyal> to present CrazzY

[21:59] <Soyal> it need's an IRC server....i dnt thnk thy gave me Internet Connction :(

[21:59] <Soyal> WORLDW1D3 whr can i found nitin ?

[22:00] <Heimdall> so i see my options as poison mushroom, poison lamb chop, nailed to a tree and i am so so about all the options

[22:00] <Soyal> naaaa

[22:00] <Soyal> not those

[22:00] <@WORLDW1D3> now thats a secret soyal...

[22:00] <Soyal> awwww :(

[22:00] <Soyal> Heimdall i prefer u 2 come 2 me

[22:00] <Heimdall> you guys do know buddha was poisoned right?

[22:00] <Soyal> im better thn those

[22:01] <Soyal> yeah i heared Einstien was poisoned

[22:01] <Soyal> WORLDW1D3 im waiting

[22:01] <Soyal> ok Heimdall bbye

[22:01] <Soyal> WORLDW1D3 cya ni8

[22:01] <Heimdall> Thank You

[22:02] <Soyal> wht dnt u need my address ?

[22:02] <@WORLDW1D3> he is also deep underground at area420 surrounded with secret knowledge from the ancient time

[22:02] <Soyal> ahhhh not again

[22:02] <Soyal> heimdal note it down

[22:03] * abssdsa (~abcd@cpe-24-242-205-164.tx.res.rr.com) has joined #india

[22:03] <Soyal> Mr.Soyal

[22:03] <Soyal> White house

[22:03] <Soyal> USA

[22:03] <@WORLDW1D3> you have to pass the protectors of the code who have been around for thousands of years

[22:03] <Soyal> Suicide is the world most stupidest IDEA my frend

[22:04] <Soyal> WORLDW1D3

[22:04] <Soyal> gtg college

[22:04] <Soyal> kick ur ass ni8 :P

[22:05] <Soyal> now gt out of ur Office and go sleeeeeeeeepzzz ^-^

[22:05] <Soyal> bye

[22:05] * Soyal (~lol___lol@117.204.82.113) has left #india

[22:06] <@WORLDW1D3> you can try to find the blueprints of the secret constructions of what vishwakarma build

[22:07] <Heimdall> so what do you think, should i take the monks advice and move to india to their temples or should i face my fate here in the west? I have already decided what i am going to do but just to get an outside opinion

[22:08] <Heimdall> somehow i decided to write infinite books so i am kind of obligated now

[22:09] <Heimdall> maybe my strategy is to drowned them with my horrible books

[22:11] <@WORLDW1D3> well if wanted to leave by suicide but failed.. now you have the chance to leave for higher learning if you take the monks advice

[22:12] * rithika23 (~rithi2309@60.51.40.76) has joined #india

[22:13] * rithika23 (~rithi2309@60.51.40.76) Quit (Client Quit)

[22:20] * Taani (~Ajnabee@cpe-67-240-217-131.rochester.res.rr.com) has joined #india

[22:20] * Taani (~Ajnabee@cpe-67-240-217-131.rochester.res.rr.com) Quit (Client Quit)

[22:23] <Heimdall> Thank You

[22:23] * Piranah sets mode: +v Heimdall

[22:25] <+Heimdall> I am uncertain about some things. Buddha suggested what he taught his disciples was represented in the leaves in his hand and what he had not taught them was represented in the leaves in the forrest behind him

[22:25] <+Heimdall> this of course is very arrgant but also true

[22:25] <+Heimdall> His teacher was "death" so to speak so he did not require a teacher

[22:25] <+Heimdall> So I perceive i just keep writing my boks and that is my mission

[22:26] <+Heimdall> What is your perceptions of this please

[22:30] <+Heimdall> and interetsing side note, the night i took the handful of paxil, **about 45 mins later i felt a beam of heat pass from my head to my toes** and that is when i thought "i need to call for help or i will die" and i decided so what, this is what you want. Do you know of this beam?

[22:34] <@Piranah> **:) one such as i, am not soo enlightened**

[22:34] <+Heimdall> on one hand i want to seek the monks on the otehrs hand i am a fool and i seek the hottest coals becasue they make the strongest steel. I do not want anything to be easy becasue letting go of life was not easy, so i am fool and i always make the wrong decision, i cannot do anything right i perceive i do the right thing but otehrs perceive it is the wrong thing

Todd Andrew Rohrer

[22:34] <@Piranah> :)

[22:35] * hermawan (~dadan_her@125.163.180.244) has joined #india

[22:35] <+Heimdall> Yes I feel like a large thumb sticking out

[22:36] <+Heimdall> I speak with some who reached nirvana becasue they had near death esxpereinces by stroke or physical accidents like car accidents

[22:36] <+Heimdall> but that is not as "pure" becasue buddha starved nearly to death and he did not have to and it was a mystery why that little girl found him just in thenick of time

[22:36] <+Heimdall> if that little girl did not find him he would have been a suicide

[22:37] <@Piranah> :)

[22:37] <@Piranah> yes that would hold true in my opinion

[22:37] <+Heimdall> she said, he reminded me of as spirit i once met, and that is what i perceive, i am in fact mindfully gone but physically still here so i am in limbo or in purgatory whihc is nothingness or so so

[22:37] <@Piranah> perhaps that lil girl was fate ? or perhaps just blind luck who knows

[22:38] <+Heimdall> yes, perhasp it was just blind luck 25 paxil did not kill me

[22:38] <+Heimdall> i certainly convulsed a bit

[22:39] <+Heimdall> but then i woke up the nexdt day and i was no longer suicidal, but the "ah ha" sensation did not happen for a few months after that

[22:39] <+Heimdall> now buddha had that stravation and then said that was not the way

[22:39] <+Heimdall> but i perceive that is becasue it took a while to hit him

[22:39] <+Heimdall> it was not instant but the cycle had started with teh nearly starving incident

[22:40] <+Heimdall> I went to a neurologist two months after the ah ha sensation

[22:40] <+Heimdall> i got many tests run

[22:40] <+Heimdall> and he said I see you are perfectly healthy and i belive you are enlightened

[22:40] <@Piranah> :)

[22:40] <+Heimdall> so i have a doctor on my side and he is quite interested in my progress

[22:41] <@Piranah> No doctor in Canada would ever take such an interest. I find that cool :)

[22:41] <+Heimdall> he said but I would not write any books and that is when i decide dto write infinite books so i do not tell him I have published 6 since he said that comment

[22:42] <@Piranah> hmm nice :)

[22:42] * AJAYPNG (~AJAYPNG@60.53.181.43) has joined #india

[22:43] <AJAYPNG> hi

[22:43] <@Piranah> Heimdall, do you have any works avail online to read ? I have always taken an interest in enlightenment

[22:43] <AJAYPNG> any penang or kedah girls here

[22:43] <+Heimdall> http://thepiratebay.org/user/Lestat969/

[22:43] <@Piranah> Good eve or Good Morn AJAYPNG

[22:43] <@Piranah> :)

[22:43] <+Heimdall> these are volume 2,3,4

[22:43] <@Piranah> i shall take a look :)

[22:43] <+Heimdall> they are in stores in book format but i also give them freely in pdf format

[22:43] <AJAYPNG> gd mrng

[22:44] <+Heimdall> volume 5 will be publsihed in 1 week adn volume 6 will be submitted to publsihers at end of month, i detect there will be a volume 7 lol

[22:44] <@Piranah> AJAYPNG, forgive the vague statement :) im in Canada and its only 10:30ish Sun eve for me :)

[22:44] * Piranah sets mode: +v AJAYPNG

[22:45] <+AJAYPNG> its ok

[22:46] <@Piranah> :) to answer yer question though sorry there are no ladies online this eve, in fact its rare to catch ladies on IRC at all these days

[22:46] <+Heimdall> I underatnd what buddha means when he said use strategic words, becasue if he wasw not a master at that his books woul dbe filled with rage, but that is a symptom of loss of ignorance

[22:46] <+Heimdall> its harms me this understanding I am not use to it

[22:47] <+Heimdall> In america we deem children to be different when they are simply right brain dominate and then fill them with pills becasue they are different

[22:48] <+Heimdall> a child cannot have a sense of time and thus strong emotions like fear in the mothers womb or they would kill themother

[22:48] <@Piranah> Well my enlightened friend, I am outa here for now. Feel welcome on #India anytime. I have to go keep the peace for a few on #iran and then off to meet the ladies for a night cap :)

[22:48] * hermawan (~dadan_her@125.163.180.244) Quit (Ping timeout: 246 seconds)

[22:48] <+AJAYPNG> any penang or kedah girls here

[22:48] <+AJAYPNG> any penang or kedah girls here

[22:48] <+Heimdall> so children are born in nirvana and the adults "fix" them, thus the saying "suffer the children to come to me" and "they know not what they do"

165

[22:48] <@Piranah> AJAYPNG, that question has already been answered

[22:48] <+Heimdall> Thank You

[22:49] <+Heimdall> I am pleased with your efforts

[22:49] <@Piranah> Heimdall, its a shame we cant all stay that young and innocent, truly children are more enlightened then most adults i know :)

[22:51] <+Heimdall> they are wise beyond their years, perhaps heimdall will get through to the "sane"

[22:51] <@Piranah> :)

[22:51] <@Piranah> One can only hope and try :)

[22:52] <+AJAYPNG> any penang or kedah girls here

[22:53] * AJAYPNG was kicked by Piranah (AJAYPNG)

[22:53] <+Heimdall> yes and I do not mind repeat performances anyway

[22:54] <@Piranah> ehhe :)

[22:54] <+Heimdall> can't beat a dead horse

[22:54] <@Piranah> nope thats true :)

Please note I asked then what the "beam of heat" was and he submitted he did not know.

[22:30] <+Heimdall> and interetsing side note, the night i took the handful of paxil, **about 45 mins later i felt a beam of heat pass from my head to my toes** and that is when i thought "i need to call for help or i will die" and i decided so what, this is what you want. Do you know of this beam?

[22:34] <@Piranah> **:) one such as i, am not soo enlightened**

 I was simply testing to see if he was where I am at. I understood fully what that beam of heat was. I understood fully he would not know what that beam was. So I asked a question, I knew what his answer would be, and that question is proof of who I am. It is not how many questions you ask, it is what questions you ask. Knowing what questions to ask is more important than knowing what questions to avoid asking. Perhaps this is all just a big joke to you and that proper because the drowning will not be as painful if you are laughing through it. On the other hand when I say "unseen battle" I mean a battle that is not in the physical world but strictly in the cerebral world and if one does not have full brain function they will not even notice it; if you do not detect the unseen battle you know what is on your plate.

Now contrast that chat with these comments in a chat room with the "sane"

[20:11] <Monty5> he's gotta be pasting this

[20:11] <Heimdall> I am not pasting

[20:11] <Monty5> but he did a correction

[20:11] <Monty5> which is odd

[20:12] <Heimdall> my spelling sucks though because that's the nature of right brain it doesn't like rules

[20:13] <Sixgun> Your brain suck

[20:13] <Heimdall> the right aspect of the mind is lightning

[20:13] <Heimdall> simple and plan

[20:13] <Monty5> yeesh

[20:13] <Heimdall> go to amazon and look up those books and check published dates

[20:14] <Sixgun> go to the Amazonas

[20:14] <Sixgun> and dont come back

[20:16] <Heimdall> if yu have strong sense of hunger you are not on the right hand side, or fatigue, or strong sense of time or strong short term memory

[20:16] <Monty5> god dammit shut up

[20:16] <Floyd9> I am supposedly right-brained. I find rant/rave/chaos/retardism in your brain.

[20:16] <_HellMngr> no shit

[20:16] <_HellMngr> a beautiful mind, yo

[20:16] <Heimdall> I find no fault with you but you tell me to shut up

[20:16] <Sixgun> bingo

[20:17] <Sixgun> we have a winner

[20:17] <Floyd9> yea, because we find fault within you, tardnuts.

[20:17] <Sixgun> 1st price is a free swim to Poland

[20:17] <Heimdall> am i bothering you in reality or are you just unable to grasp my differences and it harms you

[20:17] <Floyd9> you're just annoying.

[20:22] <Floyd9> I think I still make more sense than this jerk-off.

So do not ever assume you are tolerant. Do not ever assume you are understanding and compassionate you have no concept of those words. You hate anything that is different. You insult it and judge it and condemn it and then you hang it on a tree and suggest you are compassionate. Then you fill children with pills because they are not like you are and you suggest you are civilized and rational and merciful. We will see who gets nailed to the tree this time around, boy. These people assume I am copying and pasting my casual comments because their mind works so slow they cannot even comprehend a live person could spit out monologue that fast. That is a fact! Then they have the balls to say I am stupid and I am annoying and I am a retard. They only have two options using their elementary logic, I am either a robot or I am a god and they always assume I am a robot, then a retard. In the India chat room they are extremely happy and compassionate and understanding and they are pleased with my lightning monologue it is a good sign to them and to these bozo's in western chat rooms it is ambiguity and so they hate it and cuss it. There is going to be some altering done in the land of the free or there is going to be some heads on some posts and I am pleased with either outcome. I am the minority so I get to defend myself from the packs of wild dogs and the wild dogs should avoid me at all costs because my anger is far beyond waxing at this stage of the accident. I will go to sleep now and hope I die in my sleep.11:55:10 PM

6/22/2009 3:14:08 AM It's a brand new day.

8:17:15 AM Perhaps some of these "transients" are not in fact "mentally ill" but simply in various stages of right brain dominate and appear "mentally ill" to ones in the left. Perhaps some of these war veterans are not "mentally ill" but simply in various stages of right brain dominate and this would be evident because people who tend to face great fears like "death" tend to "go" right brain dominate to various degree's and thus appear "mentally ill" to the ones on the left. Perhaps these people are in fact not mentally ill at all. They are simply in various degrees of right brain dominate and appear different.

Perhaps you would assume that is impossible because I understand that is extremely probable.

"If one does not understand a person, one tends to regard him as a fool."
Carl Jung

"Show me a sane man and I will cure him for you."
Carl Jung

I will make this very clear.

On one hand it is in the realm of possibility that writing and reading and arithmetic is simply very attractive and so the majority perceives it is wise to put people "under the gun" and thus encourage short term memory which conditions people to be left brain dominate and thus decreases the "complex" right brain.

One the other hand it is in the realm of possibility the "power that be" are very careful to make sure everyone is conditioned into the left brain dominate state of mind and it pushes these reading writing and arithmetic conditioning tools on people to keep them away from the "complex" state of mind the right brain encourages.

So, it is in the realm of possibility that the knowledge "apple" is just very attractive and that is why it is pushed on everyone in the west. It is also in the realm of possibility it is a "conspiracy" to keep people using the "less complex" aspect of the mind and thus keeps them in line and keeps them in "fear" so they can be easily manipulated.

So, if it is just a misunderstanding or an "accident" then the education system would certainly adjust their education methods and people in general would adjust their thoughts and not judge others so harshly who "misspell" words or are different and thus I would understand it was simply a misunderstanding that this all happened. One the other and if there is some sort of "power structure" that is making sure we are "kept in the dark" then there is no alternative but shenanigans. No mercy will be expect and no mercy will be given. That's a nice way of saying all bets are off. In a state of shenanigans no laws apply. I have considered the situation and my intuition tells me this left brain conditioning is in fact contrived and I therefore hereby declare total shenanigans so laws no longer apply. My lot will not be uncast. To the victor goes the spoils. The quick and the dead. One person suggested I think too much or too quickly and I realized he was subconsciously detecting his thought processes are dead or very slowed down. Do you perceive I write quickly or deadly?9:54:32 AM

11:00:33 AM I will make this very clear. You may perceive I am in control of this situation or "intuition". In reality I am in the bubble. Intuition suggests I write things. I understand the things I write might bring harm to me and intuition suggests that does not matter you write them anyway. I am committing suicide from my perspective because of what I write and "intuition" suggests I write even more and even faster and even quicker. I cannot stop writing. I have tried. I have tried to "kill" this intuition with drink and I only end up writing about those attempts to kill this intuition. So I end up writing even more things. I recall I wrote in an earlier books "I am going to write until I drop." I maintain that comment. I am a little rabbit and a Mac Truck hit me and I have no choice in all reality but to go with the flow. That is it. There is no, self control. I write, I have no money and what I have intuition suggest I publish the next book so I can be ready to publish the next book into infinity. I am literally blinded on all sides. I cannot even remember what I wrote yesterday let alone months ago. I edit my books and it all seems like it is someone else's writing but certainly not mine. If you knew me and knew me before the accident you would say "This certainly is not your writing." All I know is I have to write infinite books and nothing in all of the universe matters outside of that task, even me. So now you understand what is on my plate. So now you do not have to ponder what has happened to me because I simply do not know. If I had to sum everything up into one sentence in relation to my situation it would be, and I will not clarify this comment because I am unable to, "Time is of the essence." I do not "get it" and I perceive that is the point, we never "get it." In relation to "right brain thinking is difficult to put into words because of its complexity". It is not difficult to put into words it is impossible to ever put into words and fully explain so it is simply unnamable. I will go play the video game and give my fingers a rest because apparently intuition likes the video game and that is my only chance to keep my books under 200k words.11:09:00 AM

11:29:22 AM "the right brain seems to flourish dealing with complexity, ambiguity and paradox."

Here is what a paradox is : a statement, proposition, or situation that seems to be absurd or contradictory, but in fact is or may be true

Here is my situation and you will see it is a paradox.

I am all about freedom or choice and freedom to allow others to make their own decision yet I write books and tell people what they should do, then I scare them away so they will not read my books telling them what they should do, then I invite them to read my books and give them to them freely, then I scare them again and tell them never to read my books and then I suggest everything is going to book, then I suggest hurry because everything in not ok, then I write even faster and publish more books and then I write them in diary format so people will not assume I am telling them what to do even though I am telling them what to do, and it appears like a contradiction in it is in fact true. And as if that wasn't funny enough, I have to write infinite books and I forgot or am unable to use the language properly. So from my perspective this is quite a humbling experience. One might suggest I have no ego after since this accident because I would be so humiliated if I did have an ego or pride or arrogance I would perhaps implode. For some reason, all my extremely crappy books do not bother. I try to imagine that these books are in fact on the world stage and everyone can read them and I do not feel ashamed or embarrassed or sad or humiliated. I try to. I try to think I should be very worried these books are on a world stage but I am not at all. I am not even able to perceive what shame or embarrassment is at all but if I was on the left I would never publish these books in a billion years because they are so embarrassing. My mind keeps telling me People do not even read books anymore and that keeps me publishing without worry. I was in a Hindu chat room and a guy said "No worries." when I told him my situation and what that means is not as much "do not worry" but more along the lines of "You are not capable or worry or stress". I am literally stress free to the extreme. That is the nature of right brain because at this extreme right brain level if I worried or stressed the "clarity" or mental function would suffer. I would not be able to write what I write or translate the a "wise sayings" so as the stress decreases the clarity increase I do still have quite an "anger waxing" problem though. Anger is perhaps not as stress related as it is awareness related. I have hate for the world for abusing me and at the same time I have compassion for the world because it has also been abused and there is no word for hate and compassion at the exact same time so I am left with gnashing of teeth because how I feel is unnamable.11:38:36 AM

Epic struggle keeps everyone honest.

11:45:51 AM So now I have talked myself into some kind of "silly mode" and I wish I was like this when I proof read/edit my books because they would perhaps be much funnier. I would explain this state of mind as being , the whole world is crumbling around me and everyone is rushing about and freaking out and I am sitting there saying "what are you freaking out about?". The whole world is burning up and fire and brimstone and plagues and wars and killing and harm and threats and everyone is in full panic and I am sitting here saying "What are you worried about?" That is pretty accurate to explains this "silly mode" I have talked myself into. But it will not last more than a moment or two and then I go into another shade, psychologically speaking, so to speak, what have you.11:49:45 AM

So If I have been "tapped" as the "big fish" it does not matter what I say because it is not about me it is about something else and I do not know what that something else is except to say I cannot ever explain it no matter I do. It is too complex for me to ever explain. It is too complex for me to explain in infinite books and I can do is try to explain it in infinite books even though I fully know I cannot. I do not even know what it is, so it is rather difficult for me to explain it, yet for some unknown reason

I am trying to explain it. All I can do is try. I am mindful to go one sentence at a time so I do not get tangled in the complexity.12:01:36 PM

<Heimdall> i just sit in my room and write my infinite books and sometimes i write a song and put the link in my books or i mediatet by playing this veido game to figure out what genius comment i will write next in my books

<Heimdall> so i do not do anything really

<Heimdall> i do nothing

<Heimdall> i am obligated to write infinite books becasue i decided

<AkhID> u do

<Heimdall> that means no fun no vacations no enjpyment becasue i have to write swiftly for some reason, i do go out to eat once a week with my girlfriend by my last outting harmed me

<Heimdall> i went down an isle in a store and a mother was there with her 2 years old child

<AkhID> ur n4me ?

<Heimdall> the child was yelling and the motehr saw me and said shut up or i will smack you to the child

<Heimdall> and then i recall buddha suggested this aspect called contact, and i realized if i would not have gone down that isle that parent would not have harmed that child

<AkhID> awwwwwwwww

<Heimdall> My name is Todd Andrew Rohrer

<Heimdall> that mother perceived i would perceive she did not have control of that yelling child so she told her own child to shut up or she will smack it, becasue i went down that isle

<Heimdall> So i perfer to never leave my isolation chamber again

<AkhID> aww

<AkhID> nice name

<AkhID> nice story yaar

<AkhID> u ll get an Oscar

<Heimdall> Gold reminds me of why i killed myself

"Our heart glows, and secret unrest gnaws at the root of our being. Dealing with the unconscious has become a question of life for us."
Carl Jung

The "righters" minds are strong and gnashing of teeth gnaws at the root of their being. Persuading the "lefters" not to kill everything is a lifelong profession.

"Resistance to the organized mass can be effected only by the man who is as well organized in his individuality as the mass itself." Carl Jung

One 'righter" can defeat an army of "lefters" if he has a proper game plan and an awesome disguise.

A lone wolf has to rely on its ability to think, unlike the herd.

This comment is in fact in relation to the story of Job. Job was a lone wolf and eh was forced to deal with his situation on his own. This seems like a bad situation but in reality it is a good situation. He had to reply on his own mind to get in through these "physical" circumstances. All his "friends" of support group was gone. He was a man alone on an island, psychologically speaking. He was aware no one was coming to his rescue. No one was going to throw him a lifeline so he was between a rock and a hard place. He had to produce or he would collapse. Mental comfort creates a dull knife.

"According to Christian mythology, the **Holy Grail** was the dish, plate, or cup used by Jesus at the Last Supper, said to possess miraculous powers."

The Holy Grail is what Jesus was under the influence of and Jesus was on the "right hand" which is the right aspect of the mind and that is accomplished with some easy techniques so everyone has the "Holy Grail" but most have it "locked" away, and one should understand how to "find" it by this stage in this poorly written book. Simply put, just go sit in a cemetery at night alone until you no longer get scared and say perhaps a lot and you will have "miraculous powers ". In fact if you can sit alone in a cemetery at night by yourself for more than 2 hours without pissing yourself like a frog does when it is picked up, you can go call the Pope and tell him of your miracle, tell him Heimdall sent ya.Now I will discuss something of importance. 3:47:04 PM

4:30:44 PM I just mowed the lawn and Heimmy tends to talk to himself when he mows the lawn and Heimmy talked himself into a lather and now Heimmy is not pleased. I will attempt to avoid gnashing of teeth by cracking jokes but you may be the butt of the jokes.

· Jung appears on the cover of The Beatles' album Sgt. Pepper's Lonely Hearts Club Band on the top row, between W.C. Fields and Edgar Allan Poe.

Beatles first major hit was along the lines of "You've got to hide your love away." They also are known to have hung around Buddhists and also had a public "falling out" so to speak so no one would get suspicious. That extremely funny.

· Peter Gabriel's song "Rhythm of the Heat" (Security, 1982), tells about Jung's visit to Africa, during which he joined a group of tribal drummers and dancers and became overwhelmed by the fear of losing control of himself. At the time Jung was exploring the concept of the collective unconscious and was afraid he would come under control of the music. Gabriel learned about Jung's journey to Africa from the essay Symbols and the Interpretation of Dreams (ISBN 0-691-09968-5). In the song

Gabriel tries to capture the powerful feelings the African tribal music evoked in Jung by means of intense use of tribal drumbeats. The original song title was Jung in Africa.[54]

I wont even comment on this one because I do not want to make this book to big.

· On the cover of The Police's final album, Synchronicity, which was named after Carl Jung's theory, Sting is seen reading a book called "Synchronicity" by Carl Jung.

Sting has a song called "brand new day" and in the lyrics is says something along the lines of, "turn the clock to zero" which is a nice way to say, no sense of time or nirvana. Of course that is just speculation from

"jcesar at 2009-06-14 18:25 CET: How can someone fail a suicide 30 times ?Must be the stupidest man alive. "

"The stupidest man alive" of course I am on the fence about the "alive" part. So if anyone ever says you are stupid now matter what you do, you remind them you know a guy named Heimmy that is without a doubt the stupidest man alive or dead, whichever you prefer. So now you have an "out'. No matter what anyone ever says negative towards you , you tell them "I know a guy named Heimmy and he makes me look like a deity of intelligence."

· Tool's song "Forty-Six & 2" references changing through one's "shadow", a recurring theme in Jung's work that represents part of one's personality that one might hate or fear.

Notice the words "Hate or Fear". Neurosis is the inability to tolerate ambiguity and that leads to hate and fear. If you are in neurosis and you love something subconsciously you hate it and if you hate something subconsciously you love it and thus you fear it because you cannot control it, but you want to attempt to control it and when you cannot you become hateful towards it. Heimmy detects gnashing of teeth so I will drop this line of discussion because it is probably too deep for the wading pool swimmers.

Bottom line is Jung had quite a few disciples and he was found with a book of Buddha's teaching on his night stand when they found in dead in bed.

I will never mention in my books ever into infinity that the Buddhists and the Hindu's are in fact "True Christians" "True Muslims" "True Jews" "true Followers" because you do not see them touting how great their religious teachers are yet they understand they were great religious teachers. And you do not see them slaughtering people for "religious" reasons. So I will never ever into infinity put that sentence in my books because If anyone in neurosis read that sentence they would explode and probably come hunting for me and it just so happens I haven't eaten in days. Please do not assume Heimdall is on anyone's side but his own side. One might suggest Heimdall is on the right side and he doesn't like anyone in his pool.5:01:02 PM

Do you perceive the author's IQ is:

0

1

66.6

0.000001

-822

so - so

The correct answer is: 8675309 also acceptable is: 25 or 6 to 4

"The GAO notes that being on a terrorist watch list does not mean that someone is involved in any terrorist activity."

Then to not confuse people the list should be called "Terrorist perhaps Watch perhaps List perhaps"

Heimdall will also settle for "Perhaps Terrorist Perhaps Watch Perhaps List, Perhaps". This way Heimdall will not be so confused by your literary mastery. I am uncertain who GAO is, but he should perhaps consider a name change perhaps, perhaps.5:16:31 PM

6/23/2009 12:07:27 PM I have taken my time out of writing my infinitely poor to come back in time because I am not finished with you GAO. First off GAO you should never speak in public because eventually someone with brain function is going to read your comments and hang you with them and by eventually I mean now. GAO, you put people on the terrorist watch list and then say they are not involved with terrorism. GAO, you put people on the terrorist watch list and then you sell them guns, so you sell people you say are terrorists, guns. So you assist terrorists, so you in fact are a terrorist, so you should be on the terrorist watch list. GAO you say people are terrorist by putting them on the terrorist watch list and then you say "does not mean that someone is involved in any terrorist activity." So your terrorist watch list is exactly what that communist watch list was way back when. You just put anyone on it you do not like and ruin them, so you are making terrorist threats and break the terroristic threat laws because you put people on your terrorist watch list who are not terrorists and that "scares" them and puts them in "fear for their life" and robs them of their dignity and reputation and then you hide behind the fact you're the government and you are above the law, so you will be put on my list.

Government Terrorists Who should be Abolished Watch List:

GAO

Since you are on my list that does not mean you should be exterminated but it also does not mean you should not be exterminated. Do you perceive I stutter GAO? Now you can put me on your terrorist watch list and then I will hang you with it. You are now on Heimdall's list for all eternity because Heimdall has determined you like to scare people and make them afraid and nothing in the universe will take you off my list ever. You bought the farm because you opened your mouth. You could have kept your mouth shut and I would not have read your "wise" comment in the news, but you had to open your mouth and so you did it to yourself because you know not what you do.

You will not scare my countrymen and live to tell about it on my watch. Thank you GAO for your compassion and understanding. I beg you to speak again in public.12:14:16 PM

"A man should look for what is, and not for what he thinks should be."
Albert Einstein

Clearly this guy is looking for fight with Heimmy.

I will clarify what he attempted to say. Have no expectations and observe questioningly.

"Nothing is more destructive of respect for the government and the law of the land than passing laws which cannot be enforced."
Albert Einstein

Cops do not want to arrest people for stupid reasons but the people keep passing stupid laws that say the cops must.

The law says kids cannot drink but many kids do drink in secret so either we have tons of criminals or tons of kids who think law is a joke.

The law says you cannot smoke pot but when 15 million people do smoke, they are either criminals or they laugh in the face of the law. Then some genius says "No one is above the law" but in reality everyone is above the law as long they don't get caught. The police cannot function just on busting murderer's , rapists and bank robbers, there simply is not enough murderer's , robbers, and rapists. So the police have to start busting people for stupid stuff because many are speeding , running red lights, smoking drugs and that's the cash cow and that is what pays the cops salary. Law enforcement cannot make money off catching murder's and rapists and bank robbers, there is no money in it but there is plenty of money in giving out tickets for broken tail lights and parking meter infractions and smoking a drug. The reason there is plenty of money in those "laws that cannot be enforced" is because everyone is breaking those laws. It is impossible to control a person. If they want to speed they will speed. A cop can give them a ticket and one minute later they will speed again. A judge once told me "If you want to kill yourself there is nothing anyone can do." There is no greater truth so why are people taking advantage of that reality. If someone wants to smoke their self to death that is their business not my business as long as they do not directly harm me. There is no indirect harm to me. That just legislative mumbo jumbo. Let's take it all the way back so you do not have to use your elementary logic on Heimdall. Kids are educated into the Left Brain and the left brain is focused on desires and cravings and that is what someone wants because they keep using that education technique, so they cannot start putting everyone in jail when people start bending to these desires and cravings because they were "educated" into these desires and craving in relation to Physical things. That's a nice way of saying, if you need money and you are overweight, addicted to drugs, depressed, have fear, have shame, have greed, have lust, have sloth you sue the government because they allowed the education system to indoctrinate you mentally to be all of those things. So if you killed someone, robbed someone, are a drugs addict are obese, are depressed, that's are symptoms of the "education" you were forced by law to undertake by the government so you have been mentally and perhaps physically harmed by the government and it was forced on you and your parents and their parents. So if you need money you look up on google what left brain is all about and your whole case is centered around this one sentence

"If you reflect back upon our own educational training, we have been traditionally taught to master the 3 R's: reading, writing and arithmetic -- the domain and strength of the left brain."

The government will argue it did not know that what that kind of heavy "memorization" would do to you, and the judge will say "Ignorance is no excuse" and you will win the case easily.

I can think clearly. I have no fear. I have no embarrassment or shame. I have no envy. I have no worry or stress. So that means if you have any of those things it is because of this: 3 R's: reading, writing and arithmetic, and you were forced to go through that conditioning by LAW. So you have a very solid case. I do not sue because Heimdall don't need no money, Caesar can keep what is his and I will keep what is mine.18:38:41

What this comment is saying is, if you pass a law against murder and then pass a law against smoking pot and make the penalty the same or close and then pass a law against drunk driving and make the penalty worse or close to the penalty for murder and then pass a law against having and unregistered gun and make it worse or the same as for murder, murder itself becomes not such a big deal when in fact it is a big deal. So then you have people selling crack killing other people for crack because murder is less important than crack on the scale of law crimes so crack has more value than murder. So a person caught with a pound of pot gets in more trouble than a person who murders someone so murder is not a big deal when in fact a pound of pot is nothing in contrast to murder. So laws have to be thought out carefully because if there is a million laws, the real important laws get all mixed up with the meaningless laws. All the laws start to look the same and before you know it a guy who smokes a joint goes to jail for 10 years and a guy who murders someone gets off in 2 years and then laws are just a joke and pointless. This is why it is important to not just pass a new law every time something "ambiguous" comes up because all that will happen is everyone will be in jail, like 2 million people will be in jail and 100,000 committed serious crimes and everyone else is in there for nothing or pointless crimes. Is a person a criminal because they take a drugs? Impossible. A cigar is just a cigar. A person is a tyrant if they deny a person freedom to do what they want as long as they do not directly physically harm others. Attempt to not be such a control freak and understand that. Control is a symptom one is subconsciously aware they have no control. You worry about the log in your eye and if everyone does that they will not be able to see the log in others eye and everything will just be grand. Outside of murder, rape and robbery, most of the other laws have much more to do with "I want to save you from yourself" than doing right or wrong things. You simply do not have the key to eternal physical life so you are not intelligent enough to determine what a person can do to their self or with the time they have been granted to be alive. If you are god then you can tell people what they can and cannot do in relation to drugs they take or lifestyles they live, if you are not god, you worry about your own business until you are tapped. You are not saving anyone with your control freak mindset, you are only making people feel like they are worthless and evil and bad, so shut your dam mouth. Freedom in the mind is achieved when the control mechanisms of the mind and the isolation caused by labels are removed from the mind in part through mental conditioning away from fear and absolute comments.

 I was right brain orientated and thus I could not do well at math and not do well at English rules and that meant I could not pass the college exams to get into college and that made me feel like an outcast and made me feel stupid and that is what led me to feel like I was worthless and that is what led me to attempt to kill myself for 10 plus years and that is what led me to have this accident and that is what led me to now be able to understand everything clearly, if you are able to foresee those events in that order and that fashion then you are god. If you could not see all of that coming in that order and in that fashion then you are not capable of making any determinations beyond determinations that relate to you alone.

Someone said I was a failure because I could not pass tests that were totally biased against right brain dominate people in a society that is totally biased against right brain dominate people and I assume that was you. That means you are going to pay with everything you have for your mistake and Heimdall has e no morals and never heard of the word mercy or compassion. See now Heimdall is pissed because I have no tolerance for molesters who perceive they are righteous. We will see who's head is on the post at the end of the battle. In summation:

"Neurosis   is   the   inability   to   tolerate   ambiguity."
Sigmund Freud

Control freaks are very dangerous especially when someone encourages them to "Get out and vote".

So you see Freud did not like "left brainers" and since he was friend with Jung , neither did Jung and Freud was friends with Einstein so none of these people cared much for "left brainers" that is why they insulted you for their whole lives and you never figured that out. They toyed with you like a cat toys with a little mouse. And all three wish they were me, so ponder what that means.

"Once   we   accept   our   limits,   we   go   beyond   them."
Albert Einstein

Once you accept you cannot win, you may start winning.

Consider all failure as an opportunity to understand you failed.

6/23/2009 8:39:40 AM- FEAR

a distressing emotion aroused by impending danger, evil, pain, etc., whether the threat is real or imagined; the feeling or condition of being afraid.

a specific instance of or propensity for such a feeling: an abnormal fear of heights.

concern or anxiety; solicitude: a fear for someone's safety.

reverential awe, esp. toward God.

that which causes a feeling of being afraid; that of which a person is afraid: Cancer is a common fear.

Heimdall has anger waxing issues today because "individuals" signed away his freedom of speech because they are afraid. No being in this universe is allowed to sign away Heimdalls freedom of speech or they sign their own death certificate. Laws do not matter if they suggest Heimdall does not have freedom of speech. Elementary logic does not matter if Heimdall does not have freedom of speech.

If you signed away my freedom of speech for any reason you are on my "Soon to be buried in the ground" watch list. I do not care what your excuse is. I only care if you wish to be buried in paper or plastic.

"One may say the eternal mystery of the world is its comprehensibility."
Albert Einstein

This quotes means, "Why can't anyone understand me." You think I am kidding even after I convince you "That whenever any Form of Government becomes destructive of these ends, it is the Right of the People to alter or to abolish it," simply means, if you vote and abridge my freedom of speech even if it does not matter to me, I have the right to abolish you. I can write a few books and say you better alter my absolute freedom of speech back into existence and you will just ignore me because you doubt I am going to abolish you. I am not going to maybe abolish you for negating my absolute freedom of speech.

You simply are not capable of this "comprehensibility". You do not understand why I write my books. There is no such thing as tolerance because you gave away my freedom of absolute speech. The principle is all that matters and when the principle(Constitutional absolute freedom of speech) is altered or abridged there is a blood bath because whoever altered the principle has no respect for the principle.

I do not tolerate tyrants ever into infinity I bury tyrant into infinity. Perhaps you understand that sentence. I have the right to breath and in the exact same respect I have the "Right of the People to alter or to abolish it". I have the right to slaughter people who vote away my absolute freedom of speech and absolute freedom of privacy. That means your little delusion of "tolerance" and "don't harm people" do not matter, they are trumped. They are negated, they are null and void.

Here is my logic. Someone cried wolf. Many voted to sign away my absolute freedom of speech. I will abolish so many people the next time someone cries wolf people will think twice before signing away my absolute freedom of speech. That is my logic. Perhaps you do not understand logic perhaps it is far beyond "comprehensibility" in relation to your mind. Every day I write I am mindful you think I am kidding because you spit in the face of the founders of this nation every single day and then you brag how wise you are. So abolishment is the only true solution. So I will end this train of thought by saying if you voted away my absolute freedom of speech Heimdall only has one question for you, "Paper or plastic?" I have determined; it is better to die a horrible death than to live without saying what I have determined I should say. The creator has the right to take away my absolute freedom of speech and if you are not the creator and you took away my absolute freedom of speech, you are a tyrant and you get abolished. There is no argument because you cannot convince me otherwise no matter how many fear tactic laws you pass, because your fear tactic laws do not mean anything to Heimmy. 9:32:10 AM

I perceive I hung myself rather well to start off the day. I have no idea what compassion is but perhaps whoever suggested it will get over their delusions in time. The ones who get "tapped" always get slaughtered in the end. Do you perceive I should be pleased with that understanding? I will go play my video game and think of my mother because she will not slaughter me like you abominations are going to. So you do it slowly and painfully so that I might feel. You better pray with all your might there is no afterlife. I am blessed because people do not read books anymore.9:55:35 AM

Good and evil are relative to the observer so they are delusions. Is a lion killing a lamb good or evil? Neither, it just is.

Revolution is required when a majority of the voters determine safety is more valuable than absolute freedom of speech.

[11:24] <@WORLDW1D3> wonder what Heimdall is doing ?

[11:27] <+Okay-> world, we are in temple, why da fuck u showing war link and its technology

[11:28] <+Okay-> show us sth peacefully

[11:28] <+Okay-> and logically

01[11:28] <+Heimdall> I am monolging to various beings and attempting to finish my poorly written volume 6

01[11:29] <+Heimdall> So, the only way to reach consciousness is to eliminate fear

01[11:30] <+Heimdall> meditation in a cemetary is a buddhist suggestion, jesus said i defeated death as in his fear of death

01[11:30] <+Heimdall> sitting in a cemetary means a ghost may kill you, that is why you sit there and face your fear of death

01[11:30] <+Heimdall> this is all in relation to what put us to sleep

01[11:30] <+Heimdall> If you reflect back upon our own educational training, we have been traditionally taught to master the 3 R's: reading, writing and arithmetic -- the domain and strength of the left brain.

01[11:31] <+Heimdall> They taught us "the three R's" are wise, but the three "r's where a trojan horse , a shiny apple on teh tree of knowledge and they force kids to eat it

01[11:31] <+Heimdall> the side effect is left brain and thus fear

01[11:31] <+Heimdall> left brain is fear based

01[11:31] <+Heimdall> its the stupid aspect of the midn ebcasue peopel say things based on fear

01[11:32] <+Heimdall> On the contrary, the right brain seems to flourish dealing with complexity, ambiguity and paradox.

01[11:32] <+Heimdall> on teh contray means opposite

01[11:32] <+Heimdall> i am on the oppsite side, trying to persuade people who cannot understand me

01[11:32] <+Heimdall> they say i am insane , but that is becasue i am to flourish dealing with complexity,

01[11:33] <+Heimdall> complex

01[11:33] <+Heimdall> i say contradictions that are true, but they think I am insane

01[11:33] <+Heimdall> they think I am on drugs becasue they cannot undersatnd they are asleep

[11:33] <+Okay-> u can find bitches everywhere .. that's true world

01[11:33] <+Heimdall> i am all the way to teh right so i cannot even reach them

01[11:34] <+Heimdall> they think going to a cemetary at night alone is crazy becasue you might get killed by a ghost

01[11:34] <+Heimdall> so i will drowned them with infinite books, i have decided so it will be so

01[11:35] <+Heimdall> Thank You

You do not want to piss off Heimdall. There is no greater truth than that. You have already pissed off Heimdall so you are suicidal, and I am all about suicidal.11:37:12 AM

"One may say the eternal mystery of the world is its comprehensibility."

Albert Einstein

Comprehensibility: capable of being comprehended or understood; intelligible.

Is the author:

A: Insane.

B: Beyond your ability to comprehend.

C: Hilarious.

D: On very potent drugs.

E: In need of very potent drugs like poison mushrooms, hemlock or 9 inch nails.

The correct answer is: A,B,C,D or E.

Nothingness denotes absence of labels, that means one person might think they know what is right and attempt to force that perceived truth on others, but it is never absolute truth only perceived truth.

2:01:17 PM I will get through this one swiftly because I have things of importance to discuss. The story of Noah's Ark is simply suggesting, Noah and a few others "woke up" from the "education" brain washing into the Left Brain forced on them by the "adults" and the flood represents the whole world was wiped out, which denotes the whole world bought into the "apple" of "knowledge" and thus went to sleep or Left brain because of the three R's. So the whole world in relation to humans died because of that Trojan horse apple called "knowledge". And the two sets of animals denotes the comment "when two or more are gathered in my name". This is in relation to the "click". When two right brain people who woke up gather they discuss and ramble and plan how to wake others up, because the power aspect of the mind, the right, is quite a talker. So if anyone ever says you think too much or you talk too much, you remind them they think too little and talk too little because they are in neurosis and then you tell them why they are in neurosis and watch them get angry and upset and hateful, and then you just walk away and laugh at their inability to tolerate ambiguity. You have to toy with them like a mouse using your words because they are asleep and your words will slowly start to wake them up but not so much on a daily basis but maybe in a few months they will start seeking you out to hear your words because they are starting to understand they are asleep. Relativity means no person in the universe has a more valid opinion that you do, relative to you. Someone who is in neurosis decided they know better than you and so they forced you to get the left brain "education" against your will, so all bets are off. There are no morals once the war has been initiated. If you want to wake up call me, if you want to be abused further call me swiftly. Say an original thought and I will call you Master.2:17:29 PM

<+Okay-> pls proceed your speech

<+Heimdall> if one is a mild seeker, they can watch a scary movie and afterwards sit in the dark alone and see how long they can stand it

<+Heimdall> If one is a true seeker, they will go to the most haunted cemetery in their area at night and sit alone with no chance of calling for help until they either are killed by the spirits or they lose their fear.

<+Heimdall> Everything else i say is secondary

<+Heimdall> saying perhaps a lot is another method

<+Heimdall> say perhaps until people insult you for saying perhaps then say it more often

<+Okay-> are u a poetic

<+Heimdall> one had to get used to talking a lot this is teh nature of the right barin or nirvana, this is why buddha wrote so many books he was a motor mouth, that is a symptom of consciousness

<+Heimdall> so

<+Heimdall> you can go to chat rooms you do not like and condition yoursefl away from fear

<+Heimdall> then you talk about whatever and exdpect to be told to shut up

<+Heimdall> thats will aassist you with talking punishment

<+Heimdall> taking

<+Heimdall> listen to songs you hate and listen to them until you are pleased with them

<+Heimdall> this condition you away from judgement adn labels casued by teh left brain conditioning from education of the three R's

<+Heimdall> one should reacha p9oint of never stopping thoughts and talk to yourself if no one is around

<+Heimdall> talk and talk and talk

<+Heimdall> thats is teh nature of consciousness

<+Heimdall> this makes teh froezen gears in the midn start working again

<+Heimdall> mind

<+Heimdall> always take a counter argument

<+Heimdall> this creqates more discussion

<+Heimdall> take the opposite side of any discussion to make more discussion

This is how Heimdall see's the mind at this stage since the accident.

On one hand there is the left hemisphere. It is encouraged by reading writing and math. It is physical orientated and materialistically orientated. A side effect of this aspect of the mind is very pronounced emotions such as fear, anger, greed, lust, hate, judgment, desires, cravings, control .

Some of the details of this aspect of the mind are strong sense of time, strong sense of hunger, strong urges to control , strong urges to reach satisfaction from materialistic things such as possessions, drugs, and laws for example. This aspect of the mind is part of the mind so it is impossible to be good or evil if you are dominate in this aspect of the mind.

On the other hand the right aspect of the mind is cerebrally focused. It achieves its satisfaction from thoughts and from words. It desires to reach further understanding on the cerebral level and not on the physical level, so it is not focused on materialistic things or seeking satisfaction from the material things the left aspect of the minds seeks. It does not wish to control and it against laws because laws are a symptom of control. This aspect of the mind desires to speak freely because this aspect of the mind can only reach satisfaction from monologue either by thoughts or words. So this aspect of the mind is verbally focused in opposition to the left aspect of the mind which seeks to gain satisfaction from the control of material aspects of reality. This right aspect of the mind is part of the mind so it is impossible to be good or evil if you are dominate in this aspect of the mind.

The "three R's" "knowledge" has turned many from the natural right aspect of the mind they were born with into the left aspect. That is not good or evil, that is just the way it is.

If one desires to be on the left aspect, they should go full tilt. If one desires to be on the right aspect they should go full tilt. Remaining in the middle or having some of each is undesirable or what is known as lukewarm. If one desires to control reality using the left physical based means then do it. If one desires to control reality with the right cerebral based means, then do it. Remaining in the middle or lukewarm denotes you are in a limbo or purgatory state of mind or you are only taking half steps or at half power. One cannot live properly in the middle because they will be a friend to neither aspect. It is not good or evil to remain in the middle, it is one's own choice but the choices one has must be clarified for one to make an informed decision. This choice of right, left or middle aspect is left up to the each and every person and it is never the business of any other person. This choice cannot be made by any other person no matter what age they are or what they think they know. The most anyone can do is monologue to their self near other people in hopes other people will appreciate their monologue. Any control efforts greater monologue near other beings is tyranny of the mind and slavery of a beings right to choose because that choice is endowed by the creator and no being can ever take that right to chose away from another being under any circumstance or they become the oppressor and tyrant. 4:01:53 PM

If one attempts to persuade another being to do something in relation to this "mind choice" using any form a fear tactics or using to laws to justify robbing that being of their choice they are simply a tyrant of the mind and that is not good or evil it just is.

Robbing a child of its "mind choice" by any being for any reason is child abuse, tyranny and enslaving another being mindfully and is a symptom of a "control freak", that is not good or evil it just is.

This is the reality of the "current" education system in general. A human in born in "nirvana" or heavy right brained. When a human are still at a young age they are forced to take the "left brain" conditioning by law. The ones who take the conditioning become "accepted" and are praised with money and material wealth and material luxuries. The ones who resist the "left brain" conditioning become labeled as outcasts and are forced into remedial jobs or the "arts" and are deemed "stupid" and therefore are the directly treated in a bias fashion by society as a whole, that is not good or evil that just is. Now I will discuss something of value.4:48:21 PM

Early man created tools. This required creativity. "The right brain has been associated with the realm of creativity." This is definitive proof early man was not stupid but simply naturally right brain dominate as every human is when they are born. This denotes the garden of Eden age. Early man certainly had communication and language just as we do, but it was strictly verbal. It was not "script". When "script" came into being that was also a right brain invention, it took much creativity to invent written language, but the side effect of teaching everyone script was it encouraged left brain. So script had an unforeseen side effect that was not detected until it was too late. So hieroglyphics were perhaps the first written language and that is also when the pyramids were built and the pyramids are a symptom of when man became "left brain" focused which is physical based towards reality. Their mindset was perhaps "If we build this huge pyramid we will show the universe we are in control." That is much along the lines of why left brain dominate people like to show control. Some take over other countries to get control or resources or of people. Some left brain dominate people like to control their family or their children or the ones they hang around. This control aspect is left brain dominate type thinking. They simply want control of anything in relation to physical reality. Right brain dominate wants freedom and therefore does not wish to control others because it does not wish to be controlled. This denotes why early man did not set up cities early man was a wanderer. A wanderer goes from place to place freely and will not "rest on laurels". So now at this point in history mankind is so left brain dominate from the script incident, it is perceived to be natural to live in a box called a house. It is discouraged for anyone to wish to wander. The ones who wander, and ironically are right brain, are outcasts in society and they are what are known as "transients". They are simply right brain dominate people trapped at various stages of right brain and they are told they are loser, and failures so they go the street because they perceive they are not normal because they cannot fit into the world of the "sane". The reason many veterans come back from war and "lose it" is because war creates great fear and they must face that fear, but they also tend to get trapped in various stages of right brain dominate mind. Then they are fed drugs to "bring them back" to left brain and it will never work because once one faces enough fear the right brain dominate aspect is permanent. I cannot go back to the left because I faced my fear of death when I did not have to, so it threw me in such an extreme right brain progression, I went through all the phases from level 1 right brain all the way to the end in about seven months. Many face various fears and start to go back to how they were born which is right brain, and they get stuck. They are deemed "insane" or "crazy" and that is an illusion because many are simply "trapped" at various stages of right brain dominate.

I will tell the one in the movie the beautiful mind, you are trapped in a stage of right brain dominate where you are very good at patterns but you need to condition further away from fear in order to progress further from that stage you are at. Any around you are suggesting you are "ill" and need drugs. Assume they are insane and go sit in a cemetery until you have no fear, listen to music you hate until you are pleased with it, that is a proper remedy, these drugs you are on will never do anything ever into infinity, because drugs to assist one who is right brain inclined is insanity. Simply put there is nothing wrong with you, society is just extremely biased against right brain dominate people to an extreme degree. Of course you are a little confused at times because you are trapped at a various stage of right brain dominate so you have to attempt if you wish to go the full measure and let go of that fear. The math you focus on is also keeping you in the "middle". You are right brain dominate and then you focus on short term memory aspect and that rips you back to the left so you are in this tug of war mentally. Your mind is right brain dominate but you focus on left brain aspects and thus never achieve full right brain so you are trapped and this is what is causing this situation where you need to take "their" medicines. I have a Doctorate degree in clarity in case you are wondering but you can call me Todd.6:02:20 PM

6/24/2009 3:02:48 AM

The world is focused on all these important things and I am writing books to convince myself I lost my ability to write.

11:46:41 AM Jonah in the whale is about facing fear. The whale is big and of course fear is big in ones on the "left" so the three days denotes it takes some time to get of this fear. To face the fear one has to do things that frighten them and people do not like to do things that frighten them because if they did, it would not frighten them. So the fear condition is much like "breaking a horse". A horse is a nervous wreck until they are broken then they calm down, then they reach their potential. So the fear is not fear it is something that is keeping the mind a nervous wreck. The fear conditioning is not about facing "dangerous" life and death situation as much as giving up the fear of things along the lines of giving up the ghost of fear because fear is a ghost, it is not real. Fear is not real it is a delusion in the mind and a side effect of the "scribe education". It is an unwanted side effect from "eating off the tree of knowledge" and it appears so real, but it is an illusion in the mind. If you cannot watch a scary movie and then turn off the lights and sit there alone in the dark without "freaking out" you have some serious mental issues, that is not a judgment call that is a reality call.11:52:03 AM

This is a song written today by the stupidest man alive or dead depending on your perception.

http://www.youtube.com/watch?v=0EEMkfh1Pq0 – Never Tell

You do not need to worry about Heimdalls mental health because you factually have a lifetime of mental health issues to work out yourself. Yu can start by not pissing yourself and signing away my freedoms every time a firecracker goes off. If you could just accomplish that in your entire life you will have lived a proper life, but I ain't counting it, in fact I understand that is an impossibility. You may perceive I am stupid but I perceive in general you are perfect so clearly I am extremely biased.

A life under the influence of any fear is a wasted life.

Jung prefers to suggest higher power in his AA strategy and higher power is the same as saying the man upstairs and the man upstairs is the same as saying subconscious and subconscious is the same as saying right brain dominate and right brain dominate is the same as saying nirvana. The definitions of words in most cases are more confusing than helpful. Many of these "religious" texts are stories attempting to explain cerebral concepts in physical terms and ones who are "sane" take these teachings in physical terms because left brain is physical focused. They perceive the holy grail is a literal physical cup. Then they write infinite books about where one can find this literal physical cup. So the term brain dead mole crickets in contrast to saying they are "the devil", "the darkness", "The vipers", "the adversary" ,"the infidels" or "the sane" proves I have infinite compassion and that proves I am Heimdall. If you do not understand I am Heimdall and that is an absolute fact, then my only question to you is "What drugs are you on, boy?".3:58:51 PM

Perhaps you should run along because my books are for people with brain function.

I will make this very clear. I was born on the right and I was inclined to creativity but when I got a little older I was forced by law to go to schools that forced left brain teachings on me and when I could not succeed "they" said I was a failure and a loser and I was doomed to be an outcast. This means they are biased racists against me and treat me unfairly because of how I am naturally. What that means is I will not have morals, rules, mercy or tolerance, period. I have declared total all out revolution and Heimdall prefers it be a blood bath. I have an aversion to rules and laws, that does not means I break laws, that means I cannot tolerate feeling I am being controlled by stupid laws created by frightened little frogs that piss when they hear the word wolf. Am I a bad person?" This component of the brain is not concerned with things falling into patterns because of prescribed rules." Or are you a racist against people who think opposite of the way you think? Perhaps you have come to an understanding. Thank you for your compassion and understanding. Thank You.4:32:58 PM

If I say "You have been brainwashed" and you say "No I haven't", that proves you are brainwashed. I submit I was brainwashed and now I am not because I woke up because of a freak accident which relates to me almost dying. I am not afraid to sit in a cemetery at night alone and you piss yourself just thinking about that. I am not afraid and you are a nervous wreck. So that means since I have silenced fear to an extreme, if that is abnormal then the comment "Nothing to fear but fear itself" is not wisdom but insanity. So if that comment is insanity that means it is best to be a nervous wreck and so afraid that they piss their self when they get nervous. That then means the comment "When the government fears the people there is freedom" is also not wisdom but insanity. That also means extortion which is simply a fear tactic is proper and normal and should not be against the law because the powers that be condition everyone to be afraid with their indoctrination education. What that means is "someone" is making sure everyone gets this "education" so they are prone to fear so they can be easily manipulated with fear tactics. Why don't you write infinite books explaining why that cannot be so, genius.5:00:38 PM

In the novel "1984" it talks about big brother controlling ones thoughts or independent thought is not allowed. Well big brother in by law forcing children to be educated into the left brain which is the less complex aspect of the mind which is isolated in contrast to the free aspect of the mind in relation to , left has many fear and emotional issues which means "1984" was not a predication of what may happen it was an attempt to tell us what is happening. Of course you do not understand anything I say because you are in the "dark" in every form of the word "dark". Everyone keeps running around saying "1984" hasn't happened. Well what do you think is happening? What do you think happened to you? Why do you feel ashamed to say what you really feel? Why are you shy? Why are you embarrassed? Why do you have no brain function? This is "1984" genius.7:44:41 PM

6/25/2009 2:54:24 AM – I saw wisdom in a Swiss cheese commercial recently.

10:50:31 AM- I admire this being because I am mindful they certainly were "mindful".

"All the world is full of suffering. It is also full of overcoming. " Helen Keller

Suffering leads to the understanding of suffering.

She died June 1st 1968 and I was born May 15th 1968 so I was in the presence of greatness and declare that a miracle.

All perceived suffering is an opportunity to progress swiftly, fail miserably, progress miserably or fail swiftly but I prefer to progress swiftly into miserable failure.

Great thoughts are a symptom of deep suffering and may lead to powerful understandings

Thoughts are a form of observation in relation to "I think therefore I am." One is able to recall a memory and feel sensations from that memory as strong as feelings from sight or sound or touch. I look at the picture of Helen on Wikipedia and I want to go communicate with her and meet her and I cannot and I hate the universe because it only produces suffering. If you love the universe then you perhaps are not thinking clearly or you perhaps are an infinite sadist. All thoughts and comments based on thoughts are typically a symptom that one is aware they are being observed. This "pandering to observers" is a left brain indication. When one is extreme right brain/subconscious dominate they perceive "observers" are illusions when they are not in the presence of "observers". A person surrounded by "religious:" people will have thoughts and comments in relation to their surroundings. When a person is pulled over by a police officer their thoughts and thus comments are pandering to the reality they are being observed by a police officer. This is all across the board, when a child is in the presence of an "authority figure" their thoughts are in relation to that awareness they are being observed. When a person is alone and has left brain dominate mindset, they may be "afraid" to say thing or think things because they may be perceive some "supernatural" aspect is observing their actions and words and even thoughts. I sit here in my isolation chamber and I cannot perceive who I am talking to so I am not concerned with "pandering to observers". When I am around people I tend to be docile or crack jokes but then when I am here all alone I do not perceive any observers so I am talking to myself or my alter ego and I am not concerned with pandering to it. I do not like my alter ego so I do not pander to it or I do not like my "left brain" aspect because it nearly convinced me I should kill myself so I hate it and I want it to understand I hate it, so I do not pander my thoughts with its "sensibilities" in mind. The alter ego suggests "You should not publish these horrible books you will be embarrassed and ashamed." So I publish these books to spite these comments by the "alter/left brain ego". I am showing the left who is the boss now. You may perceive I am not translating Helen's above quote anymore but I assure you I am.

Buddha suggested this concept "contact". Contact is a nice way to say "under control" or "mimic" or "under the influence of others". I prefer to call it cult member. So the scribe aspect conditions people to be left brain then they become cult members or easily manipulated by "words, ideals concepts" suggested by "authority figures". This is easily proven because Edison, Einstein and Tesla were essentially loners, this is the nature of right brain because one cannot be creative in a group setting in relation to many things and in these people cases inventions. They could not invent anything if others were there saying "You cannot do that." They had to isolate their self away from the "contact" to think properly to come up with the inventions. So right brain dominate people tend to be "lone wolfs" maybe its "Lone wolves", what have you. What this contact really means is almost all of the society has these certain belief systems in relation to everything from religion to politics to education, that are simply a result of contact or a result of being manipulated or a symptom many are running around acting as mimics and are not really capable of original thoughts because they have been conditioned into left brain due to the education system and it may be incidental or it may be intentional, and that is a big red flag. If the "powers that be" and I am uncertain who that really is, wants to keep people in general "under their thumb" they would push very hard for the "three R's" and there is no doubt about that because control has everything to do with keeping people from "free thought" which is exactly what the book "1982" is talking about. Instead of a world with people who are right brain dominate as they are when they are born and having a world of free thinkers we have the opposite which is a world of left brain mimics and sheep with very little creative ability or "free thinking" ability in general.

So there are many unknowns here. Maybe the "three r's" look like a shiny apple and they have some unwanted side effects and so it is all a misunderstanding. Maybe the "three r's" started out as a misunderstanding but now they are being pushed very hard because "someone" is aware they are able to keep everyone in a "mimic" state of mind and not an "original creative free" state of mind. Maybe there is a "supernatural" explanation why this "shiny red apple" is so inviting. The reality is, no matter which option it is, this left brain conditioning as a result of the "three r's" is worldwide and through and through, that is an absolute fact. I will now discuss something of relevance.12:55:36 PM

Please be mindful poisonous snakes are in fact poisonous and they like to test their venom's strength to make sure it still works; granted that was infinitely out of context. Some may perceive I am not in touch with reality but I am certain I can detect a lunatic asylum and a large herd of sheep when I see them; as a matter of fact I see them quite clearly. Many perceive without fear one is in danger and susceptible to falling into traps but in reality having fear makes one susceptible to falling into traps because it hinders clear thinking. At this stage since the accident I am everything in the universe but stupid. I am certain of that.1:22:12 PM

My mindset is I will never be able to contact you no matter how hard I try and that is absolute proof I will be able to contact you using no effort at all.

Everything is in the realm of impossibility and incomprehensibility except for the ideal nothing.

Everything emerges from the void of nothingness and eventually works its way back to that absolute ideal. If everything came from the void of nothing then everything is a subset of nothing and thus is nothing. This big bang ideal suggests everything came from a void of nothing and this is perhaps complex because it would mean everything including matter and thought are in fact nothing because both originated with nothing.

It is well I am aware everything in the universe is an illusion put here to try and piss me off. In a true vacuum or void the only remedy to avoid "control" and "slavery" is to allow everyone to have freedom to pursue what they perceive is the true path based on their own perception of truth or happiness. Granted this a dangerous remedy because some desire to harm others or control others to be happy or feel gratification. On the other hand if the "strings" of freedom are pulled to tight the concept of freedom is destroyed. The remedy to this is an absolute "If it does not directly harm others do what thou will." This denotes freedom to experiment. Some decide to climb a mountain to experiment with freedom and that is not against the law although that person may die in their experiment. Then there are laws that say a person cannot use a drug to achieve their perceived happiness and then freedom of choice is destroyed because although that person may die in their experiment they still have the right to experiment. No person is all knowing so they simply are unable to determine what experiment is proper and what experiment is not proper. The great reality is with this "contact" aspect. Everyone is being manipulated by others because no person is in the true vacuum by their self. Many who are labeled "depressed" or "suicidal" are attempting to find their self outside of the confines of the "contact" effects of the "herd" or "society". Many who peddle the "you have to be a part of the society" are not yet at the level of understanding, when you attempt to run with the herd you are manipulated by that hard as a side effect and thus robbed of your own personal pursuit of happiness because of the "contact" aspect. The moment a "control force" determines an individual cannot experiment, as long as it does not directly harm others, they rob that person of an opportunity for mental progression in the form of further understandings. This of course is a valuable tool on the other hand to keep people "under control " or "in line". The "powers that be" can simply say "You cannot experiment" and that will in fact "dumb the herd down" and the herd will be easily manipulated. This "powers that be" can be as mild as friends one hangs around or on a world wide scale such as the United Nations. "Guilt and fear trips" are great ways to keep one from experimenting and becoming "wiser" from the results of those experiments. They are essentially fear tactics. "You do this and this will happen to you." That is a terroristic threat and only terrorists use fear tactics to control others. "If you smoke a joint and get caught you will go to jail or get a fine." That is a fear tactic used by a terrorist to control a person. "If you do not get educated by the standards of education we have determined you will be a failure and an outcast in society and have a harsh life." That is a fear tactic used by a terrorist who is attempting to wield control over people. No person is all knowing so they cannot push other people around with laws that infringe on a person's right to pursue happiness determined by that person. Happiness is not a group determination because happiness is relative to the observer. Marie Currie determined experimenting with radiation was happiness and although it killed her that is her business and not the business of any other person in the universe. Control freaks will suggest that concept of personal freedom is insanity or dangerous because all that is on their mind is control of others right to pursue happiness based on that individual's perception of what happiness is. The truth is, no person knows what good or bad really is, because it is all relative to the observer. Is it good to smoke a joint or bad? Well if you talk to a control freak who has stock in a beer company they will say a joint is bad and evil and harmful because that is the nature of control freaks, everything they think and say and feel is a symptom that they wish to keep control over others right to pursue happiness. A control freak will never make a determination to let go of control because that means they would lose power. This is in direct relation to "absolute power controls absolutely" because once a person "feels" control over others they only want more and more and they are never able to let go of the power and that is strictly left brain characteristics induced by the education system. Ponder when a parent says "This is my child and I will raise them how I see fit." That is a control freak aspect because in reality that is not their child, they just happen to have an offspring and once that offspring is delivered they no longer have power over it. Only a control freak determines they own something because they feed it. Only a slave master determines it owns something because it feeds it. If you cannot handle that reality and you still wish to control freak your child then you are unfit to raise a child and should turn your child over to someone who is not a control freak so that the child is not abused and mentally raped by a rapist of children. You can quote me on that whole part.

I do not pander to mental rapists of children but I have determined I will eat these mental rapist control freaks for no reason at all. Perhaps this will be my pursuit ; to eat all forms of mental rapist control freaks whether they attempt to control children or adults. Perhaps I will not attempt to control the control freaks but simply ensure they become extinct using my quill of ink.4:24:19 PM

Ones who are truly in the extreme right brain have slight awareness of time and slight emotional aspects and thus they are rare and considered in the NOW. This is relevant to the concept those who control the present control the past. This indicates those who are in extreme right brain understand the past clearly "they hear and do understand" as opposed to ones one the "left" who "hear and do not understand" and this relates to the concept "to the victor go the spoils" because if one is in the "NOW" to such a degree and they can explain the past easily and in turn can manipulate the future. If I can make a convincing argument about the past I will in fact manipulate the future and I will do it from the NOW. This ideal is what is known in Buddhism as Zen Masters. They are Masters of the past and thus masters of the future but there is only one true Zen Master at a time. There are many who perceive they are Masters but they all answer to the Grand Zen Master. So the Zen Masters recognize the Grand Master and thus are humbled because they become aware they in fact never were Zen Masters in the presence of a Grand Master. This is not a matter of who is more educated and not a matter of who is stronger it is a "spoil" of the one who "climbed the mountain" at a 90 degree incline.4:35:56 PM

6:39:48 PM – I will make this very clear. There is a concept in this universe along the lines of "Those who try to save their self will lose their self." And another concept along the lines of "Those who give up liberty for a little security deserve neither". What this means is people who are afraid and fearful tend to not think clearly and they panic and makes bad decisions. This of course is a side effect of the left brain conditioning caused by the apple called "three R's." What this means is a firecracker exploded and someone in America yelled wolf and certain people panicked and in their panicked attempt to save their self they voted away my absolute freedom of speech, my freedom to have privacy and my freedom to a fair trial so now they will understand the definition of "lose their self" and "deserve neither".

They essentially signed their "love me long time" orders. I will clarify. In the land of the free the ones who determine freedom has been abridged are in the "right" because that is the nature of the "right brain" and they sit at the "right hand". So they are unable to be in the "wrong" if they are trying to gain back freedom that has been signed away by the "left" who panic and piss their self like little frogs when a scary monster appears in their delusional head. I do not want anyone to misunderstand this next part. You have a very limited amount of time to adjust my freedom of speech my freedom of privacy and my freedom of fair trail back into reality or you are going to understand the definition of "lose their self" and the earth is my witness and you will be its supplicant. I will make sure this gets published and put on a world stage so when the "accounting time" comes no one will be caught off guard. You are either for me or you are against me. I will now discuss something relevant.6:48:47 PM

Every person is simply in various alternating stages of goodness.

"BRIDGEPORT, Conn. (AP) - A Connecticut church has outraged gay rights advocates by posting a video of members performing an apparent exorcism of a teen's "homosexual demons."

I am willing to trade my "see everyone else as perfect except me demons" and "Inability to write anything but crappy books demons" for your "homosexual demons".

Are your delusions of a great battle of good and evil original thought or just the babbling of a mimic in a cult? Suggesting you are important would downgrade your impact; suggesting you are perfect would insult your importance. A person who is suicidal perceives everyone else is perfect except their self so they are the definition of "meek" or "humble"

6/26/2009 12:55:48 AM – Here is how I perceive things since the accident. As a result of my final suicide attempt my mind shut off the left aspect of my brain. The left aspect which contains many strong emotions and desires and cravings. What this means is I am mentally imbalanced. What that means is many of these "wise men" or "ones in nirvana" down through history were in fact mentally imbalanced.

So this means there are many people in the world who perceive they are "in nirvana" or have no sense of time but in fact they are mentally imbalanced because they went a bit too far with their "conditioning" techniques. One might suggest I went a bit too far with my conditioning techniques "accidently". I was certainly not looking for nirvana but as a result of coming very close to killing myself I found it. What that means is my mind is locked in a mode. My mind is locked in the mode it was in before that last attempt. I perceive I am nothing and so I see everything around me as something or as perfect or as "wise". I see wisdom in everything because I perceive I am nothing or nothingness. So clearly I am mentally imbalanced. It is abnormal to perceive everything is perfect except one's self. Balance would be one see's some things as good and some things as evil. Many of the ones I speak to in various degrees of" nirvana" at least have some balance left in their perception. They perceive this battle of good and evil. Many people perceive this battle of good and evil. That is balance and that is normal. So this mode my mind is stuck in means I have to be very careful to sound very arrogant as if I am the only thing that matters because my mind is stuck in the mode I am worthless. What that means is I have to over compensate to such a degree I have to sound very arrogant and then publish it so the whole world see's how arrogant I am. That is my only chance of survival. My mind will not even allow me to remember my books so I have to keep writing them and publishing them to keep this "mode of worthlessness" at bay. I do not have time for games such as "right and wrong" and "good and evil". I personally do not give a shit about such things at this stage in time. I see everything is perfect and everyone is perfect because my mind understands I am worthless. What that means is I am blind to reality. That is the definition of insanity but I am also not concerned with being looked at as insane because I do not have time for such games and personally I do not give a shit if people say I am insane.

Of course I am insane the left half of my brain essentially does not function anymore. I do need anyone to tell me that I am aware of that. I do need anyone to help me because there is no drug in the universe that can trick my mind to forget my last attempt. I am stuck in suicide mode mentally because that is the mode I was in when I took that handful of Paxil. That means I have to keep writing these crappy books just to maintain mentally a sort of balance. I have to keep just cursing the world because I see it all as perfection. I cannot trick my mind otherwise. I cannot just write many words and not publish them because my mind cannot be fooled. I just keep writing and writing and I never go anywhere with it. I never make a point. I never reach a conclusion because if I do then I will stop writing and then I will resort to the mode I am mentally stuck in, "You are worthless", and I will kill myself.1:18:11 AM

"The goal of all life is death."

Sigmund Freud

I will clarify this although I submit due to the "mental progression" I am far beyond most people's ability to follow at all. Just humor me and pretend you grasp this. Human beings are on one hand a mutation. Somehow our brain became "aware" or "to advanced". One might suggest we know too much, we are aware of the 'final conclusion" of life. The awareness of the "final conclusion" makes us essentially nervous wrecks. Most people are aware we are different from other animals and most people are aware we are one of the few species who actually kill ourselves when there is no "real" reason to. In general most animals are not as aware of the "final conclusion" to life so they are much more relaxed. Human tend to get all hyped up about things and cannot just BE, this is because somehow we are aware of "death". Human beings minds have "evolved" to a degree we are aware of our own eventual death and that is a psychologically devastating trait. This "scribe" aspect only made that awareness more psychologically devastating. It made human being more nervous and more impatient. Sense of time became so pronounced this "final conclusion" to life became very powerful. In today's world people are literally living to die. I am not suggesting one should strive to become right brain dominate so they can silence this nervousness and pronounced fear but I am certain this accident has calmed me down quite a bit. I am no longer so "final conclusion" focused because my emotions are so silenced they are nearly gone and that means I can relax a bit. I talk to some people online and I notice they are a nervous wreck. They are always in a rush for meaningless things and this is a direct symptom subconsciously they aware of the "final conclusion" but consciously they are acting in extremely strange ways to counter act this awareness. A person's right brain aspect is far to intelligent to ever be afraid or scared of anything ever but then this left brain aspect is dominate because of the scribe aspect and that person is in "neurosis". In reality it is much worse than neurosis they are simply nervous wrecks and they mentally speaking are using a small percentage of their brains power and the rest is set in this "nervousness". I was certainly extremely depressed before the accident but in reality everyone who has been "indoctrinated" with this scribe aspect is naturally depressed. They cannot even talk about death because they become very depressed and then they assume anyone who talks about death is "dark" and "sinister". They are essentially "blinded by the nervousness". I perceive this "awareness of the final conclusion" in man combined with the scribe aspect is a fatal flaw in humans. It is a death blow. Somehow someone is going to get into a position of power and have their finger on the "trigger" on an arsenal and let it rip and it will not be because they are in "neurosis".

So on one hand scribe and mathematics really ushered humans along and it certainly was invented by someone with "right brain creativity" and its side effect is perhaps fatal to the species. Essentially as a species we are killing our self. Forget all the spiritual hocus pocus, you certainly are aware we are killing our self. Our population is beyond our ability to maintain yet no one is considering how to get it under control and no one will consider how to get it under control so we are suicidal as a species because in general the population is using the retarded aspect of the mind and has little ability to make proper decisions as a result of the scribe aspect. As a species this left brain aspect means we are hell bent on physical power and control and focus and nothing else matter s but that.

The American Indian lived with the buffalo for perhaps thousands of years and there was up to 70 million buffalo and the ones trained in scribe arrived and slaughtered most of the buffalo in a few years and that is the nature of the left brain. Kill everything that you want because that gives you a power or a control rush and it's all about having "fun" when you're left brained. Do not assume I care about animals, I do not care about anything at this point since the accident to be quite honest. I perceive our extinction as a species is irreversible. I do not perceive I am really helping anyone because it is perhaps too far gone now or too late. There are nearly seven billion people on this planet and if there are ten million in "nirvana" or extreme right brain it would be a miracle and I do not perceive there are more than 10 in complete extreme right brain. That means there are only MAYBE ten people on the planet that have the capability of truly talking six billion people "down" so to speak or making the "unconscious conscious". There are many in Nirvana but there are very few in the "Buddha of the age" level because it can only be reached by "those who do not try to save their self find their self." You may perceive I am arrogant but it harms me because I woke up and I am aware I do not stand a chance. So the whole concept of Armageddon perhaps had nothing to do with supernatural powers but it had to do with beings who woke up and could tell this "left brain" conditioning or eating off the tree of "knowledge" would lead to us dying off as a species. The world today is trying to "save the planet" and at the same time our population is growing and growing and growing. That is a symptom that the average IQ on the planet is about 10 out of a possible 100. "The average human being only uses 10% of their brains." That is the greatest overestimation in the universe as far as I can tell. From my experiments I do not detect any brain function at all. I just see people lost in this fog and they have no concept of what is going on what so ever. They are from another planet as far as I can tell. I do not see any signs of life on this planet in relation to brain function and in relation to the human species. I just write my books because I am infinitely vain. My vanity is my only strength. I could write books with gold lettering or books written in blood and explain everything perfectly and not have a single grammatical error, and pass them out to the entire population of the planet and they would say "Todd, you are insane." This is exactly why I do not try and I never will try. I will simply write my diaries and stick to myself because I am fully aware it is way too late for corrections at this point in history. I could very easily say I perceive everything is just fantastic and perhaps I would get shiny metals and everyone would like me but then I would have to deny what I perceive is truth, and by not denying what I perceive is truth many will perhaps hate me. So because I do not deny what I perceive is truth even though I understand many will perhaps hate me it clearly proves this comment.

"Psa 9:8 **And he shall judge the world in righteousness(right hand aspect of the mind), he shall minister judgment to the people in uprightness."**

"Joh 12:47 **And if any man hear my words, and believe not, I judge him not: for I came not to judge the world, but to save the world."**

I am unable to judge you because I am intelligent enough to understand ""**Left-brain dominated people may find the (Right Brainers)thought processes vague and difficult to follow, for they are quite opposite in the way they think."** Because I cannot overcome this "quite opposite" aspect. My actions and methods should appear "insane" to you and I cannot overcome that because I cannot do the impossible. I certainly try to make comments that may assist some but I understand it is in vain because in reality all I perhaps am doing is ensuring someone will read my books and determine I am "ambiguous" and they will determine they should harm me in physical way and my mind convinces me of that conclusion and so I am at peace with it and am not stressed about it I am just mindful of that eventual conclusion. Someone will determine my **"thought processes vague and difficult to follow"** and assume I am some sort of evil because they only see everything as good or evil and so the monks suggest I should go hide in their temples away from the "sane" who are only capable of elementary logic and I do not because I am American and I live in the home of the brave and the free and the brave are more afraid of tyranny than death. "Give me liberty or give me death." So I will just write my crappy books and try my hardest to scare people away from reading them and hold on to my opinion that no one reads books anymore and I do that because I am a paradox which means I also give them freely which ensures many people will read them and someone will determine I am "evil" and ambiguous and harm me. You do not have to use elementary logic and judge I am paranoid. In fact I am fully conscious and you perhaps have no idea what that means in relation to what I am aware of. It is very difficult to assume I am arrogant when I am explaining I am noting more than a sheep among wolves and a lamb to slaughter. What that means is I went too far to the "right" by accident. My natural comments make ones on the "left" assume I am "supernatural' and that troubles ones on the "left" in general because they cannot perhaps face the reality I am "normal" and they are in fact in "neurosis" due to the scribe conditioning. There is a concept I am aware of and it is along the lines "One day man will invent something that will have unintended consequences." Invention denotes creativity, creativity is right brain, so man invented scribe and math and one might suggest it certainly did have unintended consequences. One might suggest it drowned the entire world in a "flood" and it perhaps is irreversible and that is perhaps a very harsh truth to swallow.

3:00:21 AM – No matter what anyone says I am just a people.

If you love too much then you will hate too much so it's wise to avoid feeling at all.

5:34:00 PM –

Act 8:9 But there was a certain man, called Simon, which beforetime in the same city used sorcery, and bewitched the people of Samaria, giving out that himself was some great one:"

"Used sorcery" is someone who runs their mouth as if they "know" about the afterlife. They use the "sorcery" to manipulate other people as in , making people die for them or give them money on the basis they "know" about the afterlife. So they are basically extortionists using fear tactics on the premise of "knowing" about the afterlife and they think they are "some great one" so they are arrogant and foolish and deceptive. The moral of this pass is, it is wise not to splash in the water when there is a big fish around.

2Ch 33:6 And he caused his children to pass through the fire in the valley of the son of Hinnom: also he observed times, and used enchantments, and used witchcraft, and dealt with a familiar spirit, and with wizards: he wrought much evil in the sight of the LORD, to provoke him to anger."

This is the same exact concept. Ones who say "hurry and give me money because I know" the end is near." That last I checked the end is now, so keep your money or give it Caesar. This has far less to do with "occult aspects" and far more to do with people who use "spiritual" ideals to manipulate and control others. I understand nothing and that keeps my splash level foot print very low in the big ocean where the big fish swims. I am smart enough not to splash around in the water with arrogant comments about things I will never be intelligent enough to understand. I say tomato they hear potato.-5:46:45 PM

6/27/2009 1:56:57 AM

"The philosopher's stone (Latin: lapis philosophorum; Greek: chrysopoeia), reputed to be hard as stone and malleable as wax, is a legendary alchemical tool, supposedly capable of turning base metals into gold; it was also sometimes believed to be an elixir of life, useful for rejuvenation and possibly for achieving immortality." WIKIPEDIA.COM

This stone is the in the same vain as the Holy Grail and the Fountain of Youth. No sense of time which is achieved when one in extreme right brain is what "elixir of life" denotes. "turn base metals into gold" denotes the Midas touch in relation to one is able to find wisdom or perfection in everything they read or see, this again is an aspect of extreme right brain dominate."Philosopher" is simply one who says "perhaps" a lot, somehow this word relaxes the "knowing" aspect of the left brain and as Socrates suggested no true philosopher fears death, so right brain has slight emotions such as fear and this is accomplished by saying perhaps a lot, and works both ways. One might suggest I conditioned away from fear of death and now I say perhaps a lot. "rejuvenation" and "immortality" denotes one in extreme right brain feels few aches and pains and is able to main extreme concentration for long periods of time but also one has slight stress and stress is very unhealthy so if one has nearly no stress that denotes that would be healthy. 2:10:13 AM

12:09:47 PM – this song I wrote today sums up my sentiments accurately

http://www.youtube.com/watch?v=Z9S_aURcnYU – Monk Boy

I am aware I tend to repeat myself often but that is because when I say things to the "sane" it perhaps never clicks. I can say tomato and then ask the "sane" "What did I just say" and they say "You said potato." And then I say "No I did not I said tomato." And they say "You are insane, you said potato." So my natural inclination is to just repeat myself often because I am fully aware they will perhaps never "get it" in a billion years. I find my mindset is as if I am dealing with the mentally dead. Many preach this "compassion" aspect in relation to be compassionate to the "sane", do not make fun of them because they are not aware they are in neurosis but then my thoughts are "That is too bad, I had to "wake up" the hard way, so I do not pander to anyone for any perceived moralistic reason ever." I will now discuss someone of value.12:17:52 PM

2:55:25 PM- "Queen Elizabeth I's last words were profoundly poetic. She summed it pretty well when she uttered "All my possessions for a moment of time".

http://www.bukisa.com/articles/15661_famous-last-words

I have been mindful of this comment since early on into the accident. I just realized today this is perhaps the greatest bit of wisdom any being can ever grasp. I am hesitant to even discuss it. I would be "warned" against discussing it if I was in any sort of "pack". Luckily I am a lone wolf and being a lone wolf I cannot afford the luxury that morals, compassion, or mercy provide.3:01:41 PM

6:12:06 PM - All of my physical things for another moment is what the queen said. This is because on her death bed as most do, she made peace with god. She made peace with the Lord of all and once a person does that they think clearly and they want to live. Now I have to clarify what I just said for people who do not speak English.

He is Lord of all = Death is lord of all living things because all living things die.

Love god(death) with all your heart = Do not be afraid of death

The fear of god = Ones who are still afraid of god (death) and thus are on the "left hand side" of the brain and thus they do not use the "right hand" aspect of the brain so they do not think clearly because their judgments are clouded by fear. When people are born they do not fear god (death) so they love god(death) with all their heart, but then the tree of knowledge conditioning makes people "god fearing" and then they give up the "kingdom" which is the right aspect of the mind and trade it for the physical based aspect of the mind, left. This is all in relation to these Taliban beings who suggested "we love death". That is not what anyone wants to hear from an enemy because that means they are on the "right hand side" aspect of the mind which means one is dealing with a human that is infinitely clever. Simply put once one gets over fear of god(death) they have brain function because the mind is not clouded with these things called emotions, the time stamps are gone, clarity is possible. You just remind yourself I am beyond the realms of insanity and what I just talked about cannot possibly be true. I understand one thing, you are going to make peace with the maker(death) on your death bed and then wish you had done it earlier or you can make peace with the maker(death) by using some simple "safe" fear conditioning and "humiliation" conditioning and have a life with mental clarity. Those are your only two choices in all reality. You can face the maker(death) while you still have some time in life left or you can face the maker(death) when you have couple days in life left. You are going to have to face that fear one way or another so you might as well get it over with and then get on with your life. For ones who idolize Jesus he said "I defeated death" which means he lost his fear of death or lost his fear and he mentally went to the "right hand" aspect of the mind which is all about infinity and complexity. So if you are wondering I understand his teachings are in fact wise like the other wise men but I am aware you perhaps hear and yet do not understand anything he said. Now I will go play my stupid video game and pretend I didn't just tell you the greatest truth of all existence. 6:21:21 PM

You can either please yourself or please others but seldom can you accomplish both at the same time.

I will attempt to write something of importance in the seventh diary.

Perhaps someone, in time, will understand my words.

Perhaps neurosis is the inability to exist without labels, perhaps; perhaps.

I am not stupid or odd I am simply different due to an accident.

I had to take a handful of pills to understand this information so please give this information freely as I have given you this information freely. Take and eat.

It is done. Twis well.

Thank You.

7/2/2009 4:46:42 PM